LONDON'S
OLYMPIC
FOLLIES

GRAEME KENT

LONDON'S OLYMPIC FOLLIES

The Madness and Mayhem of the

❧ 1908 ❧ London Games

A CAUTIONARY TALE

The Robson Press

First published in 2008 by JR Books, 10 Greenland Street, London NW1 0ND

This edition published in Great Britain in 2012 by
The Robson Press (an imprint of Biteback Publishing Ltd)
Westminster Tower
3 Albert Embankment
London
SE1 7SP
Copyright © Graeme Kent 2008

ISBN 978-1-84954-290-6

10 9 8 7 6 5 4 3 2 1

A CIP catalogue record for this book is available from the British Library.

Cover photographs © Press Association Images

Set in Minion Pro by SX Composing DTP, Rayleigh, Essex
Printed and bound in Great Britain by
CPI Group (UK) Ltd, Croydon CR0 4YY

Contents

Acknowledgements

Anyone attempting to write about the often obscure recreational and social events of a bygone age must necessarily depend to an enormous extent on the help of dedicated sports enthusiasts and researchers. I have been most fortunate to find many willing guides through the labyrinthine ways of amateur sport in the first decade of the 20th century and owe much to both their kindness and willingness to share their discoveries.

Boxing historian Larry Braysher was a fund of information about the amateur boxing scene of this era. Malcolm Fare, archivist of the British Fencing Association, provided me with useful information on the life and career of gold medallist Edgar Seligman. Tim Peake, of British Gymnastics, filled in the background of Walter Tysall. Ashley Wickham was very helpful with his explanation of the development of competitive swimming in general and of the Australian crawl in particular. Amy Terriere of the British Olympic Foundation was most helpful. Allan Best, historian of the British Wrestling Association, delved deep into his archives to produce the Olympic documentation for gold medal winners George de Relwyskow and Stanley Bacon and much other material besides.

The staff of the Boston Public Library in Lincolnshire patiently provided me with an almost endless supply of out-of-print biographies and autobiographies of competitors and officials from that White City tournament.

Two indispensable histories set me firmly on my path. The official report of the 1908 Games, *The Fourth Olympiad*, drawn up by Theodore Andrea Cook, is a massive document and, considering the speed with which it was published after the event, is a treasure trove of information about the period. It has been meticulously updated and annotated by Bill Mallon and Ian Buchanan in *The 1908 Olympic Games: Results for all Competitions in All Events, with Commentary.* Anyone attempting to study the international athletic events taking place between April and October of that year will be left in the starting blocks without the aid of these seminal works.

As usual I have been assisted beyond measure by the work of dozens of unknown contemporary journalists toiling in the heat of the day, or more often in the drizzle of the mornings and after- noons of that awful Edwardian spring, summer and autumn of 1908. The accounts in the columns of their newspapers, sometimes biased, at times inaccurate but almost always colourful, have done much to paint a picture of a most unusual and fascinating time. In their hyperbole and exaggerations can often be discerned the real truth of an era.

I am very grateful to Lesley Wilson, my editor at JR Books, for her constant enthusiasm and support for this project, and her meticulous guidance and editing.

Introduction

The 1908 Olympic Games were a watershed in the history of modern athletics. Previous Olympiads were open to everyone who could make the journey. They were held on rough tracks or in fields. The swimming events were held in rivers or even the open sea. The Games of 1908 changed all that.

A superb stadium was specially built at the White City site for the events, which took place between 27 April and 31 October. For the first time all contestants appeared as members of their national teams. Some 2,035 athletes were reckoned to have taken part. Britain furnished over 700 competitors and France more than 200. The USA, concentrating on track and field events, provided 122 handpicked athletes. At the other end of the scale, Argentina and Switzerland each had a solitary representative. Irish-born athletes won gold medals for Great Britain, the USA and Canada.

There were other innovations. Qualifying heats were introduced. The Winter Olympics, added in 1924, were heralded in London with the staging of ice-skating on the programme. The marathon distance was extended to 26 miles, 385 yards, which eventually became the official distance for the race. The relay race was introduced and in the winning US team was John Taylor, the first black athlete to secure an Olympic gold medal.

Other experiments were short-lived, with powerboat racing taking place for the first and last time. Field hockey, diving and ice-skating lasted longer. It was the end of an era at the London Games for the standing high jump and standing long jump events – effectively putting an end to the international career of the multi-medal winning Raymond Ewry, variously known as 'the human frog' and 'the rubber man'.

Families were represented at the highest levels. The first brother and sister to win Olympic medals were the British archers William and Charlotte Dod. The Swedish father and son team of Oscar and Alfred Swahn won medals in shooting events. Husband and wife team Edgar and Martha Syers took bronze medals in the pairs skating.

World and Olympic records were broken in the track and field events, although not in the sense that modern competitors would understand. This was a period in which records and record-keeping were hazy affairs and there was no central validating body. Nevertheless, runner Melvin Sheppard set new Olympic records in the 800 metres and 1500 metres and broke the world best time at the shorter distance. He also secured a gold in the relay. As far as can be ascertained, world records were also established in the 110 metres hurdles, the 400 metres hurdles and the classical discus throw.

The London Games also had their share of characters. The Cork-born English policeman Con O'Kelly was tough and determined enough to win a gold medal in the heavyweight freestyle wrestling event, but probably was not as fierce as he seemed, because he received a reprimand from his superiors for allowing street urchins to steal his helmet while he was on his beat in Hull.

Some competitors were more fortunate than others. There were only two entrants in the seven metres class yachting competition and one of those withdrew, so Charles Rivett-Carnac and his wife won gold without even getting their feet wet.

The London Olympics were full of charm and drama. Yet today they are remembered, if at all, for the quarrels, scandals and international disputes which threatened to rend the tournament apart. The intrigue may have been deplorable but it kept a huge Edwardian audience engrossed for months. For the athletic achievements, human stories and plain bloody-mindedness displayed at all levels, the 1908 Olympic Games deserve to be remembered as a fascinating footnote in sporting history.

One

Dr Badger Cries 'Foul!'

'That Halswelle was badly bored and obstructed is, of course, beyond question.'

The Olympic Games of 1908 in London: A Reply to Certain Charges Made by the American Officials

There were two finals of the 400 metres in the 1908 London Olympics. The first took place on 23 July at 5.30pm. It was the last athletics event of the day to be held at the newly constructed White City Stadium. The arena was capable of holding 150,000 spectators, with seating for 68,000, 17,000 of them under cover.

There were four runners on this drab day. Representing Great Britain was Lieutenant Wyndham Halswelle. A few years earlier he had served with the Highland Light Infantry in the Boer War and taken part in several skirmishes in South Africa. His embryonic athletic ability had been noted by a veteran Scottish athletics coach called Jimmy Curran, who was also serving with the Highland Light Infantry during the South African war. He had urged the young Halswelle to take running seriously when he returned to the United Kingdom.

Known to everyone except, presumably, the men under his command as 'Jock', Halswelle won silver and bronze medals in the 400 metres and 800 metres respectively in the unofficial 1906 Olympiad held in Athens. At the Scottish championships held later at Edinburgh's Powderhall Stadium, on one afternoon Halswelle had won the 100, 220, 440 and 880 yards championships. He also set a Scottish record for 300 yards that was not beaten until 1961, when Menzies Campbell, later for a time to be the leader of the Liberal Democratic Party, took it away from him.

In the semi-finals of the London competition he set a new Olympic record of 48.4 seconds. This established him as the favourite for the final. He had won his two heats by 10 and 12 yards.

A few days before the race the *New York Times,* referring to the runner's achievement in the Amateur Athletic Association (AAA) final had said, 'Lieutenant Halswelle is the man England expects to see win the 400 meter run and his 0.48.2-5 on a poor track would seem to put the event at his mercy.'

The other three finalists were all Americans. John Carpenter represented Cornell University and was a former star Washington DC high school athlete. The *Nebraska State Journal* called him 'a bright and quiet young American'. William Robbins ran for Harvard College. The third member of the team, John Taylor of Pennsylvania University, was one of the first African Americans to represent the USA at any sport. He was frequently bumped and bored in races by less talented white athletes, as they tried to elbow him to one side or push past him where there was no room, because of his skin colour. To counter these ploys he had taken to running his races from the rear of the field, relying upon a surge of pace to take him to the front in the later stages. He had graduated from the Pennsylvania School of Veterinary Medicine only a few weeks previously and had hardly practised his new profession at all. In his class's year book for 1908, his entry had read, 'We of the class of 1908 are proud and can boast of having one of the greatest athletes the world has ever known.'

Already a cloud hung over the proceedings. For some days before the race there had been rumours that the Americans, accustomed to a more robust running style than the English, were going to try to hustle the dignified Halswelle out of the competition. The horseshoe-shaped track would lend itself to such tactics because it was not marked into lanes by strings. Accordingly, British judges were stationed ostentatiously around the contours of the arena at 20-yard intervals, to the considerable annoyance of the American officials.

Trouble started in the British dressing room as Halswelle tried to prepare for the final. He was bombarded with conflicting advice by the dozens of officials and hangers-on who had crowded into the room in an effort to give their man moral support. Some urged him to sprint from the line, while others urged caution and told the lieutenant to tuck in behind several of the Americans. In the event Halswelle took this last piece of advice, with unfortunate consequences.

Before the race started, the apprehensive American trainer, Mike Murphy, who had coached John Taylor at Pennsylvania University, gathered his charges together and warned them what a good man they were competing against – Halswelle, the son of an artist, was Mayfair-born and Charterhouse and Sandhurst-educated. The trainer noted newspaper forecasts that the Americans were out to nobble the Briton and ordered the team to avoid disqualification – they were to be fair but run their hardest.

The runners lined up with Carpenter on the inside, Halswelle next to him and Robbins on the officer's other flank. Taylor occupied the outside berth. There were none of the customary handshakes before the event. Starter Harry Goble sternly warned the competitors that the penalty for any ganging-up, illegal elbow work or deliberate obstruction could be immediate disqualification.

As soon as the starting gun was fired there were roars of disapproval from the crowd, who thought that Robbins, making a fast start in order to cut across and gain the inside position on the track, had impeded Halswelle. As the field settled into place, Carpenter slotted into the second position with Halswelle doggedly trying to cut down the lead of the two Americans ahead of him. An apprehensive Taylor, who was reported to be unwell, settled in at the back as usual.

This order was maintained until the last bend when Halswelle made his move. Carpenter edged forward so that he was running shoulder to shoulder with Robbins on the final bend, forcing the British runner to veer wide in order to try to pass the pair of them. Inexorably, Carpenter continued to muscle his way sideways across the track, forcing the helpless Halswelle towards the outer curb.

The crowd and the British officials were both infuriated by Carpenter's tactics. One of the umpires, Dr Roscoe Badger, cried

'Foul!' He later declared in his evidence to the committee, as delineated in the official report, 'I at once ran up the track, waving my hands to the judges to break the worsted.'

Badger's declaration was the signal for fellow officials to spring into action. Several of them snapped the winning tape before any of the runners could breast it. Others ran along the side of the track like angry clockwork toys, shouting irately at the runners to stop. It was later claimed that some of them had sworn at the runners. Ignored, they dashed towards the competitors, gesticulating wildly and, as one newspaper pointed out dryly, expending at least as much energy as the runners.

The innocent and inoffensive Taylor, who was running some way back out of contention in fourth place, was physically manhandled off the track. Watching was American Les Stevens, knocked out in the heats of the 100 metres three days earlier. He claimed in disbelief, 'The Negro boy was tackled.'

Ray Ewry, an American competitor, had left the standing high jump competition to watch the 400 metres final. He believed Halswelle had panicked on the final bend.

The three runners who had not been bustled out of the event crossed the finish line – Carpenter, Robbins and finally Halswelle. The winner's unofficial time, according to those who continued to study their stopwatches for anyone still interested, was anything between 47.8 and 48.6 seconds. Few were concerned with the time.

British spectators were booing the American runners. American onlookers were howling imprecations at the British officials. The four competitors, looking confused and embarrassed, were escorted off the track and down to the dressing rooms. It was taken by some Britons as a further black mark against Carpenter that he was, by then, wearing a particularly well-cut raincoat over his shorts and vest. Caspar Whitney, an American editor, claimed the crowd had started to shout, 'Disqualify the dirty runners!'

An announcer quickly declared through a megaphone that the race had been declared void. The important announcements were made by the City of London toastmaster, who was resplendent in an odd but fetching combination of uniform, morning dress and top hat. No reason was given for the decision he announced.

A great cheer went up from the home supporters, countered by uproar from the American contingent in the stands. Remarkably for a staid British athletics tournament, thousands of spectators began to flood down the aisles on to the track, some arguing, others demanding more information. A contingent of helmeted London policemen was dispatched to counter the possibility of escalating disorder.

The AAA convened an immediate meeting to discuss the matter. Photographs of the footprints of the runners on the muddy, puddled surface were ordered. The track officials and Wyndham Halswelle were called before the meeting, but American athletes and officials were not invited. In his evidence, Halswelle refuted rumours that Carpenter had beaten him back savagely with his elbow, but asserted the American had impeded him by forcing him some distance across the track with his arm. The committee deliberated for several hours. Most of the spectators had left the stadium by then.

Transport had been set up, optimistically, by the organisers to disperse 80,000 fans at the White City Stadium in an hour. Some visitors to the Franco-British Exhibition that summer were less sanguine. Herbert Shaw, a journalist, commented: 'It is a terrible fighting, that struggle which begins outside the Wood Lane entrance and is continued for many miles beyond the ken of Wood Lane. It is more terrible on Saturday night, when half-a-million people, about the hour of nine or ten, suddenly remember that they have homes.'

Fans travelled by carriages, motor omnibuses and on foot. Many of them would be using the new Wood Lane tube terminus from which trains pulled by electric locomotives would take them to Bank station via Shepherd's Bush. Tourists intending to visit the Games had been advised, 'American and colonial visitors staying at the principal West End and Central hotels will find the Central Line (Twopenny Tube) the most direct and quickest route; book from Tottenham Court Road, Oxford Circus, Bond Street or Marble Arch Station to Shepherd's Bush (Exhibition Station)'.

Horse cabs, for the more affluent visitors, cost two miles for a shilling within the central four miles of the city. New-fangled motor cabs charged eight old pence for the first mile and another eight for each succeeding mile.

An official statement was finally received by the damp spectators who remained huddled against the cold on that grey, drizzling afternoon at the White City. It said that the race had been declared void and that the final would be re-run the following Saturday, the last day of the athletics tournament. John Carpenter, however, had been disqualified for his action in deliberately denying Wyndham Halswelle racing room. The announcement 'No race' was flashed on to the telegraph board.

Matthew P. Halpin, the manager of the United States' athletics team lodged a protest as soon as the announcer had declared through his megaphone that the final had been postponed. This action was followed up by James E. Sullivan, the Commissioner to the Games of the US team. He held a meeting of his senior officials at a London hotel that evening. Sullivan, who was still only in his 40s, had been a founder member of the American Amateur Athletic Union, and was influential in Olympic circles. His detractors doubted his total impartiality, claiming that he was on the payroll of the Spalding sporting goods company. For this reason he was commonly known as the Spalding Man. On this occasion he made no effort to pacify his colleagues, causing his former friend Baron de Coubertin to sigh, 'I just could not understand Sullivan's attitude...he shared his team's frenzy and did nothing to calm them down.'

There was no doubt that the organisation of the London Olympiad was already providing something of a culture shock to the visiting Americans. At the last official Games, held in St Louis in 1904, American officials had it all their own way. In total there had been only about a hundred foreign competitors; the Games had been little more than an extended version of the United States championships. The American officials were accustomed to running matters as they saw fit. Now they were being thwarted by equally determined and insular British judges.

As a result of the meeting chaired by Sullivan that evening, it was decided to protest strongly against the disqualification of the American runner. The stakes were raised suddenly when William

Robbins, the Harvard competitor, announced that as an act of solidarity he would not compete in the final either. That put the onus on John Taylor, the remaining runner in the final. Robbins made it clear that he was exerting no pressure on the African American competitor. Taylor was free to make up his own mind what to do. The pressure was intense.

Taylor was accustomed to being treated with indifference by athletics administrators. He felt strongly that athletic supremacy should be expressed on the track rather than in a committee room. On the other hand, when the former Pennyslvania University man saw the degree of satisfaction covertly expressed by Sullivan and his fellow committee members at Robbins' decision, reluctantly he knew how unpopular he would become if he insisted on running. Instead he threw in his lot with the others and stated that he too was withdrawing from the event.

An official announcement was made to the effect that the three American runners would not compete in the re-run of the 400 metres final the following Saturday. To make up for their disappointment, the committee issued the American runners with special medals.

Sullivan went on to complain about the overall organisation of the race. He was particularly incensed about the positioning on the line of John Taylor, who, he stated, had to run yards more than the other starters. He denied that there had been any orchestrated plot on the part of the Americans to stop Halswelle running: 'It is ridiculous to talk of a team boring or packeting as good a man as Halswelle in a quarter-mile race. No team could do it. We had nothing of the kind in view, we just raced him off his feet and he couldn't stand the pace.' ('Packeting' consisted of athletes surrounding a runner so that he could not breakthrough.)

Sullivan said if there had been any collusion it had been among the British officials, whose protests, in his view, had seemed suspiciously orchestrated: 'When Carpenter started leaving Halswelle behind, the officials cried "Foul!" in unison' he said accusingly, 'and the announcer also ran, yelling "Foul!"'

The next morning, newspapers around the world were full of stories about the previous day's race and the subsequent ramifications of its being declared void. *The Times* gave the British version of the action on the final bend. Referring to Carpenter's tactics, the newspaper said: 'He appeared to run diagonally, crossing in front of the Englishman so that he was obliged to lose several yards.' The American newspapers, not unnaturally, took a different view of the proceedings. *The Daily Kennebec Journal* summed up the feelings of many Americans when it stated of the first running of the 400 metres final: 'The unfortunate state of disputes which has arisen since the opening of the Olympian games…culminated this afternoon in an occurrence which threatened to wreck the inter-Olympic meetings.'

The Cleveland Plain Dealer, referring to the disqualification of Carpenter, said: 'It is impossible to imagine Americans adopting towards visiting athletes the tactics which have already made these British games odious.'

The *Pittsburgh Press* concurred: 'There is neither the spirit of true sport, nor the spirit of ordinary courtesy and hospitality in the attitude of the Britishers, which has called forth vigorous complaint from the American contestants.'

The Syracuse Post added, 'Athletes from other countries are completely at the mercy of the English officials who are conducting their events.' On the other hand, the respected American writer Caspar Whitney was of the opinion that the decision of the judges was final and that the Americans should have kept their mouths shut and abided by the official decision.

He was almost alone among his countrymen in his view. Mike Murphy, the American coach, was particularly bitter. '"Highway robbery" is pretty strong language, but there are no other words for it,' he growled.

Murphy was a formidable character and a sports veteran. He was a former professional six-day runner who had been brave enough to assist with the coaching of the fierce and often drunken world heavyweight boxing champion John L. Sullivan; Murphy was small, deaf and feisty. He had been one of the first to introduce the crouch start for sprinters and was a particular favourite of James E. Sullivan, who more than once had publicly praised the trainer for his ability to shave and adjust the rules in favour of his athletes, almost to the point of resorting to outright trickery. It was said that Murphy could judge a sprinter's time and forecast his potential personal best just by watching him run once. One of his aphorisms was engraved on a plaque at the University of Pennsylvania: 'You can't lick a team that won't be licked.'

Several years later Murphy was to be the first conditioner to guess that the former heavyweight boxing champion James J. Jeffries was hopelessly out of shape for his comeback contest against the champion Jack Johnson at Reno. He had confirmed his theory by following Jeffries on one of his solitary so-called training runs. He saw Jeffries stop after a mile and spend the rest of the morning fishing before trotting back to his training camp. The promoter Tex Rickard had tried to bribe Murphy not to spread the story, but the tiny trainer ordered one of his large footballing friends to throw Rickard out of a window.

In the course of his globe-trotting coaching career, the 48-year-old Murphy had often clashed with the English athletics establishment and was not impressed with his experiences. Interviewed in the *Daily Tribune* about the Halswelle affair, he had been particularly incensed. 'I have been up against the English officials for years, and it has always been the same story – they would have robbed us of everything they could.'

Throughout the heated accusations and counter-accusations, Carpenter continued to protest his innocence, claiming that literally he had run a straight finishing burst, never deviating from a direct line after he had rounded the bend and headed for the tape, making absolutely no contact with Wyndham Halswelle. He told the *New York Times*, 'I did nothing to warrant my disqualification, and the action of the British officials was a big surprise to me. On the morning of the race the English newspapers printed a warning notice, advising that the race should be carefully watched by all Englishmen. All of the stories inferred that the Americans would do something to win the race, either by fair means or foul.'

Even the normally reticent Taylor expressed his feelings to reporters, 'The deal those Englishmen gave us was about the worst thing I ever heard of,' he said. 'It was simply a plain piece of robbery!'

Whatever the private feelings of the organisers about this statement, behind the scenes efforts were still made to get the Americans to change their minds and to compete in the rescheduled final. All fell upon deaf ears. Two days later at midday, Wyndham Halswelle turned up alone to compete in the rerun of the 400 metres final. He had been the subject of criticism in the press for days. Some American writers had dug up an incident in the 800 metres final of the Athens Olympics two years earlier. Halswelle, they claimed, had been muscled out of first place towards the end of the race on a track with very tight bends by a more determined runner, an American called Paul Pilgrim, a last-minute entrant who had paid his own way to Greece. A shaken Halswelle had finished third. The implication of the articles was that Halswelle could sometimes falter under pressure and that was probably what had happened at the White City.

As he approached the starting line, the lieutenant was hissed by the many Americans in the crowd. A forlorn but dignified figure, the English-born Scot completed the course in a creditable time of 50.00 seconds. In a triumph of restraint only one national newspaper used the headline HALSWELLE THAT ENDS WELL.

Four hours after the lieutenant's solo performance, the track and field section of the first London Olympics ended. Without a doubt the fourth modern Olympiad had not been the success that its organisers had hoped for. One American newspaper summed up the views of most when it told its readers, 'The Halswelle affair, coming as it did at the end of the athletics section of the Olympics, proved the last nail in the coffin of the ill-fated London Olympiad.'

There was no doubt that amid all the other noises in the vast stadium, the thud of two cultures clashing could be heard clearly by those with an ear for such things. Yet it had all started with such high hopes.

Two

The Smoke-Filled Stateroom

'We are very well aware that many shortcomings were apparent in the organisation of the most complicated international meeting that has ever taken place.'

The Olympic Games of 1908 in London: A Reply to Certain Charges Made by the American Officials

The London Olympiad had its inception in the stateroom of Lord Howard de Walden's small yacht the SS *Branwen*. It was August 1906, the time of the unofficial Olympiad, and the yacht was moored in the Bay of Phlerum off the coast of Athens. On board was the British fencing team.

Even by Edwardian standards the assembly represented a concatenation of eccentric privilege and talents. William Henry Grenfell, Lord Desborough, was the enthusiast. He was 51 years old and a prominent sportsman. He had been in the 11 at Harrow and rowed for Oxford in the celebrated 1877 dead heat with Cambridge. He also represented the university in the three-mile track race. In 1878 he achieved the unique honour of becoming president of both the Oxford Boat Club and the Athletic Club.

For good measure he also found time to become Master of the University Draghounds, taking over from fellow undergraduate Cecil Rhodes, who was about to return to South Africa to become a diamond magnate and coloniser of Rhodesia. Desborough slightly mistrusted the South African because he had a loose seat on a horse. It was typical of Desborough's organising ability that when he came to stable the draghounds near at hand he also took care to house a fox in close proximity, so that at a pinch his dogs would always have something to chase.

By the time of the Athens meeting, Desborough had been an occasional Liberal and then Tory MP, winning and losing several elections, stroked an eight across the English Channel, climbed the Matterhorn by three different routes and swam twice across the foot of Niagara Falls, once in a blizzard. He also won the national punting championship and married an heiress. All these feats were performed in conjunction with those normal pursuits of a country gentleman: deer stalking in the Highlands, deep-sea fishing off the coast of Florida, and big game hunting wherever the fancy took him.

He was not averse to newspaper publicity and usually had a ready fund of anecdotes for reporters. Describing his experiences as a war correspondent in the second Suakin campaign in Egypt in 1888, one journalist reported admiringly, 'He was surprised and chased by a party of dervishes when out alone some distance from the British camp. Lord Desborough won his exciting sprint by a few inches, thanks to the athletic prowess that enabled him, as a boy, to run his mile in four minutes, 37 seconds.' There were further reports that Lord Desborough had been clutching an umbrella at the time of his ambush and that with true British phlegm he retained a firm grip on it throughout the sprint back to the British lines.

A gossip writer said of Willie Desborough during his parliamentary days, in the following gushing terms, that he stood 'well over six feet in height, with the frame of a Hercules and with health and strength written all over his manly face'.

He had been awarded a peerage just the year before in 1905 upon his final retirement from politics. To fill the void left by his departure from the House of Commons, he threw himself heartily into public life. At one time it was estimated that he was serving on 115 different committees, in tandem with being a justice of the peace and president of the MCC. Desborough also persevered with his love of fencing, which had brought him to Athens on the *Branwen*.

A fellow member of the team and owner of the yacht was Thomas Evelyn Ellis, Lord Howard de Walden, who was putting up the team for the duration of the Olympiad. He was 24 and had been educated at Eton and Sandhurst, served in the Boer War and was the artistic dilettante of the group. He had had a difficult childhood. When he was only 12 his mother Blanche had sued his father, Frederick George Ellis, the seventh Lord Howard de Walden, for divorce on the grounds of cruelty in a notorious case. The couple wed in 1876, Blanche 19 and de Walden 46. According to the *Gazette* the court proceedings had revealed 'an extraordinary story of cruelty and debauchery'. The newspaper refused to print all the details.

The case attracted a large audience of fashionable women in gay costumes. Among the more acceptable charges levelled against the peer by his wife were drunkenness, miserliness, twisting her arm and throwing a heavy book at her in the presence of a Major Graham, 'who had intercepted the missile'.

The peer was also accused of setting fire to Blanche's bedroom, locking her out of the house, refusing to admit her mother into the building and shooting guns up the chimney. In addition, a scandalised Lady Molesworth, who had lived opposite the de Waldens, claimed to have seen the master of the house naked at his window.

Further evidence was given by the reclusive and eccentric 86-year-old Duke of Portland, who stated that he had tried to prevent de Walden from forcing his way into the bedroom of his sick wife. The Duke went on to say that he had refused to allow Lord de Walden to visit him at his home, Welbeck Abbey, because the younger man was a drunkard and disgusting in his habits. Actually, the elderly Duke rarely received any visitors because he lived in strange monastic seclusion in a series of tunnels dug beneath his estate by a team of miners, giving rise to intriguing rumours that he was either disfigured or had contracted leprosy. He spoke so seldom that he was known as the Prince of Silence. Nevertheless, his evidence convinced the jury. After the hearing, a decision was made, within five minutes, in favour of Lady de Walden. She was granted a judicial separation, costs and the custody of her son. A counter-claim from Lord de Walden for his wife's alleged adultery was dismissed.

All that was in the past as far as the 8th Lord de Walden was concerned. He had inherited his title five years earlier and now owned thousands of acres of land in Scotland and one of the largest collections of armour in the world. For much of his time he flirted with the fringes of artistic society, eagerly contributed forewords to books and wrote and backed bad plays under an assumed name. He was also considered one of Great Britain's wealthiest and most eligible bachelors, much sought-after by debutantes and their ambitious mothers. He was one of the reserves for the fencing team using the épée – a light sword with a blunted point and no cutting edges.

A third member was 42-year-old Sir Cosmo Duff Gordon. Another wealthy Scottish landowner, sheriff and magistrate, he had served with the Gordon Highlanders. He was tall and handsome, had lost an eye in a shooting accident and was dominated by his mother. For a time he had harboured aspirations to become a singer, and had trained in Italy. Giving that up, he had become an enthusiastic member of a rather odd London martial arts establishment known as the Bartitsu club, in which kick boxers, swordsmen, stick fighters, wrestlers and fencers prowled with muscular menace. He gave house parties in which he tested the courage of his younger male guests by making them wear fencing masks while he enthusiastically fired wax bullets at them.

Duff Gordon was married to an international fashion designer known as Lucille, who was the sister of Elinor Glyn, the best-selling and, for the times, raunchy novelist. He was wealthy but relatively inconspicuous at the time. Later he was to become the subject of an international scandal.

The other members of the team present could actually fence a bit but possessed neither the clout nor the connections of the three aristocrats in the vessel's stateroom. Edgar Seligman, a talented professional artist and a veteran of the Boer War, was 37 and the current British épée champion. Charles Newton-Johnson, the oldest member of the group at 52, was a published poet with *The Viol of Love* and was credited with introducing the épée to Britain as a competition weapon at an assault-at-arms display at the Steinway Hall in 1900.

The final member of the team, its captain and the second reserve was the 35-year-old Theodore Cook, a former head-boy of Radley College and an Oxford rowing blue and founder of the university fencing club. Not the luckiest of men, his athletic career was to be terminated abruptly when he was kicked in the ribs by a racehorse being paraded before the running of the Oaks at Epsom.

There had not been a great deal of competition for a place in the side. Fencing was an upper class sport, the Olympic competition was not highly regarded and few could afford to make the trip to Greece. Several months before the Games were due to start, *The Times* of 28 February reported, 'The English team for the Olympian games in Athens next April has not yet been definitely chosen. In consequence of Mr C. Leaf Daniel's having been asked to be Captain of the Amateur Fencing Association's team to Paris he cannot go to Athens and his place among the fencers from whom the English team will be chosen has been taken by Sir Cosmo Duff Gordon.'

Nevertheless, the scratch team had done well. All the members of the side were on a relative high on the evening of their meeting. In the team épée competition they had defeated Germany and Belgium and tied with France in the final, although after a fight-off which the French won 9–6 the Britons then had to be content with the silver medal, causing Desborough to write smugly, 'We have done much better than I expected and better than the score makes out, as we suffered in the judging which is more important than the fighting.'

The loyal and opportunistic Cook backed him up, 'Lord Desborough was at the top of his game with the épée,' he wrote unctuously, 'and no one has ever been worse treated by an international jury than he was in our most critical fight against the French.'

Their successful efforts in the heat against Germany had been witnessed by no less personages than King Edward and Queen Alexandra, following a slight delay in starting the proceedings due to some of the German team over-sleeping. The match took place in the enclosed garden of a gymnasium. A keen gambler, Edward was said to have laid a substantial bet on the British team to win and was so pleased with the result that he consented to become the patron of the Amateur Fencing Association.

When, after dinner on the *Branwen*, Desborough mooted the matter of the venue for the 1908 Olympics, his fellow fencers were in a mellow and receptive mood and nodded the proposal through, although they could have had no idea of what they were letting themselves in for.

The modern Olympics had been instigated 12 years earlier by an aristocratic French educationalist, Pierre de Frédy, Baron de Coubertin. Obsessed by the ideals of the ancient Olympics, he had travelled the world making contacts and propagating his theories on international sport. During his journeys he had been influenced by the work of an English doctor, William Penny Brookes, who shared Coubertin's interest in the Olympiads and instigated his own idiosyncratic and parochial mini-Olympics in the village of Much Wenlock in Shropshire.

There had been a number of attempts, of varying scales, to revive the idea of the Greek Games in Britain, dating back to the 17th century. At one of them, at the Crystal Palace in 1866, the 18-year-old W.G. Grace, later to become the greatest English cricketer of his time, won the 440 yards hurdles, in the process he had abandoned a game of cricket in which he was playing, ran up a hill, secured first place in his event and then hurriedly returned to his match.

Coubertin was greatly impressed by such examples of muscular Christianity being displayed across the English Channel. Gradually, he began to make headway with his international scheme. At an international congress held at the Sorbonne in Paris in 1894, he proposed the restoration of the ancient Olympics. Representatives came from 13 nations and a further 21 conveyed written messages of support. The baron's idea was well received and the International Olympic Committee (IOC) was formed. The official congress report said, 'The re-establishment of the Olympic Games was decided unanimously and before the Congress adjourned, it appointed a permanent International Olympic Committee entrusted with ensuring the rebirth of the games.'

It was decided that the inaugural modern Olympiad would be held in Athens. For a time it was mooted that Athens would be the venue for the Games every four years. Later this was amended to moving the competition from nation to nation.

The Greek prime minister had his doubts about the expense of the proposed Games, but he was persuaded, thanks to the support of the Greek royal family and a substantial donation from a Greek businessman, to rebuild the ages-old stadium. The first Athens Olympiad was reasonably successful. It was a modest affair. At first it seemed as if it might collapse from lack of support but a few European countries sent teams. Even so, the Games would have been largely a parochial affair if it had not been for the arrival of a small squad of athletes from the USA. It was a scratch crew, consisting mainly of some Princeton athletes, a Harvard freshman and a handful of runners, jumpers and throwers sponsored by the Boston Athletic Club. Apart from the Bostonians all the other competitors paid their own expenses.

The Americans reached Athens after an uncomfortable sea journey. A day out from New York a freak wave broke across the deck, injuring several of the athletes on board. Once they arrived they wasted no time. There were 12 track and field events in the first Olympiad. Americans won nine of them.

The first modern Olympiad was a place for versatility. An Islington-born Australian named Edmund Flack won the 800 metres and 1500 metres races and was one of the leaders in the marathon before he collapsed. Immediately he was attended to on the ground by a solicitous Greek spectator and by Mr W. Delves-Broughton, the butler of the British ambassador, who was wearing a bowler hat despite the heat of the day. When the two men came to his assistance, the disorientated Flack punched the local man. The semi-delirious runner was then transported in a carriage to the stadium to be presented with an old Greek coin by the royal family. He wrote in a letter to his father, 'All along the roads there were crowds of people. I think that almost every house and building in Athens must have been locked up and their occupants present to see the finish.' Undeterred by his marathon failure, Flack later borrowed a racquet and entered the singles and doubles tennis competitions.

Flack's partner in the doubles was Englishman George Stuart Robertson, later to become a QC. He also took part in the throwing the weight and the discus competitions, although not familiar with these disciplines. As an Oxford classical scholar, he was interested in their antecedents. He had only become aware of the Olympics when he saw an advertisement in the window of a travel agent's shop. He commented on the British entry. 'No direct appeal was made to Oxford or Cambridge athletes to compete until March, just before the Games. Thus only six British athletes were there – including one who lived in Athens.'

The energetic Robertson did his best to make up for the shortage of Britons at the competition. In addition to his throwing and tennis-playing activities he composed and delivered a Greek ode at the closing ceremony on the tenth day. He even conspired with the King of Greece in order to deliver it: 'The committee would not allow it to be recited, as they had refused sundry Greeks who had sought permission to do so,' he explained, 'so he arranged with me, that when he gave the signal, the ode should be delivered. He was so pleased with his victory over the committee that he gave me both the olive branch, the laurel branch and a valuable present as well, which was some consolation for my failure in the discus.'

Some athletes overcame the handicaps they encountered. The American shot-put winner Robert Garratt, who had taken his mother with him on the excursion from the USA, also entered the discus event. He found that the discus to be used in the competition was of a sort he had never encountered before but he still won the competition. 'I wanted as much action as I could get, because it meant fun,' he explained. 'I got into the discus thing never figuring I'd do anything but finish an absolute last.'

Baron de Coubertin insisted that the next Olympiad be held in Paris. Yet, for all his efforts, it was not a success. Barely a thousand spectators attended the five-day competition. It was an offshoot of the 1900 Paris Exhibition and was relegated to the status of a sideshow. The athletic events took place in what was little more than a field. There was no cinder running track and no jumping pits. The area was so cramped that a powerful heave of the hammer or javelin would send it right out of the field.

But despite the deplorable conditions, the standard of performance in the athletic events was much higher than that of the Athens Olympics. New records were set in every track and field event. Americans won 17 of these events, their outstanding athlete being Alvin Kraenzlein who won the 60 metres, the 110 metres hurdles, the 200 metres hurdles and the long jump. His jump defeated Polish-born Syracuse University student Meyer Prinstein by one centimetre in the final, held on a Sunday. The Syracuse authorities refused Prinstein, who had performed his leap in a heat, permission to jump on the Sunday, although he was Jewish. The opportunistic Kraenzlein went ahead and performed his winning leap on that day, although he had assured Prinstein that he would not compete then either. When Prinstein heard what had happened he punched Kraenzlein in the face.

The Americans housed the 1904 Olympics, in St Louis. These were held as an adjunct to the celebrated World Fair and turned out to be little more than a glorified American National Championships. Hardly any European athletes made the long and expensive journey to compete, so once again the Americans swept the board.

Emil Breitkreutz, who represented the USA in the 800 metres, described the eclectic nature of the entrants for the competitions: 'The two-man throwing contingent from Greece was supplemented by ten Hellenic hopefuls from the local Greek community, who entered for the marathon…Also in the marathon were two Africans who worked at one of the concessions.' The Africans were Len Tau and Jan Mashiani of the Tsuana tribe. They had been employed as runners in the Boer War. The concession to which Breitkreutz referred was in fact a mini-reproduction of the Boer War, with four or five hundred participants from the two sides recruited to re-create some of the battles they had fought in South Africa.

The two South African runners finished a creditable 9th and 12th. One of them, contemporary accounts are not clear which, might have done even better if he had not been chased off the course for some distance by two stray dogs.

The 1906 Athens Olympiad was something of an anomaly. The IOC had overreached itself by devising an intercalated series where every four years, half-way between the other Olympiads, there would be an Olympics held in Athens, as a tribute to the original Greek Games. The idea did not catch on, and although it was successful, the 1906 Athens meeting is generally considered an unofficial Olympics. The next Olympiad, to be held in 1908, would represent a return to the original four year cycle.

The 1908 Olympiad had originally been designated for Berlin, but prescient doubts were expressed by Germans about the expense likely to be incurred. The games were offered to Italy, Baron de Coubertin particularly enthused by the idea of a modern Olympiad being set against such an historic background. He said it could be recognised as 'an international homage to Roman antiquity'. However, arrangements got off to a bad start when two committees were formed and started bickering almost from the start. One of the committees was headed by Prince Colonna, the Lord Mayor of Rome and a member of an ancient aristocratic family. Its decisions were disputed persistently by a second organisation, called the Municipal Board, supervised by Count de San Martino. Both groups came under an almost continuous fusilade of sniping fire from the city of Milan, which considered itself 'the moral capital' of Italy and was jealous that Rome had been selected to host the Games. There were also complaints from the city of Turin, which regarded itself as the centre of national sport.

In some despair Coubertin, by now president of the International Olympic Committee, tried to take over the planning of the Rome Olympiad. For a year he lobbied the King and Queen of Italy, sought out potential sites, drew up budgets, attempted to raise funds and submitted hopeful but deferential papers to the Rome authorities. Unfortunately, the two committees were locked in such deadly internecine combat that its august members could spare no time for the French aristocrat's aspirations. The presidents of both boards left, but their successors merely continued the squabbles. Ominously, the Italian government constantly refused to contribute funds to their Olympiad.

By the time of the 1906 Athens Olympics, it was apparent to the exasperated Baron de Coubertin that a fresh locale would have to be sought for the 1908 Games. He reported as much to the IOC, which called a special meeting under the chairmanship of the Italian member of the committee, Count Brunetta d'Usseaux, an enthusiastic amateur rider and rower. Coubertin was not present at the discussions, which took place in Athens in April at the same time as the Games, but acting on his advice it was decided at that late date to take the Olympiad away from Rome and offer it to another city.

There were a number of influential Englishmen in the Greek capital for the intercalated Games and the IOC resolved to make an unofficial approach to Willie Desborough in the hope that the well-connected sportsman would like the idea of moving the 1908 Olympics to London. The networking to that end would begin from his berth on the *Branwen*.

It was the sort of challenge that the hyperactive Desborough loved. He immediately made contact with King Edward VII, who was still in Athens and was receptive to the idea. The monarch gave the peer permission to start the ball rolling, as long as it did not cost his government any money. The monarch reasoned that, after all, England was accustomed to organising such large-scale sporting events as Henley Royal Regatta and the All-England Lawn Tennis championships at Wimbledon. An Olympics tournament should not worry the redoubtable Willie Desborough.

Roused from its inertia by this development, the Italian government made the expected token protests about being deprived of the next Olympiad. Then its attention was diverted by the eruption of Mount Vesuvius. The volcano had been rumbling for some time, but on 7 April it exploded and continued to disgorge molten lava until the end of the month. Rocks and lava poured down the mountain's side in a bubbling molten river over a mile long and 500 feet wide. Black smoke and ash obscured the sky. Trees and vineyards were set alight. Small towns and villages on the fertile lower slopes were helpless before the inexorable progress of the threatening lava. Naples itself was scorched by the blast and houses in the city were destroyed. Hundreds of miles away in Paris, the volcano made its presence known as a yellow fog choked the streets of the French capital. Thousands of people in the vicinity of Naples fled from their homes or were evacuated by the government. Over the course of the dreadful month the official death count around the Bay of Naples rose to over 200.

Lord Desborough and his fencers had anchored in the Bay on their way to Athens, shortly after the eruption. Concerned, the party made a journey some way up Vesuvius. A subdued Theodore Cook reported, 'Soldiers were still taking out the mummified bodies of victims who had been caught in the last lara flow, looking exactly like the bodies we had seen in Pompeii of the victims of 1800 years before.'

For all its tragedy, the eruption provided the face-saving excuse for which Count Brunetta and his Italian colleagues had been hoping. It was announced officially that funds intended for the Rome Olympics were being diverted to the relief of the victims of the eruption in the Bay of Naples area and that Rome was reluctantly withdrawing from its patronage of the 1908 Games.

Lord Desborough had no trouble in recruiting the fellow-members of the British épée team on the *Branwen* to his banner. They espoused the cause vigorously and promised to do what they could to help. In fact, two years later, each one of them dutifully played his part in the London Olympics.

The remaining member of the 1906 épée team, Theodore Cook, who had been scraping a living as a freelance journalist for press agencies and writing a laboured rowing column under the nom de plume of *An Old Blue* in the *Daily Telegraph*, was released temporarily by the newspaper to represent fencing and became a member of the British Olympic Committee charged with the actual organisation of the London Olympiad. Cook was put in charge of a sub-committee supervising medals and decorations. Later, on behalf of his committee, he would write a pamphlet in the wake of the 1908 Games' controversy, refuting some of the major accusations of inefficiency levelled at its administrators: *The Olympic Games of 1908 in London: A Reply to Certain Charges Made by the American Officials.*

But all this lay in the future. In August 1906, Desborough set out on what would be a fraught and sometimes painful journey, which was to culminate in the 1908 London Olympiad. And at the time, following the obfuscation and petty-mindedness of the Olympic Italian experience, it seemed as if a bright new day might just be dawning for the IOC. As Coubertin later expressed it, perhaps a little too warmly, 'The curtain descended on the Tiber's stage and rose soon after on that of the Thames.'

Three

A Vision Of Dazzling Whiteness

'For a long time – many will think for too long – we have remained silent under the calumny and abuse which have been heaped upon the management of the Olympic Games.'

The Olympic Games of 1908 in London: A Reply to Certain Charges Made by the American Officials

The SS *Branwen* made a leisurely return to England via Ithaca, Corfu and Venice, where the fencers celebrated de Walden's birthday and then returned to London by different routes, enabling Lord Desborough to commence the not-insignificant task of organising the next Olympiad.

Theodore Cook, who was now committed to the cause and was to have a bird's eye view of proceedings throughout, wrote admiringly and with truth of the peer, 'Sheer force of personality and prestige enabled Lord Desborough to carry out a task which no one else could have attempted.' It was certainly undeniable that all through his life Desborough was someone who got things done. And there was much to accomplish.

First, enough money had to be raised to secure the building of a suitable stadium and cover the enormous running costs of the proposed London Olympiad. Upon his return to London from Athens, Lord Desborough remained true to British traditions: when in doubt, establish a committee. The British Olympic Association had been launched at a meeting in the House of Commons in the previous year, but at Desborough's instigation the British Olympic Committee was formed within that body. It was to have the sole purpose of organising the London Olympics and liaising with Baron de Coubertin and the International Olympic Committee. It had 38 members, representing the nation's different sporting bodies.

Coubertin was delighted to see the British apparently swinging into action so quickly. He had a soft spot for the country, having visited it on a number of occasions. His own views on the efficacy of physical education in schools had been influenced earlier by Thomas Hughes' novel *Tom Brown's Schooldays*, published in 1857. Coubertin embraced the full-blooded concept of God-fearing athleticism portrayed in the book, as summarised by the author's sturdy defence of individual combat:

> After all, what would life be without fighting, I should like to know? From the cradle to the grave, fighting, rightly understood, is the business, the real, highest, honestest business of every son of man. Everyone worth his salt has his enemies, who must be beaten, be they evil thoughts and habits in himself, or spiritual wickednesses in high places, or Russians, or border-ruffians, or Bill, Tom or Harry, who will not let him live his life in quiet till he has thrashed him.

Baron de Coubertin had also been impressed by the rapid growth of amateur athletics throughout the UK, starting with the first Oxford–Cambridge tournament in 1864 and reinforced by the foundation of the Amateur Athletic Association several years later and its subsequent rapid growth. A visit to Henley Regatta in 1888 had reinforced the baron's conviction that one day Britain would be ideally placed to host an Olympiad. He was particularly impressed by the rowing club's organisational structure. A core of committed workers powered the body, a second group was encouraged to devote their time to it, and a third carefully selected circle was put in place to contribute power and influence. De Coubertin was to adapt this composition sedulously when nurturing his embryonic Olympic movement

In 1905, even before Britain had been offered its Olympics, Coubertin had presented Lord Desborough with an Olympic Diploma of Merit. It was to encourage the peer, who was also a member of the IOC, in 'his great love of sporting achievement and his work in favour of sports development'.

With the British Olympic Committee (BOC) in place and William Desborough scurrying about everywhere using his contacts to publicise the Olympiad and move it forward, it was obvious that a talented and dedicated Secretary would be needed in order for the BOC to achieve its aims. The Reverend Robert Stuart de Courcy Laffan had been the Principal of Cheltenham College and was a friend and protégé of Baron de Coubertin. He was a pompous, ambitious man – he added the 'de Courcy' to his name with little apparent justification – but a workhorse and extremely gifted, especially as a linguist.

He was the son of Sir Robert Laffan, a professional soldier, and attended schools on the continent while his peripatetic father was engaged in various military engineering projects. He managed to develop a precocious gift for languages. At Merton College, Oxford, he obtained a First Class in Classical Moderations and BA, First Class, in Latin and Greek. He was ordained some years later. Laffan became a schoolteacher and a successful headmaster at King Edward VI School at Stratford-upon-Avon, where he more than doubled the school roll in seven years. In 1895, he accepted the post of Principal at the prestigious Cheltenham College. By then he was calling himself de Courcy Laffan.

It was not the successful career move that Laffan had anticipated and planned. At his previous school he had been a big fish in a small pond. At Cheltenham College he came into conflict with entrenched views and inviolable traditions. He did his best to modernise the school but met with obstructions from both the staff and the alarmed governors. To make matters worse, Laffan's wife Bertha made herself unpopular from the start. She was highly intelligent and was a successful and popular novelist, with such books as *Colour Sergeant, No 1 Company* and *A Garrison Romance*. For a time she had been on the editorial staff of the magazine *All the Year Round*, once owned by Charles Dickens and then taken over by his son. She was also tactless and something of a busybody. At King Edward VI School she had held sway; at Cheltenham, she soon found that she was fighting out of her class.

Matters came to a head when she tried to interfere in the running of the boarding houses at the college. The affronted and firmly entrenched housemasters were accustomed to a great deal of autonomy in the running of their fiefdoms. They were unwilling to allow even the Principal to have any say in the matter, let alone his outspoken wife. There were arguments, complaints and finally an unprecedented request for an official enquiry by the school governors.

Laffan tried to fight back on behalf of Bertha but found himself outmanoeuvred at almost every turn by Machiavellian pedagogues spoiling for a fight. As a final blow, his wife was even accused of contributing to the moral corruption of the pupils. In 1899, Laffan conceded defeat and resigned. Casting about for something else to do, he left teaching and became rector of St Stephen's at Walbrook in the City of London.

It was not the glittering promotion for which Laffan had been hoping, but fortunately he already had another string to his bow. Several years before his resignation he had attended the 1897 Congress of the International Olympic Committee in France. He was there as the representative of the Headmasters' Conference, the public schools' association. Although he was not an athlete, Laffan had caught Baron de Coubertin's eye at the assembly with a speech delivered at short notice in fluent French in which he stressed the importance of physical education in schools. Laffan then went up still further in Coubertin's estimation by delivering a rousing toast to France at the closing banquet.

The delighted baron went on record saying that he was convinced that 'a collaborator of the most invaluable quality has come down from the heavens to help us'. He invited the Principal to join the IOC. Laffan was already in trouble at Cheltenham and recognised a lifeline when he saw it. He accepted the baron's offer with gratitude and threw himself enthusiastically and energetically into the Olympic cause in Great Britain.

In 1904, Laffan made the arrangements for a meeting of the IOC in London. He attracted much favourable attention with its faultless organisation and his ability to arrange meetings for the representatives with such luminaries as the Prince of Wales and

King Edward VII. In the following year he helped form the British Olympic Association and became its Secretary to Lord Desborough's president. The two men undertook similar posts with the British Olympic Committee, and Laffan's new path as a leading sports administrator was marked out for him. He was to follow it for the next 30 years, until his death in 1927.

Laffan threw himself into the details of preparing for the Olympics. It was said that he wrote 11,000 letters for the cause. He certainly translated the rules of the Games into French and German. His most important contribution, however, was to conduct negotiations with the Franco-British Trade Exhibition to persuade its patrons to agree to the building of a new stadium for the Games. Both the 1896 and the 1904 Olympiads had been held as adjuncts to international trade fairs. Desborough and Laffan both appreciated that the aid of a similar commercial backer would be needed if London were to host the great sports meeting successfully.

Fortunately, one was at hand. As far back as 1905 the French Chamber of Commerce had been planning to celebrate the *entente cordiale* and strengthen Franco-British ties by building a great trade exhibition featuring the two countries in London. Officials of the BOC approached the Chamber of Commerce and made their pitch for the Franco-British Exhibition to finance the Olympiad to be held in the same year. To their surprise and delight the backers of the fair agreed to spend £44,000 on building a vast stadium and to make a donation of £2,000 to the committee's costs. In return the BOC would have to donate 75 per cent of the takings to the exhibition from the sports events held in the new arena. Desborough and Laffan knew a good thing when they saw one and agreed at once.

The fair was to be held on a recently purchased 140-acre patch of an agricultural estate at Wood Lane in London. The man selected to realise the project called it disparagingly 'a bit of farm land lying half-forgotten at the very doorstep of London'. The form that the exhibition would take and the shape of the proposed athletics stadium was not yet decided. Time was running out, but the exhibition organisers were not worried. They had done what any far-sighted proponents of spectacular events of the time would do. They had sent for Imre Kiralfy.

Kiralfy had the name of a villain in a John Buchan thriller, the obsessive determination of a hungry tiger, thick skin and the ability, if not to move mountains, then to manufacture facsimiles of them to order. He was an Austro-Hungarian born in 1845 in Pest, before it became Budapest. He was the oldest of seven children, his father in the clothing industry. He fell upon hard times and for some reason changed the family name from Konigsbaum. At the age of four, Imre Kiralfy went on the stage. For a decade he toured Europe as a boy actor, musician and conjurer with his siblings or as a solo act in third-rate travelling companies.

He stumbled inadvertently across his vocation in Paris in 1867, when he visited the International Exhibition. Kiralfy was entranced by the scope and variety of the exhibits but was convinced that he could make a far better display. He talked his way into being allowed to produce several fetes in Brussels and then journeyed to the USA, convinced that his future lay there. 'I saw instantly that the great popular want in America was spectacle,' he later wrote.

Always glib and self-confident, Kiralfy was able to persuade several producers to allow him to design magnificent scenes for such stage productions as Jules Verne's *Around the World in 80 Days*. Even this was too limiting for the eager Austro-Hungarian. He raised some money, borrowed the rest and leased an open-air site at Staten Island, New York. He caused a sensation there with historical productions like *The Fall of Babylon* and *Nero: the Burning of Rome*. There were over a hundred performers, most of them extras, in each of these lavish displays and their success made Kiralfy famous. Receptive to new ideas as long as they contributed to the spectacle, he had been one of the first to introduce electric lighting to Broadway in his production of *Excelsior*. The electrical components of the show had even been supervised by Thomas Edison, the great inventor himself.

Kiralfy was soon taken up by the elderly but still spry showman P.T. Barnum, who sensed a kindred spirit in the young and enthusiastic producer. The old man was impressed by the bustling Hungarian who refused to be deterred by any practical challenges presented by the problems of depicting scenes of burning cities and rushing waterfalls or even the discovery of America by Christopher Columbus.

Kiralfy worked in the USA for 25 years. Until they quarrelled he sometimes produced with his brother Boris. In 1892, he brought an awesome production of *Venice*, complete with canals, bridges, gondolas and a working glass factory, to Olympia in London. Having settled in England, he was approached to design the Franco-British Exhibition of Science, Arts and Industries in 1905.

The producer accepted eagerly, feeling that such a commission would elevate him from the ranks of mere showmen and bring him into contact with the aristocracy of both nations. Then, unusually, he began to have his doubts. He worried that such a commission was far beyond anything he had attempted before. He could not think of an approach for such an ambitious project.

In 1909, he told the editor of the *Strand* magazine how the idea finally came to him: 'One night I lay awake in bed and, as if by magic, I saw stretched out in my mind's eye an imposing city of palaces, domes and towers set in cool, green spaces and intersected by many bridged canals. But it had one characteristic, which made it strangely beautiful. Hitherto I had dealt in colour, in the shimmering hues of gold and silver. This city was spotlessly white.' It took Imre Kiralfy two years to realise his concept. In that time there were many problems. The main one lay in the actual building of the exhibition halls.

First, the marshy area had to be drained and then the buildings erected. The construction proceeded doggedly around the clock. More than 4,000 workers toiled on the site for long hours each day, with another 2,000 at night, The incessant noise and the lights turned the area into an inferno. It was rumoured that there were hundreds of accidents, some of them fatal, most of them covered up by the authorities determined to see the project succeed. There were timorous mutinies among the architects, objecting to the strict conditions imposed upon their creativity by the rigid Kiralfy. He issued steel outlines and permitted the architects to design only the plaster coverings for them.

Gradually, the brilliant white buildings began to emerge from the chaos. They were interspersed with lakes, fountains and caged displays of wild animals. Only France, Great Britain and their associated colonies were allowed to take part, but every display centre was filled. There was the Palace of Decorative Art, the Palace of Women's Work and the British Palaces of Industry. Britain organised the Ceylon and India Tea Houses and the French supplied a complete, inhabited Senegalese village. The British responded with the stereotypical Irish hamlet of Ballymaclinton. Among the rides were the Canadian Toboggan, the Scenic Railway and the Flip Flap. The latter consisted of two 150-feet counterpoised arms, which carried 50 visitors at a time 200 feet into the sky, giving them an incredible view of London. This was celebrated in a musical hall number called 'The White City Flip Flap Song'. It began: 'Good old London's image,/With its very latest craze...'

The song was taken up by a northern character singer and pantomime principal boy called Ella Retford. She had had a great success with her hit song 'I'm a Lassie from Lancashire', although subsequent efforts to broaden her range and occupy more exotic settings had failed with an over-ambitious followup effort called 'A Bungalow in Borneo'. 'The Flip Flap Song' was much more down-to-earth and suitable for her large and appreciative audiences.

Even the architects, with whom Kiralfy had had many quarrels during the construction process, admitted that the finished product was certainly spectacular. Writing in the *Architectural Review* of July 1908, Robert W. Carden said, 'By day it is a vision of dazzling whiteness, with its tiled court and plashing cool waters, its pointed arcades and latticed windows. At night it is equally effective with its thousands of lights and the rainbow colours of the cascade.'

Others were less complimentary. In an article in the *Manchester Guardian* a critic complained that the Court of Honour 'is neither French nor English, but Mohamedan-Hindu'.

Incredibly, the sports stadium was also completed on time. For the first time in such a large structure, steel tubes were used for the stands, reducing costs. A central area of turf was 700 feet long and 300 feet wide. On it lay a swimming pool, 100 metres long and 15 metres wide, marked out in lanes, with a diving tower which could be lowered. Unfortunately, no one had made any plans to clean or change the water and by the end of its first week in use the pool was decidedly murky and odorous. Competitors complained that they could not see more than six inches in front of them through the opaque water.

Pitches for soccer, rugby, hockey and lacrosse, however, were laid out meticulously. The entire patch of sward was surrounded by a running track which in turn was encircled by a cycling circuit. Finally, Imre Kiralfy was content with his efforts. To add to his delight, one of his sons, Edgar, was selected for the US 100 metres sprint team. Never one to under-use his employees or family members, Kiralfy also put Edgar and his two brothers to work to help decorate the stadium. When Edgar could get away from his duties in order to compete, he was eliminated when he came fourth in his heat.

The exhibition was opened by King Edward VII on 14 May 1908. It was not to close until October. In the intervening period more than eight million people attended. As the summer approached there was no doubt that the Franco-British Exhibition was going to be a triumph. There were high hopes that the accompanying Olympiad would be just as successful.

On the day that Edward opened the exhibition, the athletics track had been tried out by the Finchley Harriers, racing and jumping in the presence of the Prince and Princess of Wales. The athletes were impressed by the stadium, although the official reports mentioned that the rain had fallen pitilessly throughout the afternoon. The most promising result in these pre-Olympic trials came from the 5 feet 4 inches of Harold Wilson, who became the first runner in the world to complete the 1500 metres course in under four minutes. He returned a time of 3 minutes 59.8 seconds. A short time later the AAA gave the facilities of the White City an even harder workout by holding its annual championships there. A record entry of 254, including runners and jumpers from the British Empire and the USA, performed before a crowd of 22,000. It looked as everything was going to be in order for the big day.

There were occasional disasters. In August 1908, a soldier-of-fortune known as Captain Lovelace was about to embark upon a balloon flight from the White City when someone threw a lighted match on to the ground near the gas cylinders. The resultant explosion killed Lovelace's secretary and a male assistant, George Waite. The explosion caused a panic among the crowd and several were hurt in the resultant stampede for safety.

This did not prevent the crowds from continuing to flock to the exhibition. Lord Desborough and the other committee members hoped that the track and field section of the Olympics would be as popular. After all, as a current guidebook put it, 'Every effort is being made to make the gathering the greatest athletic meeting that has ever been held.'

The staff of *Outlook* magazine went even further, predicting optimistically, 'We have reasonable grounds for believing that the London games will help to dissipate causes of war, on the ground urged by the old class of schoolmaster that a round with the gloves was the best foundation of friendship.'

Were the boys at *Outlook* ever wrong!

Four

This Flag Dips To No Earthly King

'If by any unfortunate accident the American flag has been absent from the decorations of the Stadium, no-one would have regretted it more sincerely than members of the British Olympic Council.'

The Olympic Games of 1908 in London: A Reply to Certain Charges Made by the American Officials

Track and field events had been growing in popularity in Britain throughout the 19th century. Professional athletics had received a boost when aristocrats had started to match the fleetest of their servants for wagers against one another in the celebrated 'running footmen' races. The idea caught on with the sporting public at large and by the middle of the century, professional runners, known as pedestrians, or 'peds', were drawing large crowds in the larger cities. Walking races were also popular, with contestants seeing how much ground they could cover in 24 hours.

Further impetus was given to athletic sports with the arrival of a charismatic Native American runner known professionally as Deerfoot. His tribal name was Api-kai-ees and he was also known as Lewis Bennett. He was from the Siksika or Blackfoot tribe on the Cattaragus reservation in New York State. His running ability had been recognised at an early age and he was employed as an army courier delivering messages on foot from one fort to another in Alberta and Montana. After he had won $50 in a five-mile race at the Erie county fair, he was spotted by a professional racing consortium. Before long Deerfoot, as he became known, was racing all over the northeast of the USA

Much was made of the runner's ethnic background. He ran

stripped to the waist with a belt of feathers about his waist and a band containing a single feather around his head. As he ran he was encouraged to emit war whoops. His backers also devised a spectacular running style, consisting of powerful and dramatic surges from the back of the field.

In the 1860s, a British promoter called George Martin brought Deerfoot to Europe for a 20-month tour. It proved a great success. The athlete travelled with a group of four professional runners with a portable tent and a wooden track. Always on the road, Deerfoot would race several times a week. He won the majority of his races, usually over five and ten miles, and fast, if unconfirmed, times were claimed for him, including several world records. By the time Deerfoot left Britain to return home, professional athletics were to remain for some decades a popular and well-supported spectator-sport in Britain. It went into decline when corruption crept in and bookmakers took over. Heavy bets were laid on the results of races and professional 'ringers' were substituted for genuine amateurs, leading to some results being pre-arranged.

A dramatic example of this took place at the Lillie Bridge Stadium in Fulham, in 1887. A much-anticipated race between Harry Hutchens, who claimed the world sprint championship, and a fellow professional called Gent was called off after many spectators had taken their seats. It was rumoured that following long discussions between the two runners and their managers they had been unable to arrive at a decision as to which sprinter was to win. When the crowd heard that there was to be no race, the arena was almost wrecked.

Up until about 1875, national sports organisations were either non-existent or in their infancy. This meant that athletics and other games were in the hands of unsupervised individual entrepreneurs. The professionals did their best to run a closed shop, giving short shrift to local competitors. The full-time athletes made a practice of rushed starts at the beginning of races, bowling over less experienced competitors and getting into their stride long before the amateurs had recovered. In 1908, towards the end of the era of professional running as a major sport, full-time pedestrian Alfred R. Downer wrote of life on the paid Scottish circuit, 'The best known "peds" as a rule "stand-in" with one another, which means they agree to divide among themselves any prize money the school may win. The poor "locals" as a rule have to be content with what is left.'

Amateur athletics took over. The first tournament was held at the Royal Military Academy in Woolwich for its 'gentlemen cadets' of 1849. It was so successful that the following year a Captain Eardley-Wilmot presented a silver bugle in perpetuity for the young athlete winning the most events.

University athletics competitions were held, with considerable success, in tandem with the introduction of the competitions at Eton and other public schools which so impressed Baron de Coubertin.

For some time amateur athletics remained with the universities and public schools. In 1910, an American Rhodes Scholar writing in *Century* magazine, explained why, unlike in the USA, there was no danger of professionalism entering university athletics in Great Britain: 'It is because Oxford is not a university for poor men. It caters openly to a single class in society, the men of leisure and cultivation. A man who is an amateur athlete in England is enthusiastic enough about sport to pay for it and to pay heavily. It requires a comfortably-lined pocket to keep up one's end.'

Timekeeping records could be uncertain. In 1861, one of the fastest times for the 100 yards in Britain may have been set at the Oxford University Sports, when a Mr Poole from Trinity College was the winner by some distance. Yet newspaper accounts of the race merely gave the time vaguely as 'somewhat under ten seconds'.

The first athletics meeting between Oxford and Cambridge was held in 1864, when the 100 yards had been won in 10.50 seconds and the mile time was four minutes 50.0 seconds. The high jump was won with a 5 feet 5 inches leap and the 440 yards had been accomplished in 56.0 seconds.

The formation of the Amateur Athletic Association in 1880 and its subsequent regular open championships threw open the sport to everyone, but by the beginning of the 20th century, athletics at the highest level was in the main a middle-class sport. James B. Connolly, who had taken first place in the triple jump at the 1906 Olympic Games, wrote of the class distinctions in English athletics of the era, 'If your father wasn't a curate, or a barrister, or if he wasn't a brewer, or a wholesale dealer in jams, or in some way making his living off the Government, or if he did work with his hands for a living...be sure your entry won't be accepted.' However, the AAA recognised the pulling power of professional pedestrianism and put on its own tournaments in front of crowds approaching 20,000 at its Lillie Bridge ground.

Many athletes maintained a precarious amateur status. In an anonymous article, an Irish sprinter who represented Britain in the 1908 Olympics described how his potential had been spotted at 21 by bookmakers in his home country as early as 1906. They arranged for him to compete in handicap races all over the British Isles. The bookmakers subsidised him, allowed him to keep the under-the-counter payments he received for winning, usually in the region of ten or fifteen guineas and bought his trophies off him for an agreed price, usually about three pounds per cup. They also gave him a small cut of the money they made by betting on him to win or lose, whichever he was instructed to do. Eventually, he became too well known on the circuit. Promoters and rival bookmakers and trainers worked out that this athlete was capable of running a hundred yards in ten seconds and the 220 yards in 23 seconds and adjusted his handicap accordingly, so that he was starting off scratch and thus was of no more use to his erstwhile backers.

Timekeeping and recording was still a hit-and-miss affair. Even what constituted athletics events was open to some doubt. In *T.S. Andrews' World's Sporting Annual Record Book* of 1908, in addition to the usual sprints, jumps and longer races, were details of such events as fence vaulting with one hand, potato races, standing jump for distance with weights and one mile across tidal water with 25 turns. So many different sports were advocated for inclusion on the Olympic programme that *Punch* helpfully submitted its own list. It included swimming (one leg out of water), throwing the paper dart (Greek style) and quick shaving (both safety and danger razors).

However, in 1908 there was no doubt that Britain was ready to host the world's most ambitious athletics meeting to date and London was prepared for the influx of visitors about to descend upon the capital. With over six million inhabitants, it was twice the size of Paris and three times that of New York. The exchange rate was four dollars to the pound and it was ready to cash in on the international craze for sport.

The Olympiad was not alone in making money from sporting activities that year. In Sydney, Australia, on Boxing Day, Jack Johnson thrashed Tommy Burns to become the first black heavyweight champion of the world. In Britain, Manchester United won the first Football League Championship and England took part in its inaugural overseas internationals, defeating Austria 11–1 and 6–1 in Vienna. W.G. Grace played his last first class cricket match for the Gentlemen of England against Surrey, while future batting genius Jack Hobbs scored 83 runs in his first Test for England, but Australia still regained the Ashes. Signorinetta, a 100-1 outsider, won the Derby. As a forecast of the dreadful weather to come that year it snowed on Easter Monday. On a wider front, American explorer Robert Peary sailed for the North Pole, and in South America Butch Cassidy and the Sundance Kid engaged in their final, fatal shoot-out with the Bolivian army.

Back in England, as the opening date moved ever closer, the British Olympic Committee pressed on with its plans at its offices in Victoria Street, not far from the Houses of Parliament. There were teething troubles. One of Britain's leading athletics administrators, Charles Herbert, a civil servant who was a member of the IOC and Secretary of the Amateur Athletic Association, had started to assist Laffan assiduously. Unfortunately, in 1906 he fell from the top of a London omnibus, injuring his head so severely that he was forced to withdraw from all committee work.

The IOC at the Hague kept a close eye on progress but did not interfere too much. At a meeting in 1907 the committee endorsed the use of metric distances for track and field events. At the same assembly Baron de Coubertin was elected president for another ten years.

It was decided that the Games would take place over six months, from the end of April until the end of October. William Henry, the Honorary Secretary of the Lifesaving Society, was appointed Director of the White City Stadium. To commence the Games, racquets and tennis would be held at the Queen's Club in West Kensington and polo would be played at Hurlingham. More tennis would be played at Wimbledon, and shooting would follow at Bisley in July.

The aquatic sports in August would be divided, with rowing at Henley and powerboat races at Ryde and also in the Clyde and on Southampton Water. The home team was to be referred to as Great Britain and Ireland, but in most official and unofficial print it was usually called Great Britain.

An unwelcome distraction occurred at the beginning of 1908. The American Inter-Collegiate Amateur Athletic Association had the bright idea of holding a track and field competition between the best college athletes in the USA and a team of undergraduates from the British Empire. Crazily, the tournament was to be held at about the same time as the London Olympiad. The thought of two major competitions being held at the same time, perhaps even involving some of the same athletes, was too much even for someone of Desborough's phlegmatic nature. He wrote at once in a typically mollifying manner, saying that although the idea sounded very interesting it would not be possible to arrange it in the time available. He was then able to return his attention to more pressing problems.

The going was not always easy. With so many nations committing to enter the tournament in some strength, international divisions and rivalries had to be considered by the British Olympic Committee, some detailed by Theodore Cook: 'The British Empire itself was a slight stumbling block in 1908 to those who did not realise that Australia, Canada, South Africa, or India were just as much independent kingdoms as England herself. Then there was the usual Irish Question, reflected in the division of Finland from Russia, or of Hungary from Austria.'

Matters were not helped by the committee and its sub-committees being conducted on ad-hoc amateurish lines, with few notes or minutes taken. Hobby horses were vigorously ridden and many of the plans of action and explanatory diagrams offered up for study by the different sporting bodies proved quite unintelligible.

Suggestions for more serious events were coming in from all sides. Even Baron de Coubertin pressed for the inclusion of his own particular obsession, a forerunner of the modern pentathlon, in which competitors would take part in shooting, rowing, riding across an obstacle course, fencing and running a 4,000-metre cross country race. Not for the first time the baron was ahead of his time and it was not until the 1912 Olympiad that such a competition was included.

Another dream of the baron also failed to be realised. He wanted competitions in art, sculpture, music, architecture and literature held at the same time as the sporting events of the White City Olympics. He first floated the idea at the Fourth Olympic Congress in Paris in 1906, when he invited delegates to bring artists and writers with them in order to contribute to the discussion. 'Sport can bring joy only in a festive dress,' he declared, urging that the arts be combined with athleticism. He revealed plans for what he described as a marriage of muscle and mind.

Coubertin urged that the stadia to be used in 1908 should be based on the concept of ancient Greek gymnasia. Playwrights and novelists should produce drama and books on the theme of sport. Dance should be choreographed in an athletic fashion, both indoors and outdoors. Choirs should sing before and after athletics events. Relevant paintings and sculptures should enhance sports halls employed at the London Olympics.

Theodore Cook and his committee did their best to oblige. Although Coubertin and Cook got on so badly that the baron once referred to the Englishman with a shudder as 'that odious journalist', a special committee was formed.

Sir Edward Poynter ran the committee. He was 72 years old and president of the National Gallery. He had been born in Paris of English parents and for decades had been considered one of Britain's foremost artists and art administrators. He was famed for such massive, detailed paintings on classical themes as *The Meeting of Solomon and the Queen of Sheba, Israel in Egypt* and *Faithful Unto Death*. The last-named depicted a Roman soldier refusing to abandon his post as Pompeii is destroyed by one of the early eruptions of Mount Vesuvius. It had sold hundreds of thousands of prints. By the beginning of the 20th century, however, Poynter's themes and approach were beginning to be considered old-fashioned and out of date. The art critic of the influential *New York Times* winced that the elderly Englishman painted 'with scholarly correctitude rather than with charm'.

To the general public Poynter was better known as the husband of one of the gorgeous Macdonald girls. These were the four daughters of a humble Methodist minister, each of whom made an impressive marriage. Agnes married Poynter; Georgiana wed the famous pre-Raphaelite painter Sir Edward Burne-Jones; Alice became the mother of Rudyard Kipling; while Louisa's son was Stanley Baldwin, who was to become Prime Minister.

The brusque and self-contained Sir Edward was the first establishment person the British Olympic Committee turned to when it tried to put Baron de Coubertin's idea into practice. Almost from the start he put a brake on the proceedings. It had been Coubertin's hope that all entrants would be allowed to design their own subjects and submit them freely. Poynter would have none of it. Reluctant to abrogate responsibility, he felt that it would be much better if his august and conservative committee set the themes. This caused a great deal of time-consuming debate, as did the practicalities of transporting and displaying pictures and sculptures.

The key members of the art committee were G.S. Robertson, the thrower and scholar who had composed the ode delivered by King George at the first Athens Olympiad, and Theodore Cook. They were assisted by artists A.S. Cope and Thomas Brock. Cope was 50, a celebrated portrait painter who numbered King Edward

VII among his sitters. Brock was almost 60. He was a well-respected member of the Royal Academy and a sculptor responsible for statues of the actor Sir Henry Irving in Charing Cross Road and explorer Captain Cook in the Mall.

At the start of his career, Brock worked in the studio of an Irish sculptor, John Henry Foley. Foley caught a chill and died while working on a section of the Albert Memorial in Hyde Park and left many commissioned pieces unfinished. On his death Thomas Brock completed most of them, thus establishing himself artistically and commercially in his own right.

Carefully, almost laboriously, the committee selected the Olympic subjects in which writers, artists, sculptors and architects were to compete. One of the painting competitions was for a sketch of a frieze 10 feet long by 4 feet wide, depicting either a triumphal procession or the battle between the Greeks and the Amazons. There was a sculpture competition with the same themes. A second painting competition gave entrants the chance to select a modern football match, an ancient classical discus thrower or the wrestling match between Hercules and the Libyan giant Antaeus. In architecture, contestants were to submit designs for a swimming pool, a gymnasium and a sports hall.

But the committee moved so ponderously that at length Coubertin despaired. Fearing the worst, in February 1908 he wrote plaintively to the Reverend de Courcy Laffan that, 'the art competitions have completely disappeared from the programme'. Laffan and his colleagues were too busy with the minutia of the administration of the sports events to have much time to devote to arts and crafts. The preparation for an arts Olympiad was therefore shelved and later handed over to the organisers of the 1912 Stockholm Olympics, who made much better use of the framework provided by the London administrators.

Back with the sports, there were many problems with entries, especially from the USA. The closing date for all competitor paperwork was 12 June. The Americans asked for an extension, pointing out that their track and field trial events were to be concluded on 6 June. A stay was reluctantly permitted by the BOC, but in the event some of the details were not submitted until just before the opening ceremony, causing even more chaos in the committee's offices.

Some ideas fell by the wayside. There was a plan to present a cup to the most successful overall nation in the Olympics, but it was decided that drawing up a system of scoring agreeable to all parties would be very difficult. The suggestion, wisely as it was to turn out, was dropped.

There were also flashes of lucidity, even if they were not always acted upon. Theodore Cook protested against the proposal to have the flags of all the nations on display at the White City as this would promote nationalism and be contrary to the spirit of the Games, but he was outvoted. Other members were concerned about the possibility that the Games might not be well attended, wondering whether the British public would actually pay money to see Hungary play the Netherlands at football. A Greek official also suggested the formation of an international Jury of Appeal for the Games, in case the judges on the spot disagreed. He was outvoted.

Pressing on doggedly, by 1907 the IOC had approved the programme steered into place by Desborough and Laffan. The popular track and field events would be held at the White City Stadium between 13 and 25 July. The Games would end in October, with the finals of the association football, rugby, hockey, lacrosse, skating and boxing.

The conservative committee gave way to the IOC on some matters, such as reluctantly agreeing to their insistence on metric distances in each event and rejecting equestrian events, but it was adamant that only the host nation should provide the judges for each event. It was already becoming obvious that the entries would exceed those for any other Games of the modern era. Accordingly the committee agreed that, for the first time, numbers of competitors for each event would be restricted and that athletes would have to be sponsored by their national Olympic committees. The organisation of each individual sport in Britain would be left to the national bodies concerned.

Ticket prices at the White City Stadium were steep. A seat in an upper row was two shillings and sixpence and one with a better view fetched a guinea. A seat in a box for the Opening Ceremony would cost as much as eight guineas (£8 8s.) and this was at a time when a miner or cottonworker would be lucky to earn a little over £2 per week. Magnanimously, the committee decided to charge only sixpence for standing room for the plebians.

A lack of funds was beginning to worry Lord Desborough and his colleagues. They had approached all their wealthy friends and still there was not enough available to provide hospitality for the thousands of athletes and officials. Almost in despair, the peer approached Lord Northcliffe, the proprietor of the *Daily Mail,* and begged him for assistance. Like so many others Northcliffe was reluctant to become involved, but eventually agreed to make an appeal for funds in the pages of his newspaper. It was surprisingly successful: £10,000 was raised in the first week. Donations ranged from a few shillings to a munificent £1,000 subscribed by professional strong man Eugen Sandow, who already that year had given £1,500 to help the explorer Shackleton fit out an expedition to the Antarctic.

There was some criticism for the lateness of the call for financial assistance. *Punch* magazine agreed tongue-in-cheek with one correspondent, 'The appeal for funds for the entertainment of foreign competitors in the Olympic Games is, as you say, a little sudden and hasty, seeing that the authorities must have guessed, several years ago, that somebody was sure to want to come and compete.' Altogether, unofficial estimates put the eventual total cost of the first London Olympiad as a little over £80,000.

Britain was not the only nation struggling to find backing for its athletes. The Italian Olympic Committee succeeded only in getting the loan of a few coal ships from its country's navy to convey sports kit to London. A belated offer from the Ministry of War of 20,000 lire to help with the horse-racing events was withdrawn in disgust when it was discovered that there were to be no such competitions in London.

It paid to be adaptable. Richard Weisz, the gigantic Hungarian weightlifting champion and all-round strength athlete, discovered that his major sport was not being represented in London.

Undeterred, he entered the Graeco-Roman wrestling competition and won the heavyweight gold medal without breaking into a sweat.

Laffan and Desborough spent many hours pondering over the matter of nationalism at the Games. They knew that Irish competitors would object to being part of the British team and that the Finns hated their conquerors the Russians. Other differences could be settled by negotiation, like allowing the Commonwealth nations to compete as autonomous nations. The two organisers also had to exert all their diplomacy to persuade Bavaria and Saxony to compete as part of Germany.

There was much discussion over the continuing vexed matter of professionalism, which had different connotations among the nations. It was some time before the *New York Times* could announce that 'the threatened trouble over the interpretation of the amateur rule with France has been satisfactorily adjusted'.

Some athletes tried to take matters into their own hands. Two Irish jumpers, Con Leahy and Dennis Murray, who were visiting New York, tried in vain to represent the USA at the Games. The British Olympic Committee replied in short order that Leahy and Murray must compete for Britain unless they took out US citizenship before the competition got under way. Leahy had won a gold medal in the 1906 Athens high jump event and Britain was unlikely to allow him to defect without putting up a struggle.

Canada somehow raised £20,000 to send more than 80 athletes to London. Australia and New Zealand were competing under the banner of Australasia. Their team was equally hard up and its members had to resort to ingenious stratagems in order to take part. The Australian Olympic Committee told its athletes that as long as they had attained a decent standard in their sports, preference would be given to those who could pay their own fares to Britain or who were already living in that country.

The Australians asked all-round amateur athlete Reginald 'Snowy' Baker, on a boxing tour of Europe, to represent the country not only in boxing but also at swimming and diving. In an act of some desperation, he was also offered the position of reserve scrum half for the rugby team, but refused. The Australian rugby team, the Wallabies, had already arranged a tour of Britain, so as an afterthought the side was entered for the Olympics in October. As a final pragmatic gesture all Australian and New Zealand athletes in London were summoned to a meeting at the Polytechnic Institute in London just before the start of the Games, so that their final entries could be decided.

All over the host country, trials were held to pick the team for the Games. By 12 July, the track and field teams had been selected. At the same time a number of sporting events were held in the newly completed stadium to test it out.

As preparations continued for Games which Baron de Coubertin hoped would engender a spirit of peace and harmony among nations, it was beginning to become apparent that the reverse was going to be the case. For most nations the White City Games were to be a battlefield, a test of national resolve and ambition. The tone was set when *The Times* of 10 June reported on a meeting of the French delegation to London: 'General Picquant, Minister of War, who was present, congratulated the team and wished it good luck.

'Subsequently, the Minister, amid cheers, made a speech in which he said that the efforts of all the young men of the gymnastic societies would be in vain were not the eyes of those young men always fixed on the flag which was the symbol of the Fatherland, the symbol of all the sacrifices France had a right to demand of her children.'

Equally strongly, a British guide book specifically designed for tourists in London in 1908 pointed out, 'American Ladies will find it greatly to their advantage and cheaper to shop in Free Trade England rather than High Protection France where Heavy Duties are charged. Save 20 to 30 per cent by buying in London, and where business is conducted in our mother tongue.'

Not only the French were regarded as potential rivals. Those few organisers who were not totally immersed in their adminis-trative tasks were also starting to realise that the burgeoning hostility between the host nation and the USA was to be contested on the athletic tracks and sports fields. Britain had been the world's leading industrial and trading nation since the industrial revolution, a hundred years earlier, but by the time of the Games, it was being challenged by the emerging might of the USA and this would be played out on the field of competition. A warning shot had been fired in *Outing* magazine as early as 1907, when the editor issued a hint that the USA's chief athletic administrator for the Games was not to be underestimated: 'Sullivan is a great AAU president, who not only sees right, but has the courage to fight for it.'

He was at the head of a sporting movement that was fast developing. American track and field athletics had been developing since 1876, when Harvard and Yale began to compete against one another, and the New York Athletic Club began its annual tournaments to decide the championships of the USA. Standards had improved immensely and, going into the White City tournament, US athletes held a number of world records. A close contest between the two nations was envisaged.

Sullivan announced that regional competitions would be held in the east, west and south of the country, the winners to compete against each other for a place in the side. Entrants paid $2 to take part. Almost as an afterthought, he said that the individual sporting bodies would all be asked to nominate candidates for all the events, 'even cycling, fencing, rowing and wrestling'.

The resultant tournaments produced encouraging results for the United States' administrators. At the competition held for the eastern states athletes at Franklin Fields, Philadelphia on 7 June, A.C. Gilbert set a new world record for the pole vault with a jump in excess of 12 feet 7 inches, while Martin Sheridan broke the world record for the freestyle discus throw. Not all Americans appreciated Sullivan's stranglehold on the sport. His lawyers threatened to sue the *New York Telegraph* if it persisted in accusing Sullivan of corruption within the sport he controlled with such an iron hand.

Meanwhile, James Sullivan declared that he would introduce a bill in Congress requesting a grant of $100,000 to cover the expenses of sending a team to Great Britain. He rejected as fanciful, however, a suggestion that the US Navy provide a battleship in which to convey the competitors and officials, as such vessels 'are not built to accommodate excursion parties but for the necessity of possible sterner use'.

Most of the American track and field athletes left from New York on 27 June on the SS *Philadelphia*. They worked out on the deck during an uneventful voyage, and gave displays of gymnastics for the other passengers. One competitor defeated a member of the ship's crew in a race up a mast. The vessel was delayed for 16 hours by fog and there were no members of the Olympic welcoming committee on hand when the *Philadelphia* eventually docked at Southampton.

On 9 July, a week before the opening ceremony, the *Oakland Tribune* said, 'The greatest athletics meet of the last decade will start at London next Monday, when King Edward will inaugurate the Olympic Games in the English capital...America's prospects of winning the Olympic championship in track and field are now brighter than ever.'

Theodore Cook was slightly alarmed by the eagerness for combat being displayed by the other nations. He put their enthusiasm down to a lack of international experience, explaining it away by pointing out condescendingly, 'They have no Henley, no Lords, no Bisley, no St Andrews.'

Welcoming banquets and receptions for all sides were hosted by Lord Desborough and the Reverend de Courcy Laffan, who must have hoped that the worst of their problems were now over. The competitors were officially welcomed at the Grafton Gallery and on 24 July, 700 representatives of the athletes and officials were entertained at the Holborn Restaurant. The Lord Mayor also gave a reception at the Mansion House for a thousand guests, receiving them in the Egyptian Room. Some comment was caused when a number of athletes turned up there in flannel trousers and other items of casual attire, but the Germans and Swedes redressed the situation by attending in full uniforms, while most of the officials were in morning dress.

Those who could afford it sampled the nightlife of the city. The music halls played to capacity. Stars such as Marie Lloyd, Gus Chevalier, George Robey and Chirgwin, 'the white-eyed Kaffir', were earning £200 a week, while the Scots entertainer Harry Lauder drew in £250 a week and could command a fee of £100 for a 30-minute appearance at a private party. At the Palace Theatre American dancer and sex-manual writer Maud Allan was to play to packed audiences for 18 months with her *Vision of Salome*, in which it was rumoured among impressionable young male theatre-goers that beneath some flimsy veils she was stark naked.

There was no Olympic Village. Athletes were mainly housed in hotels and boarding houses in the London area. The American officials may have considered the bright lights of the city to be too tempting for red-blooded young athletes. Iconoclastic from the start, they made some of their charges stay in Brighton 60 miles away and be put up overnight in the capital before their events. Coach Mike Murphy, assuming control, announced that not all the American athletes would take part in the opening ceremony, as he wished to provide special training for a selected few. Because of the stream of peevish complaints soon to emanate from the American headquarters it was dubbed Camp Dissension.

Before long, a stream of carefully selected but unsubstantiated news releases were being issued from the south coast as to the high state of readiness among the US competitors. Sprinter James Rector was declared to be in the condition of his life, if a trifle nervous. Pole vaulter A.C. Gilbert was said to have broken the world record in training, while high jumper H.C. Porter, it was announced, was clearing six feet with ease in his training efforts.

The runners were based at Brighton in the charge of Matt Halpin and trainer Mike Murphy, while the throwers, wrestlers and swimmers remained in London with James Sullivan, where the training facilities were more advanced. The London-based athletes probably had the best of it, for they were allowed to look after themselves. Those stationed on the south coast had a tougher regime under the ever-watchful Mike Murphy. The sprinters trained daily at the Brighton football ground. Brighton was then in the First Division of the Southern League, but conveniently the football season was over. The American marathon runners covered ten miles before breakfast daily. Smoking and drinking were forbidden.

The suspicious American officials were soon complaining. They objected vehemently to the proposed system of points allocation for the unofficial overall team championships. The BOC had decreed that points would be allocated for positions in all the sports, not just the track and field events.

The Americans pointed out that most of their efforts were concentrated on running, jumping and throwing. In the *New York Times* of 17 July, James E. Sullivan protested about the matter, 'We came here, as we went to Paris and Athens, with a field team, and are making a fight in the field events, caring nothing for other sports. We asked that the championship trophy be put up for the field sports separately, but this request was not acceded to.'

Desborough and his fellow committee members refused to countenance the idea. Then, with the day of the opening ceremony almost upon them they were faced with a more urgent matter. When the first American officials entered the arena they were faced by a host of flags representing the participating nations. There were even the banners of China and Japan on display and these countries had not entered the tournament. But what emphatically was not being flown were the Stars and Stripes.

Actually, the Swedish flag was not on display either, but the representatives of that country were a little more understanding of the oversight. The sensitive American officials, by contrast, suspecting a deliberate slight, went berserk. Recriminations and counter-recriminations flew about like confetti at a wedding as the furious Americans made their verbal onslaughts on the committee. Willie Desborough was produced to pour oil on troubled waters but even his legendary charm could not placate James E. Sullivan and his cohorts. At one point an effort was made to place the blame on the designer of the stadium, Imre Kiralfy, but the Austro-Hungarian was too old a dog to accept any responsibility, stating smoothly that a minor functionary must have been responsible for any unfortunate mistake.

Matters were not helped when one of the BOC committee

members, in a misguided effort to look on the bright side, pointed out that at least the Americans had been provided with a borrowed flag behind which they could march into the stadium. Before anyone could actually lynch the well-meaning official, it was announced that King Edward VII and his family were approaching the White City and that the official march past would soon begin. The Americans were assured that their national flag would be erected among the others in the arena as a matter of urgency. Grumbling massively the athletes and officials began to get into position in the dressing rooms capable of holding 2,000, although the matter was not yet over.

King Edward, his wife Queen Alexandra and their children had travelled from Buckingham Palace in a horse-drawn carriage. The hedonistic monarch was quite looking forward to the ceremony. Earlier *The Times* had obsequiously announced, 'There is no-one living more fitted to open and in one sense preside over the fourth Olympiad than King Edward the Peacemaker.' The royal party entered the stadium some time after 3.30pm and took their places in the royal box by 4.00pm, where they were joined by members of other European royal families, including King George of Greece and King Haakon of Norway, together with noblemen and peers and representatives of all the participating nations. Lord Desborough made a brief speech in which he expressed the hope that the friendly competition engendered by the Olympic Games would strengthen the cordial relations among the nations of the world. The peer then approached the King and asked, 'Will your Majesty graciously declare the Olympic Games opened?'

In return the British monarch did just that, parroting briefly, 'I declare the Olympic Games of London open!'

A bugler gave a signal and the gates to the competitors' quarters flew open. The march-past began. It was the first Olympiad at which the contestants had paraded as teams behind their national flags. This was an excellent idea, which was retained for subsequent Olympic ceremonies.

The administrators may have been dubious about admitting women to the London Olympics, but the crowds on the opening day seemed all for it. A number of newspapers commented that the biggest cheer at the march-past had been reserved for the members of the Danish women's gymnastic team, who were scheduled to give a demonstration out of competition with female British gymnasts at the White City. The *Daily Mail* leered, 'The very appearance of the young ladies as they stepped into the arena in their neat cream costumes and golden-brown stockings captivated every eye.'

It was too good to last. All too soon, the impressive procession was to become a symbol of the controversies that were to follow for the next fortnight and beyond at the White City Stadium. As the athletes filed into the stadium and took up their positions on the turf, the Americans were still seething with discontent about the absence of their flag among the others in the stadium. Finland, controlled by Russia, had been refused permission by the Russians to march behind its own flag and had been ordered to parade under the Russian banner. The athletes refused to do so and walked as a separate body, with no flag at all, although there were reports that somewhere among the athletes someone was waving the flag of a Helsinki gymnastics club. The Russians were watching developments very carefully and Baron Rheinhold von Willebrand, the recently elected Finnish member of the IOC, had to use all his diplomatic skills to prevent an overt break between the two nations as the Games progressed.

Irish athletes had been ordered to compete as members of the British team. To mark their resentment a number of them boycotted the opening ceremony, while the rest marched a little apart from the main United Kingdom contingent. Symptomatic of the privileged times, the British contingent was led by a Cambridge and an Oxford blue and a former member of the Eton rowing eight. The Germans and Austrians were dressed in navy blue and the Swedes and Norwegians wore white flannels and singlets.

Some much-needed light relief was provided by the appearance of the Australasian team in the line-up. The 27 Australians and three New Zealanders marched behind their flag-bearer, the New Zealander Henry St Aubyn Murray. He had already won the New Zealand 440 yards hurdles championship on three occasions and was to do so twice more. While most of the other teams were wearing well-cut athletic uniforms, the completely unsubsidised Australasians looked more like a rag-tag-and-bob tail outfit.

Efforts had been made to supply a uniform for the occasion but obviously the clothing ordered had not reached the athletes from the tailors. Some contestants were wearing t-shirts and shorts, while others were in swimming costumes. Most were wearing ill-fitting caps. One newspaper account described them as looking 'impoverished'.

But the worst was yet to come. As the teams had filed past the royal box, each standard-bearer had dipped his nation's flag to King Edward, who was taking the royal salute. When it came to the turn of the US group, the standard-bearer, a gigantic Irish-American shot-putter called Ralph Rose, made no effort to lower the flag he was carrying.

There were horrified gasps from those spectators who had noticed the slight, followed by delighted raucous laughter from those Americans in the crowd who were aware of the missing Stars and Stripes in the stadium and guessed that this was payback time. The procession continued but almost everyone in the stadium was now discussing the insult just paid to the sovereign. Whether some of the American athletes and officials had got together to discuss the possibility of refusing to acknowledge the English king, or whether the idea was Rose's alone, has never been ascertained.

The strength athlete was an independent man and as an Irishman fiercely anti-British. He had been expelled from his university for rowdy behaviour. It might have been Rose's unaided idea to keep the banner upright, but it certainly met with the approval of the majority of the US team.

After the ceremony, another example of this belligerent attitude of the now-inflamed United States team entered Olympic folklore. Newspaper reporters of all nations were scurrying around the arena trying to get follow-up stories to the refusal of the Americans to dip their flag. They noticed many members of the US team shaking Rose by the hand and patting him on the back. A rumour emerged, never validated, but eagerly taken up as time passed, that Martin Sheridan, another Irish-American member of the US team, a New York policeman and a famed hammer thrower, had condoned Ralph Rose's action by growling, 'This flag dips to no earthly king!' Few challenged anything Sheridan said. He was tough enough to be the Governor of New York state's personal bodyguard whenever that worthy visited New York City.

Gustavus Town Kirby, an official American observer at the Games, tried to play down the reaction of the athletes, pointing out that more than 50 of the 83 athletes in the parade were either students at or graduates of universities and as such would certainly have known how to behave in such circumstances.

Whatever the truth of the situation, the pattern had been set for the rest of the London Olympics. Within minutes of the ending of the ceremony, two Americans, two Britons, a Frenchman, a Norwegian, a Hungarian, a Canadian and a Dutchman responded to the gun for the start of the first heat of the 1500 metres. The swimming pool burst into scurrying life with its first swimmers and divers. The cyclists appeared on their track. A gymnastics team started an exhibition in the centre of the stadium. The 1908 Olympiad track and field events had begun. Over the next fortnight there were to be some outstanding athletic and sporting performances returned, but with the opening ceremony over it was a regrettable fact that the serious business of taking offence and expressing grievances could also gather momentum.

Five

Preamble With Racquets And Rifles

'Before the stadium sports began, American victories had been scored in court tennis, the national rifle teams, the revolver teams, and the running deer double shot.'

The Olympic Games of 1908 in London: A Reply to Certain Charges Made by the American Officials

The London Olympics had commenced sedately several months before the official opening ceremony with a number of esoteric sports practised mainly by the well-to-do middle and upper classes. They drew small numbers of entries and hardly more abundant audiences. The events were scattered mainly over the suburbs of London and the dull, damp heaths of Surrey.

The first sport to be held was racquets, a forerunner of what became squash racquets and then just plain squash. In Britain the sport was the preserve of a few public schools and the older universities. Courts were few and far between, and the clubs owning them were exclusive to the point of fastidiousness in their membership. The sport was hardly known in the USA. In 1907 there had been only two public racquets courts in the country, one in Philadelphia and the other in Boston. As a result, there were only seven entrants, all of them British and even these were not the pick of the crop.

The official Olympic report commented disapprovingly, 'Unfortunately, so many players scratched or failed to make an appearance that the competition lost much of its importance.' Perhaps this was because that at racquets the English gentleman-amateur tradition still persisted. One absentee was Edgar Baerlein, a noted racquets player. He had won the British amateur championship in 1903, 1905 and 1908 and was to win it again on a number of occasions. He did not enter the London Olympics because, as he later told *The Observer*, 'I'd just won our racquets championships and the Olympic entry was virtually the same. In the circumstances, for me to take part would just have looked like a silly bit of pot-hunting.'

His absence left the door open for some of the players Baerlein had hitherto been defeating with ease. The singles title was won by Evan Noel, an old adversary of Baerlein. He won two matches without losing a set and then had a walkover in the final when his opponent was injured. He also won a bronze medal in the gentlemen's doubles, which was won by Vane Pennell and the wealthy American John Jacob Astor. Evan Noel later became secretary of the Queen's Club, the venue for the tournament. The tournament was the end of racquets as an Olympic event, the official report commenting sadly that as the sport was such a minority, it probably should not be included in future programmes.

The tournament would have attracted little public interest at the best of times, but in April of that year it was completely overshadowed in the newspapers by reports of a naval tragedy off the coast of the Isle of Wight. Two vessels of the Royal Navy, HMS *Tiger* and HMS *Berwick* collided with the deaths of 35 men.

Back at the Olympics, the Queen's Club also housed the indoor or covered tennis championships. With a total of six competitors, this event had even fewer in the men's singles than had racquets. There were, however, two representatives from Sweden to leaven the home-grown players. The gold medal was won by Arthur Gore of Great Britain, a 40-year-old veteran whose father Spencer had won the first Wimbledon singles championship. Arthur was a late developer, causing *Sandow's Magazine* of 1899 to write, 'for certainly 12 or 14 years he has held a consistent if not lofty place in the second or third group of players and probably no one imagined that any higher lot was reserved for him. Last year, however, he suddenly sprang into the first class, and it is no exaggeration to say that this year, if one may regard skill alone and disregard staying power, he stands absolutely at the top of the tree.'

After winning the covered courts men's doubles with H. Roper

Barrett, Gore went on to win the Wimbledon singles final in 1901 and 1908 and was to triumph again in 1909. He entered the Wimbledon championships every year from 1888 until 1927.

Dolly Lambert Chambers won the ladies' singles. She had to play three matches in her half of the draw to get that far, albeit without losing a set, while her opponent in the final, Alice Greene, had seen everyone except herself falling out of the competition in her section of the draw without playing a game. In spite of her long journey to the final, Dolly Lambert Chambers was much too strong for her opponent.

There was a break of a few days before the outdoor tennis events were held at Wimbledon. During this period the annual Wimbledon Tennis Championships were held.

A.W. Gore won the men's singles, Mrs A. Sterry won the ladies' singles, and M.J. Ritchie and the popular New Zealander Tony Wilding won the men's doubles. At the same time, London and other parts of England experienced a natural phenomenon that was to replace sport on the front pages of newspapers.

From 30 June, people began to notice red glows in the sky at night. A letter to *The Times* described them as having the appearance of a dying sunset which grew in intensity between 11.00pm and 2.30am. The resemblance to a false dawn was so great that birds began to sing at about 1.45am. Other reports confirmed this unnatural light and there was great speculation as to its cause. It is possible that the disturbance was caused by the descent in a remote forested, uninhabited area of Siberia of a meteorite weighing hundreds of thousands of tons. The resultant flash could be seen 250 miles away and the sky was lit much further.

Back on earth there was a better turnout for the Olympic outdoor tennis men's singles event than there had been for the indoor events, but the standard was still low. The Olympic report noted, 'New Zealand only heard of the Olympic Tournament from the Lawn Tennis Association of Australasia at too late a date to nominate their players.' The report also suggested that the Olympic tournament had been held too close to the date of the Wimbledon championships, which had attracted many of the better players.

Lawn tennis had been losing popularity for some years. It had never been particularly fashionable in the public schools and universities and a lack of public courts effectively barred working-class players, who were largely unable to find an entry fee combined with an annual subscription of several guineas. The game depended for its existence on the whims of an increasingly fickle, suburban middle class.

In 1899, H.W.W. Wilberforce, a former Wimbledon champion, wrote, 'There are some people who, at the beginning of every season, agitate themselves rather unnecessarily with regard to the position of lawn tennis; they see that fashionable crowds no longer flock to tournaments, in the neighbourhood of London at any rate, and they cry out, some in despair, some in exultation, that the game is doomed.'

Even Arthur Gore, who had won the indoor singles, did not bother to travel over to Wimbledon for the outdoor Olympic event. In his absence the gold medal went to Josiah Ritchie, who had played a great deal on the continent and had won the German singles championships on several occasions. He was 38 at the time of the London Olympics. In the final he came up against the dynamic and exciting 24-year-old German Otto Froitzheim. The latter had attracted interest when he defeated J.C. Parke, a former Irish and European singles champion and current Irish rugby international. Earlier in the year Parke, who played for Monkstown, had kicked one penalty in his country's losing game against England and another when Ireland defeated Scotland. In the rain, Froitzheim won a game of tennis the official report described as 'the singles match of the week, if not the match of the year'.

An interesting final was expected between veteran Ritchie and the young German. However, Froitzheim was either overcome by the occasion or simply adopted the wrong tactics. He played long-distance from the baseline, a strategy at which Ritchie excelled. The official report said, 'It was by no means an exhilarating match, and it was a positive relief sometimes to see Ritchie desert the back of the court and bring off a smart cross-volley, an occurrence, however, which was none too frequent.' Ritchie won the gold medal 7–5, 6–4.

Gladys Eastlake-Smith won the women's final title out of an entry of seven, some two days before she got married and thus became eligible to enter the soon-to-be-discontinued married doubles championship.

The men's doubles event was won by two English players who had perhaps seen better days. George Hillyard was 44. He had taken up tennis at a relatively late age when he married an established player. He displayed an immediate flair for the game and won the men's doubles at Wimbledon on four occasions. At the Olympics he could have been forgiven for seeming a little distracted. Not only was he Secretary of the All-England Club at Wimbledon, but for the purposes of the Olympic tournament he was also acting as honorary manager and a member of the committee in charge.

His partner in the final had also been a considerable player before being afflicted by poor health. Reggie 'Big Do' Doherty had been Wimbledon men's singles champion on four con-secutive occasions. At the 1900 Paris Olympics, he took gold in the men's doubles, with his brother Laurie and also in the mixed doubles. He had been drawn against Laurie in the semi-finals of the singles, but had withdrawn to allow his sibling to go through and win the gold medal. By 1908, he was not a well man but still was fit enough to help Hillyard defeat Josiah Ritchie and James Parke in the final.

If racquets had been an obscure sport, *jeu de paume* was positively recondite. Originally played by hitting a ball with the hand, it had evolved into another racquet sport played on a court and it involved a complicated set of rules. The game was also known as real tennis, royal tennis and court tennis. Said to be the sport of kings, it had not brought monarchs much luck. Louis X of France, known as Louis the Quarreller, died of a chill after a game in 1316, if he had not in fact, as some insisted, been poisoned. Charles VIII of France was in such a hurry to enter his court in 1498 that he struck his head on the low lintel of the entrance, killing himself. Fifty years earlier James I of Scotland would have escaped an assassination attempt had he been able to escape down a drain that unfortunately had been blocked to prevent loss of tennis balls.

The 1908 Olympic final was played between the American scion of a railway robber baron and a British health food fanatic. Jay Gould was the 19-year-old grandson of the famous railway financier of the same name who had amassed a personal wealth of $75 million by his corrupt business practices and had been responsible for the celebrated Black Friday of 1869, when he had attempted to corner the gold market and in the process caused a financial meltdown. He was said to have been completely indifferent to the fact that he was the most hated man in the USA in 19th-century America.

Jay's son took over the empire which included the Denver and Rio Grande Western Railroad and the Western Pacific Railroad. By the use of the courts rather than bribery and intimidation, George Gould had maintained the family fortune and had built a magnificent mansion called Georgia Court at Lakewood, New Jersey. Here he had built a *jeu de paume* court and brought in some of the leading amateur and professional players to coach his son in the arts of the game from an early age. With such a background and with so much spare time in which to perfect his game Jay Gould became the US champion on 18 occasions between 1906 and 1925, with time out only for the war years of 1917 and 1918.

His opponent in the 1908 Olympic final was Englishman Eustace Miles, an enthusiastic nutritional reformer who marketed his own brand of health supplements, a powder containing dried milk and cereals. A fitness magazine admiringly calling Miles a nutritional artist and philosopher, extolling the value of his product: 'The basis of the foods he has evolved is Emprote, which stands For Eustace Miles Protein, a special mixture of body-building energy foods, in which is incorporated many tasty and sustaining products.'

Miles was also a productive and eclectic author, with many books and newspaper and magazine articles to his credit, including *Quickness and How to Increase It* (1904) and *Power of Concentration: How to Acquire It* (1907). He also marketed a physical culture course and ran a restaurant and cooking school in London's

Chandos Street. He was not a great favourite with the medical establishment. A review of one of Miles' books in the *British Medical Journal* in 1903 referred to him disparagingly as someone 'who has published, at a comparatively early age, a formidable list of work, ranging in theme from the History of Rome to the Failure of Vegetarianism and from the Teaching of Jesus to the game of Squash. Mr Miles is a well known athlete but does not appear to have taxed himself severely in the study of physiology.'

Miles certainly displayed plenty of energy in the *jeu de paume* final. In 1906 he had defeated Gould in the British championships, in front of the largest and smartest crowd ever to attend a court tennis match in the UK. Then Gould had been in his first year of competitive play. By 1908 he was bigger and stronger.

The Englishman went ahead in each of the Olympic sets but Gould gradually overcame him to win the gold medal by three sets to nil. Afterwards Miles said, 'Mr Gould is a bit of sheer whalebone. I can testify that it is simply awful to play against him. He is so relentless. Yet nobody could wish for a more courteous opponent.'

Gould's politeness did not extend to his turning up to receive his gold medal at the ceremony but he went on playing for many years, eventually retiring to look after the family business interests and invest in New York property. As a reminder of his glory days he had a *jeu de paume* court installed in his office block.

Miles continued to write and to urge the use of Emprote as the basis for such delicacies as savoury cheese sandwiches and macaroni cheese. He probably achieved more fame from his health products than he had as a *jeu de paume* player. As one magazine wrote admiringly of his promotional efforts, 'Mr Miles is no amateur in the gentle art of self-advertisement: he would be the first to admit it.'

An American entrant who went out in the first round was Charles Sand, who had won the American title three years earlier. He suffered with equanimity the metaphorical fate of having a number of horses shot from beneath him in midstream in Olympic competitions. In 1900, he won the first Olympic golf champion-ship and lost in the early rounds of the tennis competition. These two sports, together with his 1908 choice of *jeu de paume*, were all removed from the Olympic timetable, leaving Sand technically unemployable as far as Olympiads were concerned.

While the racquet sports were taking place so modestly, the gold medal in another minority pursuit, polo, was being competed for at the Hurlingham Club. Originating in Persia, the sport was a favourite among army officers stationed in India and had been taken up by Winston Churchill, first at Sandhurst and then when he was commissioned into the Fourth Hussars and stationed in India. He continued to play the game into his early 50s. In 1908, while president of the Board of Trade in the Liberal cabinet and a freelance journalist, he wrote as a guide to parents, 'Don't give your son money. As soon as you can afford it, give him horses. No one ever came to grief – except honorable grief – through riding horses.'

The polo tournament preserved the low-key, almost anonymous approach of the other Olympic sports held before the official opening ceremony. At the turn of the century it had been estimated that to take up the sport at the humblest level it would take an outlay of over £100 and more than half that sum every year to play – only three teams were entered for the Olympics. The entrants were all comfortably off aristocrats and businessmen who had competed often with and against one another on the exclusive club circuit. To the surprise of no one, the two senior polo clubs in England were represented. The Roehampton Club had been formed in 1901 as an officers' polo club while Hurlingham had been established in 1867, originally as a pigeon-shooting club for the gentry. When the Prince of Wales, later King Edward VII, started to patronise the establishment, it expanded rapidly and included polo among the sports it offered to selected members. The third side was a scratch All-Ireland one.

The winning side, Roehampton, was represented by a bevy of sturdy, wealthy middle-class players. The two Miller brothers, Charles and George, had been educated at Marlborough and Trinity College, Cambridge. They had taken up polo to while away the time when they had been sent to India to work in their family's merchant business. The other two members of the team were both distinguished army officers and learned polo while serving. They had plenty of time in which to hone their skills between wars. Patteson Nickalls had been educated at Rugby and New College, Oxford. He was a member of the Durham Light Infantry and had been present at the relief of Ladysmith. Herbert Wilson was an Old Etonian and a graduate of New College who had been decorated with a DSO (Distinguished Service Order) during the Boer War.

The only aristocrat in the competition was in the Hurlingham side. John Woodhouse, the third Earl of Kimberley, was 24. He devoted himself to managing his family estates and playing polo. He was to become famous chiefly for being the son of a famous Liberal statesman (the second earl) and the father of the most married peer of his time, with a total of five wives (the fourth earl).

The All-Ireland side drew a bye, and so went into the final without playing a game, while Roehampton defeated Hurlingham 4–1 in the first round. The final turned out to be one-sided with Roehampton taking the gold medal by a score of 8–1 against the hapless Irish. Crowds were sparse. Across London in Hyde Park at about the same time, several hundred thousand demonstrators were estimated to have assembled to demand the vote for women. In that same month, Alliottt Verdon-Roe became the first Englishman to design and fly an aircraft. He managed a 'hop' of about a hundred feet, but never bothered to make an official claim for his pioneering effort.

The various shooting competitions started in the second week of July and continued until the 11th. Four of the disciplines took place at the Bisley rifle range outside London, while the trap shooting competition was at the Uxendon School Shooting Club.

Uxendon, situated between Wembley Park and Harrow, was still a rural area. A farm had been turned into the Lancaster Shooting Club. When the idea of using the club's facilities as part of the Olympic shooting programme was mooted, a small request railway station called Preston Halt was opened on the Metropolitan line in May 1908. This made the area more accessible and led to the first major commuter developments in the region.

Like tennis and polo, shooting was the preserve of those who could afford to participate. The sport was patronised largely by army officers and country house guests at parties which were notorious for the scale of slaughter ensuing from their organised shoots. On a single day in 1885, Lord de Gray shot 920 rabbits, while three years later Lord Walshingham bagged 1,058 game birds, also in one day's shooting. The National Rifle Association, which organised the Olympic shooting events, admitted that their sport was not one for the masses: 'Rifle shooting practice is only indulged in by the few.'

The NRA did its best to be a good host. Competitors were provided with huts in which to shelter from the wind and rain. They were given lunch in the Bisley Council Club each day and on Thursday and Friday evenings they were entertained by displays of cinematography in the aptly named Umbrella Tent – most of the Bisley and Uxendon competitions were conducted in the sort of foul weather that was to mar the White City events.

In an effort to speed matters up, some of the rifle and pistol shooting events were run simultaneously with the competitors queueing up to fire, something which could lead to confusion. The organisers tacitly admitted that the attempt to make things go quicker was because most interest lay in the international events: 'The other competitions, although not so attractive to the ordinary spectator, nevertheless aroused the keenest interest in those who took part.'

The international matches were played over distances of 200, 500, 600, 800, 900 and 1000 yards. Gold was won by the USA. Nothing was said officially, but there was a feeling among high-ranking British military officers that the Americans had taken an unfair advantage by the adoption of the deadly, magazine-fed, bolt-action Springfield M1903 rifle, modified in 1906 to allow the use of newly developed pointed ammunition. This sporting use was a dreadful precursor of World War I, which was already feared and where its ability to kill a man without hearing its report caused it to be known as the weapon of 'silent death'.

The official report of the competition loftily pointed out that the down-to-earth British teams did not fare as well in the competitions because their members did not dally with 'hair triggers, hand rests and other refinements'.

One overly patriotic Briton went to considerable lengths to get back the American gold. This was the sneak thief who entered the Victoria Hotel near Trafalgar Square and stole the medal from the room occupied by General Drain, president of the American Rifle Association, and his wife. They were out for a morning walk at the time. For good measure the miscreant also stole three diamond rings and two necklaces from a leather trunk.

The running deer shooting competitions featured two unusual entrants. In the single shot event, the individual gold medal was won by a 60-year-old Swede, Oscar Swahn. The following day he won another gold medal in the team event, and he went on to secure a bronze in the running deer double-shot event. The 'deer' consisted of targets pulled on trolleys.

The 1908 Olympiad was to prove almost literally a sighting shot for the Swedish sexagenarian. Swahn was to go on to win a shooting team gold and an individual bronze in the 1912 Games. He also finished fifth in the individual single-shot competition, which was won by his son. He went on to compete in the 1920 Olympiad at the age of 72, winning a silver medal in the team double-shot event. Four years later he was selected for the 1924 Games, but was forced to withdraw through illness.

The winner of the 1908 running deer double-shot event, in which rifles with two barrels were used, was a wealthy American called Walter Winans. He was born in St Petersburg, Russia, of American parents. His father built the Moscow and St Petersburg railway line, making so much money in the process that Walter Winans' *New York Times* obituary later said of him, 'His life was never one of idleness despite his lack of interest in business, in which he never engaged.'

Winans developed an early interest in shooting when listening to the lurid stories of his nursemaid's boyfriend, who had served in the Crimean War. As a young man he developed a reputation as a good rider to hounds and a keen exponent of horse-trotting skills, as well as being a crack shot. For much of his time he lived in England. He visited Bisley as a competitor on a number of occasions before the Olympics.

In his book, *The Art of Revolver Shooting*, published in 1901, he gave some idea of how much money was needed to follow his hobby of competitive shooting: 'I always have my Bisley sights made solid with the revolver, without any screws and have some made to shoot higher, others lower, each on separate revolvers.' Winans was also a gifted sculptor in bronze. At the 1912 Olympics in Stockholm he was awarded a gold medal in the sculpture competition, as well as achieving a silver medal in one of the running deer shooting events.

There were several administrative disasters in the shooting events. Some contestants were plain unlucky. In the small-bore prone rifle shooting, Philip Plater won the competition with a world record score. Then it was discovered that Great Britain had been competing with an extra man in its team. The unfortunate Plater was disqualified.

One story that gained some circulation regarded the Russian shooting entry. The Russians had entered a six-man team for the military rifle competition. The USA came first out of eight entrants. Originally Russia had entered as the ninth set, but its team did not turn up on the day. It was said that Russia was still following the old Julian calendar, which differed by 13 days from the Gregorian calendar used in Britain and most other countries. Adhering to their national calendar, it was reported in some newspapers, the Russians arrived 13 days too late for the tournament. It seems difficult to prove or disprove this suggestion, but it does bear some resemblance to a similar rumour concerning the US team, which arrived only two days before the 1896 Athens Olympiad was due to start. Here too there were reports that the tardy arrival of the Americans was due to the discrepancy between the two calendars. However, there are official itineraries which show that the US athletes had always intended to arrive on the eve of the tournament. Until definite proof is unearthed, perhaps it should be assumed that travel arrangements ruffled by the differences between the two calendars might be better filed under the heading of Olympic urban legend rather than fact.

Six

The Lure Of Going Pro

'We were continually reminded by the European committees that their men could not remain during the whole period of the Games.'

The Olympic Games of 1908 in London: A Reply Made to Certain Charges Made by the American Officials

In the lead-up to the 1908 Games and for some time after they had ended, several thousand athletes and officials from 21 nations arrived in and left England. Their main purpose was to do well at their chosen sports, but amid their comings and goings some found time for other activities during their sojourns in the country.

Of the group of fencers on board the SS *Branwen* who had first discussed the possibility of a London Olympiad, all were to maintain some connection with the White City Games. Lord Desborough and Theodore Andreas Cook worked flat out at their administrative jobs. Edgar Seligman was preparing to represent his country at fencing once again. Charles Newton-Johnson, now well into his 50s, had retired from competitive sport but volunteered to be a judge at the yachting events. That left Cosmo Duff Gordon and Lord Thomas de Walden who painted on larger canvases.

Duff Gordon was married, some would say over-married, to the strong-willed fashion designer Lucille, who, in 1907, had experienced an enormous success with her costumes for the London production of Franz Lehar's operetta *The Merry Widow*. Responding to pressure from his wife, Duff Gordon had invested money in the production and much against his will he was forced to drag himself away from his beloved clubs, sporting organisations and ancestral grounds and take an interest in what was going on at Daly's Theatre, just off Leicester Square in June 1907. The production was destined to run for 778 performances.

Under its original title of *Die Lustige Witwe*, the Viennese operetta had been touring the world with enormous success for several years before producer George Edwardes commissioned an English translation of the book for the first London production. The whole affair was a triumph, not least for Lucilley Duff Gordon, who revelled in her opportunity and later gloated, 'That season was a very brilliant one, perhaps the most brilliant of the series which brought the social life of pre-war London to its peak.'

In addition to the sumptuous gowns she ran up for the new young star Lily Elsie, Lucille Duff Gordon also designed the striking Merry Widow hat, a great cartwheel of the milliner's art, coveted and purchased by practically every society lady in London. The publicity made Lucille one of the leading clothes designers in the world. It was estimated that her company turned a profit of £40,000 a year.

Whenever her husband was in London, Sir Cosmo lived in his Belgravia home, which had once been a hunting lodge belonging to King Charles II. He was mortified when his wife invited in a journalist, anticipating *Hello!* magazine by almost a century, to write an article describing how Lucille had transformed the rather small house. Lady Cosmo Duff Gordon was only too eager to tell how she washed the walls white to give an impression of space and decorated arches and doorways with green ivy leaves cut from ordinary strips of wallpaper.'For to Lady Duff Gordon material is nothing,' the journalist wrote, 'taste is everything.'

Lucille may have been having the time of her life but her hapless husband was becoming increasingly adrift and miserable. Eager to take a full part in the Games, he was more and more distracted by his wife's profitable business ventures, which were helping to finance the restoration of the family home in Scotland. He was also coming under the influence of his novelist sister-in-law Elinor Glyn, Lucille's equally determined and soon-to-be even richer sister. In 1907 Elinor Glyn had published what was then a raunchy novel, *Three Weeks*. It had been a runaway success in the

US and most European countries, eventually selling millions of copies. To Duff Gordon's embarrassment, his sister-in-law's reputation as a purveyor of steamy sex had given rise to the much-quoted piece of doggerel:

> Would you like to sin
> With Elinor Glyn
> On a tiger skin?
> Or would you prefer
> To err with her
> On some other fur?

Matters were made even worse for the would-be Olympic administrator when his strong-minded sister-in-law persuaded him, much against his will, to join her backing in a popular quack medicine called *The Secret of El-Zair*, which purported to provide an elixir of eternal youth. Duff Gordon's increasingly bizarre family commitments not only kept him busy, but made him something of an embarrassment to his fellow committee members as well as a laughing stock with the public. He looked on with envy as preparations for the Olympics proceeded apace, largely without his input.

'Tommy' Howard de Walden, the host of the 1906 fencing party on the *Branwen*, also had plenty to do, even by his enthusiastic and unselective standards. In 1907 he had witnessed the end of trials in which a shopkeeper's widow, Anna Maria Druce, made claims against his maternal grandfather, the eccentric Duke of Portland. She said he led a double life as her late husband. It was asserted in court that when the Duke tired of life at Welbeck Abbey, he travelled in a hearse by a secret tunnel to Worksop railway station from where he had caught a train to London to join her and take up his commercial responsibilities at the Baker Street Bazaar.

Bearing in mind that he stood to lose his share of the Portland estate, de Walden was sufficiently stirred to call the court proceedings 'infamous'. He was greatly relieved when, after much publicity, the case collapsed in October. Two witnesses were convicted of perjury and Mrs Druce and another witness were committed to lunatic asylums.

Lord de Walden was now free to concentrate on creative matters. His first drama, *Lauval,* set in the times of King Arthur and starring Harcourt Williams as an idealistic soldier of fortune, opened in London in May 1908. Unfortunately, although de Walden's aristocratic friends came loyally to see it, the general public did not. He turned his attention to sport again.

Kenneth Grahame's classic *The Wind in the Willows* was published in 1908. The young sporting peer could have been the prototype for the character of the well-meaning Toad of Toad Hall, always hopping from one enthusiasm to another. By the time of the London Olympiad, de Walden had discovered offshore powerboat racing, which was included for the first and last time at the 1908 Games.

Motorboats had been developed before cars and after motorcycles. In 1887, a rowing boat powered by an engine developed by Gottlieb Daimler had moved sluggishly for a few yards across the River Seine in Paris. From those beginnings, powerboat racing was taken up enthusiastically as a sport, supported in Britain by Sir Alfred Harmsworth, later Lord Northcliffe, who donated a trophy to be competed for in 1903.

De Walden joined with his friend the Duke of Westminster in announcing that they were prepared to represent the UK in powerboating at the Olympics. With their connections – and because they were two of the very few men in the country who could afford to own and maintain motor boats – their nomination was a relative shoe-in. The only problem was how to fit the Olympics in to their busy schedules.

With his writing and theatrical commitments to occupy him, de Walden also continued to restore his castle and add to its collection of armour. Another minor irritation was the fact that he had been nominated in a newspaper as Britain's wealthiest and most eligible bachelor. This entailed keeping at bay the determined approaches of the mothers of London society's latest crop of debutantes.

De Walden's friend, Hugh Richard Arthur Grosvenor, second

Duke of Westminster, was married to the first of four wives, but he positively welcomed the attentions of comely young women and was usually balancing one liaison off against another throughout his long life. He was known as Bend'or, a nickname he had since a child which came from the 1880 Derby-winning racehorse owned by Grosvenor's grandfather, the first Duke of Westminster.

Bend'or's main interests away from women lay in transport of the mechanical rather than the four-legged kind. He had driven very fast round the Brooklands racing track on the day it had opened and had participated in several international speedboat competitions. This was why he had condescended to allow his name to be put forward for the motorboat section of the Olympics together with that of de Walden's.

The year 1908 did not start well for the Duke, as he became embroiled with the law and the subject of criticism across the world. Towards the end of 1907 he had given a dinner party for a number of neighbours, including the Marquis and Marchioness of Cholmondeley. Lord Cholmondeley had bored his host and fellow guests with his interminable boasting about the efficacy of a new burglar alarm system he had recently had installed, saying that he defied anyone to break into his castle now. Responding to the implicit challenge, the Duke and some of the male guests allowed the Cholmondeleys time to leave the party, get home and go to sleep. They then followed them to Cholmondeley castle in motor cars, accompanied by some of the ladies who had been at the dinner, broke in with ease and stole a silver cup and a quantity of the peer's cigars, leaving a lump of coal in their place, all without disturbing the much-vaunted alarm system.

The next morning, in the cold light of day, after the Chief Constable of Cheshire himself had been summoned to head the investigation into the theft, Bend'or and the other men in the raiding party confessed to their part in the break-in. The participants expected that their rank would absolve them from any punishment and wished Lord Cholmondeley and the county police force a Merry Christmas. The Chief Constable rolled over supinely enough in the face of so much concentrated country house rank and privilege,

What the Duke had not been expecting had been the barrage of criticism his nocturnal excursion would arouse. Times were changing and the child-like exploits of the upper classes were no longer being tolerated by the public. To the amazement and fury of the Duke of Westminster and his fellow burglars, newspapers all over the world swooped to condemn their prank. As far away as Ohio the *Sandusky Star Journal* of 2 January 1908 condemned the exploit, describing the noble participants as having weak minds. *The San Antonio Light* dealt with the news report in the same manner, remarking of the aristocrats that 'the circle of the great unemployed have taken to a fresh method for obtaining a new sensation'. It was not the response to which Bend'or, who had raised the British flag at Pretoria during the Boer War, had become accustomed. Worse was to follow. Days later he fell off his mount while hunting, sustaining injuries.

But he soon recovered. After a couple of weeks in bed he dropped in to see his wife Shelagh, who had rented a villa on the French Riviera, where he played a little polo. From there he journeyed to Paris and returned to England. After a few more weeks of rural pursuits Bend'or then travelled to Spain to stay with friends. He made use of this time to take part in a motorboat race at Palermo, before returning home to accept delivery of a new speedboat which had been specially designed for him.

Leaving his expensive new toy in the hands of his chief mechanic, Bend'or played a little more polo at Hurlingham, hosted a number of house parties and left for South Africa. By this time the date of the Olympic motorboat competition was approaching. Unfortunately it clashed with the running of an international speedboat competition in the USA. Both Bend'or and Lord de Walden wished to enter their motorboats for these races, considering them an ideal warm-up for the competition as well as an opportunity for sybaritic travel. Letters and telegrams were sent, strings were pulled, the Olympic committee cravenly gave way and agreed to postpone the motorboat races until the end of August.

Neither Bend'or nor de Walden could take enough time out from their busy social and artistic calendars to make the trip across the Atlantic, but they dispatched their vessels *Daimler II* and *Wolsey-Siddeley*, complete with captains and crews, to compete in the Harmsworth Trophy. This was also known as the British International Trophy. Both vessels were beaten out of sight in the race at Long Island Sound at the end of July by the US speedboat *Dixie II*. Lord Howard de Walden's *Daimler II* didn't even complete the course. The generous American hosts invited the British speedboats to stay on and take part in another international race on the St Lawrence River, but Bend'or and Lord Howard de Walden sent petulant telegrams to their respective captains, ordering them to return at once with their vessels to participate in the London Olympics.

The Native Canadian marathon runner Tom Longboat was having trouble. He and his manager Tom Flanagan had survived by the skin of their teeth efforts by the USA athletics authorities to have Longboat banned from the Olympics because of claims that he was a professional runner, and had set off for Europe. Longboat, sometimes billed as 'The Speedy Son of the Forest' to emphasise his ancestry, had aroused suspicion because he had no visible means of support, apart from a cigar store which soon went under due to its owner's neglect. He was living in his manager's Toronto hotel.

Naively Longboat, a minor league hedonist who had once been ejected from the YMCA for getting back too late at night, had anticipated a few weeks of living it up among the fleshpots of London before the race. Flanagan, meanwhile, knew that Longboat was favourite to win the London marathon and was eager for his charge to do well in the race, so that the pair of them could cash in on the gold medal by getting Longboat to turn professional officially. He wanted to curb the runner's worst excesses, at least until after the Olympics.

So instead of meeting up with the rest of the Canadian team at the Sussex Hotel in London, Longboat discovered that he was being spirited out of England altogether and taken to Ireland, where it was thought he would be free from the temptations of the flesh. Having no pressing desire to be relieved of these temptations, he protested vehemently against his abduction. Not without reason the runner suspected that the old walled medieval town of

Kilmallock in County Limerick, to which he was being dispatched, might have not all the attractions of Piccadilly or Oxford Circus. Flanagan tried to persuade his runner that the area was famed for its hurling contests and horse breeding, but Longboat would not be consoled.

His fears were soon realised. Not only did Kilmallock turn out to be less than socially effervescent, it rained almost every day, hindering Longboat's training. Flanagan came to an understanding with several local promoters and ensured that the Onodaga Indian gave a couple of long distance demonstration runs before large crowds, but the tedium was otherwise unbroken.

It did not help that both men were preoccupied with other matters. Longboat was planning to get married to Miss Maracle – a reservation schoolteacher – after the Olympics but could find no Protestant minister to perform the ceremony. He was deemed by the church to be a 'heathen' whose affirmed conversion to Christianity could not be regarded as a genuine one. Flanagan's problems were commercial and financial. He was considering both promoting professional wrestling in Toronto and also managing recalcitrant world heavyweight boxing champion Jack Johnson. One of those projects alone would be enough to daunt most men, and the prospect of undertaking both of them subdued even Flanagan, who was normally optimistic. It was with some relief that both men admitted defeat and left Ireland and returned to London ten days before the marathon was due to be held.

One of the first would-be Olympians to make his own way to London was a young Australian swimmer from Melbourne called Frank Beaurepaire. He was 17 and arrived in England four months before the aquatic events were due to start. His father had taught him to swim as a four-year-old by tying a rope around his waist and hauling him up and down a sea-water swimming pool. This rough and ready system obviously worked. The year before he had left for London the youth had been selected for the national team, and at the age of 16 he had won Australian titles over a quarter mile, half mile and mile.

Beaurepaire sailed to Britain with his coach Tommy Horlock, a South Melbourne barber. The Victorian Swimming Association could only afford to send the pair in third-class steerage accommodation, although the ship's captain allowed Beaurepaire to train on the first-class decks when there were not many passengers around. There had been a breakdown in communication and the Australian officials had made no arrangements to meet or house the new arrivals. For the first month they existed in the home of one of Beaurepaire's relatives on £16 between them. Beaurepaire could not afford to train in heated swimming pools, so uncomplainingly he did his preparations in the freezing waters of Highgate Ponds. He lived on a diet of bread and cheese and ginger beer.

While he was waiting for the Olympics to start, Beaurepaire illadvisedly decided to include a 16-mile race up the River Thames in his training. He was not ready for such a gruelling event so early in his stay. He collapsed and had to be pulled out of the water close to Hammersmith Bridge. The young Australian mule-headedly entered the English five-mile championship in the Thames. Again, he could not finish the course.

Gradually, however, Beaurepaire did become acclimatised. At Bradford he caused a considerable stir by winning the English halfmile championship from the highly regarded British champion Henry Taylor. He then entered the 220 yards championship at Nottingham, where he happened to mention that the water at Bradford had been almost unbearably cold. To accommodate their Antipodean visitor the Nottingham officials cranked the heating of the water up to 82 degrees, causing the race to be conducted through a cloud of steam. An almost parboiled Beaurepaire won the title.

Even after they had joined up with the rest of the Australian squad, Beaurepaire and Tommy Horlock had no money. In their spare time they were forced to take advantage of the less expensive London attractions available at the time. The British Museum, completed in 1845, did not charge admission. The busy life of Covent Garden market could be witnessed getting under way at midnight as hundreds of boxes of fruit, flowers and vegetables were unloaded and carried by porters to the stalls. There were firework displays at Crystal Palace on some Thursday evenings. There were the celebrated green walks to be undertaken through 5,000 acres of Epping Forest, which could be reached on the Great Eastern railway service at Leyton. Henry VIII's state apartments could be viewed free at Hampton Court every day except Friday.

But most of Beaurepaire's time was spent training as the Olympic swimming events grew closer. These sessions running up to the White City Games were not without excitement for the teenager. On one occasion he was training in the Thames when he developed cramp and sank. Vic Aitken, a member of the Australian marathon team, had to dive in and save Beaurepaire from drowning.

Jean Bouin became one of France's most celebrated athletes, known for always chewing a toothpick while he ran. He had a chequered time at the White City. In the three-mile team event he won his heat in an excellent time. Then the night before the final he was arrested after a pub brawl in London. He was rescued from a police station by French officials and entered for the final. However, the events of the previous evening had been too much for the 19-year-old and all the fight had been knocked out of him. He did not finish the race.

The combined Australian and New Zealand Rugby Union side was touring Britain before the Olympics. The Wallabies were under attack from the creeping virus of professionalism, which was proving to be a particularly insidious foe. In Britain, the so-called Northern Union had split from the Rugby Football Union in 1895 over the matter of payment for broken time. Unlike most of their middle-class counterparts in London and the South, the Rugby Union players in Lancashire and Yorkshire were mainly miners and factory workers. If they had time off to travel to away matches they claimed from their clubs the sums they had lost for what would otherwise have been holiday.

The RFU deemed this unacceptable. The Northern Union broke away from its governing body and set up the forerunner of what became Rugby League. At first it adhered to the structure and laws of the RFU. Gradually, however, it took on its own distinctive shape, with paid players, teams of 13-a-side and abolished the lineout where opposing lines of forewards jumped for the ball at a throw-in. In 1907, a similarly professional form of the game was mooted in Australia. To the dismay of the authorities, the best Australasian Rugby Union players were soon poached to join these 13-a-side teams. The following year, a professional New Zealand Rugby League team left to tour Britain.

This meant that the professional Kangaroos found themselves playing in the United Kingdom at the same time as the Wallabies. As the teams criss-crossed the country, the players met up increasingly often on trains and in hotel bars. Some of the Wallabies even went to watch the Kangaroos play. Herbert Moran, the captain, discovered that most of his team members were being 'tapped up' to join the burgeoning Rugby League set-up when the tour was over and they returned to Australia.

Even worse, scouts for the English professional Northern League clubs began to report back to their owners that many of the Wallabies players were of an extremely high standard and that, unlike the Kangaroos representatives, they had not yet been secured to cast-iron contracts by Australian Rugby League teams. Signing-on fees of £100 were offered to the better Australian amateurs to abandon the tour and turn professional. The beleaguered Moran and his associates suddenly discovered that in addition to pursuing a punishing travelling and playing itinerary, they were having to ward off the attentions of both the Australian Rugby League agents and lurking scouts from the English Northern League. The scouts brandished wads of pound notes under the noses of the Wallaby players, who were existing on a controversial expenses allowance of a meagre three shillings a day.

Matters came to a head at West Hartlepool over the weekend of 30 October–1 November 1908. On the Thursday, the Wallabies travelled up from Portsmouth to St Pancras Station in London after defeating the United Services 8–6 and had transferred to a train taking them to West Hartlepool via Sheffield. The players and officials then took up residence in the Grand Hotel. Friday was spent on a light training session and then the players were taken on an excursion to see the town, including its fish market and the extensive shipbuilding yards.

Moran had then hoped for a restful Friday evening before the following day's game against a selected Durham County side on the Saturday. Instead, he found the hotel and the pubs and its environs invaded by a concerted rush of professional rugby agents. Not only were there representatives of most of the Northern League clubs such as Bradford, Leeds, Wigan and Hull present but there were also rumours that the notorious J.J. Giltinan had been seen in the vicinity.

James Giltinan was an Australian entrepeneur who had got in on the ground floor of Rugby League in his home country and had backed the touring Kangaroos. He was also secretary of the newly-formed New South Wales Rugby League and seemed in a position to offer Wallaby players a good deal to change codes when they returned home.

Herbert Moran did his best to keep Giltinan away from his players but there was little that he could do to stop them listening to the blandishments of the persuasive businessman and his representatives. There was little doubt that over that long weekend in West Hartlepool a great deal of harm was done to the Rugby Union movement in Australia and that great changes were to take place in the lives of most of the players in the Wallaby shirts.

The damage was not at first evident, because soon after Giltinan's pre-emptive raid on the Wallabies the Kangaroos' tour of Britain went belly-up. Dreadful weather that was plaguing the Olympics had the same effect on gates for the Kangaroos. The tour soon began operating at a loss. After playing 46 games Giltinan had lost so much money that the Northern Union had to pay for the return fares of the Australian professionals. A few of the Kangaroos stayed on to play for such Rugby League clubs as Hull and Wakefield Trinity.

With fingers so badly burned financially by the failure of the tour, J.J. Giltinan drifted out of professional rugby. But the seeds he had planted in West Hartlepool bore fruit when the Wallabies returned to New South Wales. Out of the 31 players, 14 turned professional.

Seven

Boots, Somersaults And Swords

'The policemen who pulled in the tug-of-war against the American team in the Olympic Games wore their ordinary duty boots, as it is their invariable custom to pull in such boots which have gone too shabby to be worn on street duty.'

The Olympic Games of London in 1908: A Reply to Certain Charges Made by the American Officials

With the official opening over, the White City tournament proceeded with all the dubious panache and showmanship of a Wild West rodeo, albeit one organised by British civil servants. Morning events began at 10.30am, while the afternoon got under way at 3.30pm.

At any given moment down in the arena, three or four events were often taking place at the same time. One feature of the entertainment was the movement of the diving tower of the swimming pool. It was retractable and could be raised and lowered to facilitate easier viewing of what was going on around the pool.

The *New York Times* of 15 July complained of sporting congestion: 'The games were as bewildering to watch as a three-ring circus. At any one time a dozen cyclists were wheeling along the outer edges over the oval, while 20 runners were racing on the cinder path just inside of it.'

Three days later, the *Ohio Evening Telegraph* confirmed, 'One needed a dozen pairs of eyes to keep track of what was going on, with events proceeding simultaneously in every part of the arena.'

The weather did not help. It rained incessantly almost every day for the duration of the track and field events that June. Most existing photographs of the tournament seem to feature depressed-looking officials sheltering under umbrellas while being ignored by the preoccupied athletes for whom they were responsible.

The bad weather coupled with the high prices kept many visitors away. And there was confusion with the Exhibition next door. Arguments and even scuffles broke out as those who had paid to see the Exhibition then tried to get into the arena for nothing, while sated sports enthusiasts attempted to make their way in vain into the halls and sideshows. The location of some of the turnstiles rendered passage between the two areas difficult, even for those willing to pay twice. Ever-helpful, *Punch* suggested that disillusioned visitors to the Exhibition be allowed in free and charged a shilling to get out. In the face of such burgeoning ridicule, reluctantly Lord Desborough agreed to lower the prices of seats in the arena.

The *Glasgow Herald* crowed that it served the BOC right for confining most of the events to London and not dispersing them around the country. For the benefit of those who did attend, *Punch* also offered a series of translations of all-purpose phrases likely to be of general help to those less well-informed spectators in the stadium: 'The show is a bit slow', 'He does a bad time and won't have an earthly' and 'They carried off the winner to the mixed bathing tank'.

One thing was certain. The Americans were starting as they meant to go on in the track and field events. By the fourth day, their strength athletes had already picked up two gold medals, with Ralph Rose winning the shot put and Martin Sheridan outclassing the field in the Greek-style discus throw. In the former event the crowd was upset when unsubstantiated accusations went the rounds that Edward Barrett, a Kerry-born English policeman fancied by some seriously to challenge Rose, had been injured when an American had dropped the shot on his ankle. It was, in fact, more likely that the Irish constable had succumbed to sheer exhaustion.

In addition to the shot, Barrett entered the javelin and discus competitions and was to go on to win a gold medal in the tug-of-war and a bronze in the free-style wrestling as well as competing in the Graeco-Roman style grappling. Obviously restless as well as multi-talented, five years earlier Barrett won a medal with the victorious Irish hurling championship side.

The American officials kept up their litany of complaints. They were upset when their team manager was not allowed on the track for the first couple of days. Some runners were offended by the knee-length shorts that they were asked to wear. In a display of defiance some of the Americans ostentatiously rolled their shorts up above the knee. James E. Sullivan was disturbed by bowler-hatted British officials running alongside the track coaching British athletes – sometimes, it was claimed, through megaphones. He was also outraged by what he considered to be the fixing of the preliminary heats, when, he declared, the best US athletes were drawn against one another, thus eliminating a number of potential medal winners.

A much more august reproof, and one which struck chill into the hearts of the organisers hoping to be rewarded with honours in the future, came from King Edward himself. He had withdrawn after the opening ceremony in high dudgeon to Buckingham Palace. The monarch let it be known that he deplored the 'barbarous cries' coming from the US supporters at the various slights being heaped upon their competitors and was extremely vexed about the whole matter. Still shocked by the refusal of the American athletes to dip their banner, the sulking Edward had nothing more to do with the Games. When the closing ceremony arrived it was performed by his beautiful, long-suffering wife, Queen Alexandra.

It was plain that apparently already unbridgeable gulfs were widening still further between the staid hosts and the free-spirited Americans. James Connolly, covering the Games for the US *Colliers* magazine, referred to this when he praised the successful athletes 'who are shaping the future rather than living in the past'.

However, all criticisms of the organisation of the Olympiad were dwarfed by the events of 17 July, the fifth day of the Olympic track and field events, and the occasion of the first round of the tug-of-war competition. Although it was to lose favour later, the sport was extremely popular in the first decade of the 20th century. It could trace its origins in Britain to inter-village free-for-all competitions in the 16th century. Its emergence as a competitive team event is believed to have taken place on the tea-trading vessel the *Cutty Sark* towards the end of the 19th century. Its captain introduced the pastime to his crew as a means of keeping them fit and honing their competitive instincts. This team competition was observed and taken up by army officers on their way to India, where it was used as a military sport. From here it spread to fire brigades, police units and other muscular institutions.

No one expected such an uncontroversial event to spark off an Olympic furore, but it all had to do with the footwear of one of the teams. Rudyard Kipling's poem about a foot soldier's lament, 'Boots (Infantry Columns)', had been published, with its well-known refrain, in *The Five Nations* three years before the London Olympics:

> We're foot-slog-slog-slog-sloggin' over Africa –
> Foot-foot-foot-foot-sloggin' over Africa –
> (Boots-boots-boots-boots-movin' up an' down again!)
> There's no discharge in the war!

By 1908 the poem was still a music hall favourite, both as a recitation and song. On the fifth day of the White City track and field events, the title was to achieve a totally different and devastatingly controversial connotation. It happened in the first round of the tug-of-war competition. So popular had the sport become among athletic members of the country's constabulary that at the London Olympics all three British teams came from police forces – the Liverpool Police, the City of London Force and 'K' Division of the Metropolitan Police.

Four national eight-man teams entered – Sweden, Germany, Greece and the USA. Germany and Greece withdrew without competing and lots were drawn for the preliminary pulls. The City of London and Metropolitan Police sides received byes to the semi-finals, leaving the Liverpool force to compete against the USA in the first round of the competition. The rules were simple. If one team could pull its opponents a distance of six feet it was declared the winner. However, if after five minutes neither team had pulled the other six feet, then the team which had pulled the other side the furthest emerged as the winning eight.

The US team was a formidable one as far as size was concerned, but a scratch side in experience and skill. It consisted of a job lot of very talented throwers. Ralph Rose and John Flanagan had already won gold medals in their respective events, while between them the other members were to win two silvers and a bronze before the track and field events were over. Typical of their number was Marquis 'Bill' Horr, All-American football player, who was to win a bronze medal in the discus throw and a silver in the discus, Greek style. He finished in sixth place in the hammer and the shot.

Such expertise was of little help as far as the tug-of-war was concerned. The US big men certainly looked the part. The *Warren Evening Mirror* of 18 July commented approvingly, 'When the stalwart Americans, neatly dressed in their athletic costumes, made their appearance they received great applause from all sections of the stands.'

The Liverpool policemen may not have looked as smart, but one item of their apparel certainly attracted the attention of their opponents. The Englishmen were wearing heavy duty, official issue police boots with steel tips. One American spectator complained, perhaps with some exaggeration, that the footwear of the Liverpool competitors was so heavy that the policemen could hardly lift their feet from the ground. The American *Evening Telegraph* enlarged upon the theme: 'The shoes or boots were enormous calf affairs that could not by any stretch of the imagination be called ordinary shoes.'

American officials present, with Matthew P. Halpin to the fore, at once complained, quoting the relevant passage from the official rulebook, 'No competitor shall wear prepared boots or shoes, or boots or shoes with any projecting nails, tips, point, hollows or projections of any kind.' Halpin was not a noted trouble-maker. Some of the Americans considered him almost too acquiescent and conciliatory. At the 1896 Olympics he had carried the Stars and Stripes and had dipped it with gusto when he passed the Greek monarch. At the closing ceremony he had called enthusiastically for three cheers from the American team for King George. However, after only a few days of the White City shenanigans,

Matty Halpin now seemed as convinced an anti-monarchist as the most belligerent of the Irish-Americans under his shaky command.

The Liverpool policemen were not impressed, nor were they to be moved. They replied with hauteur to the official's protests that these were their working boots, worn out from long use on the beat and so currently reduced to mere athletic usage. The judges were called upon to adjudicate and finally decided in favour of the policemen. They ordered the tugs to commence. The disgusted Americans made only a token effort to compete. In a slow-motion travesty of action they refrained from digging their heels into the ground and the anchorman did not even bother to follow the practice of wrapping the end of the rope around his body. Not surprisingly, the Liverpool Police team was successful with its first desultory grunting heave. The Americans promptly withdrew from the competition and walked angrily off the field, to howls of condemnation from the British crowd.

At the St Louis Olympics, a form of compromise had been reached over a similar problem. The contestants had not been allowed to wear cleats on their shoes but the field on which the tug-of-war had been held had been dug up to afford better footing for the teams. There was no suggestion that the hallowed new White City turf should be treated in this manner.

In his official reply to the stinging criticisms by the Americans, Theodore Cook later suggested that the Liverpool policemen had then contemptuously offered to pull against the Americans in their socks, although this challenge seems to have emanated some time afterwards, when the policemen suggested that both teams participate in a post-Olympic shoeless competition in aid of charity. In any case it was too late. As far as James E. Sullivan and his fellows were concerned, another nail had been hammered into the coffin of British officialdom. Again writer Caspar Whitney, who seemed to be occupying the unpopular role of a prophet crying in the wilderness, begged his fellow countrymen to bite on the bullet, pointing out unsympathetically that 'trying to bulldoze umpires and judges out of making decisions unfavourable to you, or sulking when an unfavourable decision is made against you, is not losing like a man'.

There was one brief family meeting that passed almost unnoticed in the rumbling run-up to the match. Martin Sheridan, who was in the American side, noticed his cousin Jim Clarke, a Liverpool policeman, competing against him. Both men came from the same 20-house village of Bohola in County Mayo.

Over the next few days the City of London Police, including the ubiquitous Irishman Edward Barrett, went on to win the gold medal, overcoming the Liverpool Police 2–0 in the final. Their success did not come as a surprise. For the past five months specially selected members of the inner-London constabulary had been training full-time under the supervision of the dreaded Inspector Harry Duke, a Cross-Channel swimmer and police wrestling champion.

While the tug-of-war was being disputed, in more senses than one, the gymnastics competition was taking place in another part of the arena. The sport was very much an amateur one in Great Britain, as exemplified by Henry Cain. He was presented with a medal after winning the national championship in 1897, but returned it because he already possessed one. Before the competition began, the sports governing body issued a statement warning its members not to be complacent, because at the White City for the first time they would encounter the cream of continental opposition.

There were two events, the individual and the team. Teams could contain between 16 and 40 members and were given 30 minutes to display a series of voluntary mass exercises or drills. In the individual disciplines there were a number of sub-competitions involving floor exercises and apparatus work. First place in the individual event was contested between two very different characters.

Antonio Braglia, an Italian who was to win the gold medal, was a fiery, slightly scatterbrained athlete. At the age of 12 he had started to teach himself gymnastics in a barn. His precocious ability caught the eye of Carlo Frascaroli, one of many peripatetic athletic 'professors' and showmen who abounded at the time. The coach allowed Braglia to train in his gymnasium but the young gymnast still had to fit in his training around earning his living at a number of menial jobs, including portering at a tobacco factory, something he resented in the light of what became increasing success. He began to win local and national championships and was selected to represent Italy in the 1906 intercalated Athens Olympiad. Braglia was runner-up in two individual events. Even after King Vittorio Emanuele III took an interest in the young tumbler, Braglia's circumstances did not improve appreciably and he continued to struggle to earn a living.

At this time he started to flirt surreptitiously with professionalism. Later this aspect of his *curriculum vitae* was to expand into theatrical and circus appearances, billed variously as the Bullet Man and the Human Torpedo. It was a practice that later was to get him into trouble with the authorities and briefly threaten his chances of appearing at the 1912 Olympiad. He developed a stage partnership with a dwarf – Braglia carried a suitcase onto the stage from which the dwarf would emerge to join him in a display of gymnastics. The Italian Gymnastics Federation disqualified their gold medalist for accepting money for his displays but prudently reinstated him in time for Braglia to win another gold medal in the team competition at Stockholm in 1912.

In the end, though, the gymnast did not have a happy life. He suffered a nervous breakdown upon the death of his four year-old son, sustained serious injuries after a bad fall during a performance and lost most of his money after a serious of bad investments. He ended his life as a hired labourer, sweeping out the gymnasium he had once owned.

But in the open-air competitions at the White City, Braglia shone. He performed with spectacular ease on the horizontal bar, parallel bars, pommel horse, rings and ropes and was adjudged a clear overall winner.

In second place came one of the great unknowns of British sport. His name was Walter Tysall and he was an Englishman. He came from Birmingham, where he was a member of the Athletic Club team. He was the British gymnastics champion in 1906–07 and in 1908 and was an enthusiastic exponent of the art of club swinging. He retired not long after the White City Olympics and disappeared from gymnastics history.

Eight teams entered the combined team exercises for men at the White City. Their smart turn-outs and spectacularly co-ordinated displays, together with those of the women's demonstration teams, caused general admiration. The *New York Times* commented, 'The displays of 25 men entered from Germany, France, Italy, Norway, Sweden, Finland and the 25 women from Denmark was a revelation to many Americans present.'

The teams of between 16 and 40 competitors were required to perform mass voluntary co-ordinated exercises. The official requirements for this event were: 'The exercises may be those known as free gymnastics or exercises with hand apparatus, or any combination of both or either.' Each team was allowed a maximum of 30 minutes in which to perform. The Scandinavian teams excelled. First place was taken by Sweden, with Norway second and Finland in third position.

Out of competition, a number of clubs and nations put on gymnastic demonstrations for the crowds. There were complaints when one such exhibition was poorly attended because of the lateness of the hour. There were more protests because, due to an official dinner that evening, no representative of any of the Olympic committees turned up. Meanwhile, the German team had fallen out with its official national body, the Deutsche Turnerschaft, and a number of its competitors were banned from competition when they returned home, because of so-called 'unGermanic' behaviour. There was nothing new in this. As early as the first Athens Olympics in 1896 the German authorities had tried to recall its gymnasts; again the athletes stubbornly defied threats of suspension and stayed on to compete.

At the beginning of the 20th century, Hungary was one of the leading fencing nations in the world. At the 1908 Olympics it showed. There were four events in the competition: the individual and team sabre competitions and the individual and team épée matches. In the épée competitions, points were scored with the point of the sword all over the body of an opponent. Points in the sabre competition were also accrued by hits on any part of the body and strikes could be made both with the point and the flat of the blade.

The fencing events took place in an arena adjacent to the White City ground, in the exhibition hall of the Franco-British Exhibition. The official report of the 1908 Olympics referred to the fencing hall as a tent. The Hungarians won the sabre team gold medal, with Italy second and Bohemia third. In the individual sabre competition, Jeno Fuchs of Hungary won the gold medal, while other Hungarians came second, fourth and fifth. The impressively named Vilem Goppold von Lobsdorf, representing Bohemia, won the bronze medal.

Dr Jeno Fuchs was the outstanding fencer in the whole tournament. He was small in stature but skilful and agile. He won golds in the individual and team sabre events in the 1908 and 1912 Olympics but never won a national title because he did not belong to a club and so could not enter the annual Hungarian tournaments.

In the épée events, France won the team event. Great Britain came second, with a team including Edgar Seligman, who had helped give birth to the London Olympiad on board the *Branwen* several years earlier. Belgium won the team bronze medal. In the individual épée competition, France took the gold, silver and bronze medals with Gaston Alibert in first place and Alexandre Lippmann and Eugene Olivier behind him in that order. An Englishman, Robert Montgomerie, came fourth.

Representing Denmark in the team épée event was Ivan Osiier. His team came equal fifth but this was only the start of a long Olympic career for the Dane. He competed in the next London Olympics, in 1948, 40 years later.

Still the newspapers continued to fan the flames of the disputes occurring in most of the competitions. One or two of the more serious writers tried to ease the situation. In the *Illustrated London News,* G.K. Chesterton attributed the differences to the ways in which the two main disputants approached sport. The British, he claimed, regarded it as prominent and pervasive, but not important, while the Americans considered sporting activities as akin to patriotism and theology.

Eight

Malevolent Mendacities

'We are not used either to making all our evidence public in case of athletic disputes, or to interviewing our competitors and officials as to the facts of competitions with which they were personally concerned. That is one reason why no detailed answer appeared, before now, to the malevolent mendacities uttered by some of our American visitors.'

The Olympic Games of 1908 in London: A Reply to Certain Charges Made by the American Officials

It was not long before a newspaper-fuelled hate campaign was in full spate around the Olympics and its beleaguered officials. Both American and British reporters knew a good, long-running story with front-page potential when they saw one and did their best to keep the international feud going.

Typical of the American reaction to events was that of the *Ohio Evening Telegraph*, which reported gleefully, 'American athletes of all kinds and degrees have reported difficulty in getting a square deal while on English soil.'

If editors hoped for a full-blooded response from British officials and former athletes, they were not disappointed. George Stuart Robinson, who had represented his country at the very first modern Olympiad, took the bait. In a speech at the London Athletic Club the choleric young barrister called the leaders of the American contingent 'liars and no sportsmen'.

It was not a good time to tweak the lion's tail. The suffering British government had political problems with the Irish question, female suffrage and attempts to reform the House of Lords. The

Boer War had proved a great threat to the nation's cherished imperialism. At this time, no one in authority wished to become embroiled in an international incident sparked off by a bunch of sweaty runners, even if one of them, Lieutenant Wyndham Halswelle, held the King's commission. The unfortunate Scot was made to feel by his superior officers that the trouble over the 400 metres might, in some undefined manner, have been his own fault.

The British Olympic Association tried to remain aloof from controversy and did not respond to the baiting from the Americans. This was seized upon and led to the American magazine, *Truth*, sneering in its columns at the secretary de Courcy Laffan, 'The eloquent and reverend Mr Laffan has been silent.'

Baron de Coubertin was also treading warily. The founder of the modern Games could have been forgiven for feeling slightly disillusioned about the whole concept. He had been elbowed aside at the first Athens and the St Louis meetings, snubbed at the intercalated Games of 1906 and now the London Olympiad seemed to be getting out of hand. He was powerless to control it. To make matters worse, a senior official called the baron publicly 'a fussy little Frenchman'. It was almost too much to bear.

Even within the various camps themselves, not all was well. Matthew P. Halpin, one of the senior American officials, was fighting for his professional life. An exact, withdrawn, well-organised man, with a great dislike of sham amateurs taking payments under the counter, Halpin had had an undistinguished career as an athlete. A New Yorker from the Lower West Side, he had been a good enough sprinter and hurdler to join the New York Athletic Club, but the highest level he had attained there had been as a pacemaker for the more able athletes. He had soon turned his ambitions to administration, becoming captain of the club at the turn of the century.

It had proved a bad time for a precise and meticulous man to try to bring order to such a free-wheeling sport of the time as amateur athletics. The young Halpin soon found himself in conflict with the boozy, easy-going ethos of the celebrated Irish-American Athletic Club, with its cornucopia of extroverted star athletes and a relaxed atmosphere towards its members accruing 'expenses'. The Irish-Americans trained at Celtic Park on Long Island, then regarded as a wilderness far from the city. When Halpin protested publicly that the rival club was shielding semi-professionals among its ranks, he laid down the foundations for a mutual animosity that was to reach a peak when he was promoted to manage the US Olympic team in Athens in 1906.

Fake-amateurism in athletics was rife in most countries. It was common practice for a well-known runner or jumper to be presented publicly with a trophy after winning it after an event, only to return it surreptitiously at a later date in exchange for a handful of banknotes. The prize could then be polished up and offered at the next tournament. However, knowing that this went on was one thing, proving it was quite another. Just before the 1908 Olympics, perhaps as an example of bolting the stable door after the horse had fled, the US Olympic Committee issued its definition of an amateur athlete as one who had never competed for money or monetary consideration, or for any wager or side bet, or who had accepted money for any coaching activities.

Among the US team bound for Athens in 1906 under the inexperienced administrator's notional command were many outspoken members of the Irish-American Athletic Association, who remembered the prissy Halpin's previous unsuccessful attempts to curtail their lavish lifestyles and his complaints against the loose way they conducted their sporting activities. They did their best to make their manager's life a misery on the trip over to Greece, to such an extent that Halpin complained, 'It is almost public property that before the American team left New York the antagonism of some members of the team reached such a state that Martin J. Sheridan was requested not to permit any of his club mates to use personal violence on me during the trip to Athens and return.'

Things got worse. Halpin found Sheridan and Rose drinking late at night and had to get an unnamed Irish-American athlete out of trouble after the latter had insulted women and smashed the furniture at the Hotel de Napoli. Even at a celebratory dinner after the 1906 Olympics were over, Halpin's problems did not diminish. A letter of congratulations from President Theodore Roosevelt was read out to the celebrated athletes and then passed down the table for all to see. It got no farther than two burly members of the Irish-American Athletic Club, and was never found again, although as Halpin reported petulantly, 'I have repeatedly demanded it from the athletes in whose hands it was last seen.'

Yet the diminutive manager was nothing if not tenacious. Even in the run-up to the 1908 Games he continued to rail at illegal payments to amateur athletes in general and the Irish-American club members in particular. For months he hounded Ray Ewry, accusing the jumper of giving paid exhibitions at circuses in 1907. He also tried in vain to prove that Martin Sheridan had accepted payment above the normal expenses for appearing at tournaments. Crowds for athletics meets in the USA at the time could exceed 10,000, so there was plenty of money to be had in the game by top competitors. The matter was brought before the Registration Committee of the Metropolitan Association of the AAAU in December 1907.

Halpin assured reporters that he was sure of his ground. 'I am free to confess that when this matter is thrashed out before the Olympic Committee that not only will I be able to make good for my seeming harsh treatment of these certain men, but will also be prepared to prove many things to their detriment.'

Both Halpin and Ewry gave evidence. Other administrators rallied to Halpin's support, including Charles H. Sherrill, former captain of the New York Athletic Club, who assured the committee of Halpin's probity and fair-mindedness. 'I would regard it as a severe criticism of his ability as a manager if he should have charge of a team none of whose members did criticise him, for it would show that he let them do pretty much as they pleased.'

After much debate it was established that Ewry had indeed competed at unregistered meetings and had probably been well-paid for so doing. However, when Halpin pressed for the erring athlete to be suspended, the committee, probably holding that Ewry was almost certainly a stone-cold certainty for a couple of gold medals at the forthcoming White City Olympiad, replied tartly that the jumper would not be suspended until it saw fit to do so and that at present it most certainly did not see fit. The case was then declared closed.

The decision was a shattering blow for Halpin. By the time the US team arrived in London, many of its senior athletes were completely ignoring their manager and regarding the much more sympathetic, even biased, AAAU president, James E. Sullivan, as the man to turn to in times of crisis, which soon were recurring with almost monotonous regularity.

Halpin certainly could not rely upon the British officials for any show of sympathy. During the long jump final of the 1906 Olympics, he insisted on continuing as the sole judge in the face of protests from Irish jumper Peter O'Connor that his opponent was an American, Myer Prinstein. What was more, Halpin refused to announce the distances covered by the jumpers until the end of the competition, when it was declared that the American had won with his first leap. Halpin was ostracised.

Matty Halpin had not been the only one trying to stem the flow of semi-professional athletes in the USA. At the beginning of 1908, Stanford University president, David Starr Jordan, accused coach Fielding 'Hurry up' Yost of Michigan University of using agents to bribe young athletes to join his team, and of offering them up to $1,500 each to do so. Yost, famed as the coach of the celebrated Michigan University 'point-a-minute' football side, replied indignantly that Jordan had been persecuting him in this matter for years. He offered to pay the sum of $1,000 to any charity if Jordan could prove that he recruited runners and jumpers illegally. Yost did not buckle under pressure. At Michigan in 1904 he had been urged to include the gigantic Ralph Rose in the starting line for the university football team. Rose was notorious for being one of the 'tramp athletes', itinerant sportsmen fully aware of their worth, who were not above allowing colleges to bid for their presence on their sporting teams. To have the throwing champion's name in the programme would add greatly to the gate receipts. The sceptical Yost had taken one look at Rose's efforts on the gridiron and had dismissed him out of hand as being too slow and would have no more to do with him.

At first Professor Jordan, a noted ichthyologist, stood his ground in the debate over amateurism, arguing that not only were Yost and other coaches giving athletes secret payments, they were also allowing them into their universities with sub-standard qualifications. Among the examples he cited was Ralph Rose, who had been accepted for Michigan with only a high school diploma. The AAAU considered the case but rejected Jordan's accusations, saying that they had not been proved. David Starr Jordan went back a wiser man to his university administration and the still waters of the study of fish.

British administrators were suffering almost as grievously. The members of the épée team who first discussed the possibility of a London Olympiad had mixed results in the 1908 competition. Lord Desborough and Theodore Cook became heavily involved in the administration of these games and the accompanying obloquy. Edgar Seligman won another silver medal in the épée team event, although surprisingly he was eliminated in the first round of the individual competition. However, there were 99 entries for the event and the competition was tough. The versatile Charles Newton-Robinson, now in his 50s, had abandoned fencing for the time being and was a judge in the yachting competition.

Nine

Field And Water

'In the stadium itself, the American team won 15 out of the
27 events that came out of the single heading of "athletics",
besides seven seconds and nine thirds; and during that
same fortnight in July they won the 100 metres swimming
and two classes in wrestling. Several of these events were
not only victories over the world of amateur sport at the
largest meeting of the kind ever held, but were also records
of the very highest merit.'

*The Olympic Games of 1908 in London: A Reply to Certain
Charges Made by the American Officials*

The official Olympic motto '*citius, altius, fortius*' was not introduced as the Olympic motto until the 1924 Games in Paris.
Nevertheless, at the London Olympiad, athletes were certainly
proving that they were 'faster, higher and stronger' than most who
had gone before them. Time after time they rose, sometimes
literally, above the squabbles and disputes to produce performances
of stunning merit. The best were rewarded by the introduction of
the three Olympic medals – gold for the winner, silver for the
runner-up and bronze for the third place. The medals were designed
by the Australian Bertram MacKennal, who later was to make
George V's coronation medal and was to become famous for his war
sculptures. One side of the medal showed two young women
crowning an athlete with a laurel wreath, the obverse side depicted
Saint George slaying the dragon. They were presented in boxes and
not designed to be worn.

Britain hoped to match the Americans in the track and field
events. The first Briton to win an 1896 Olympic final had been

bodybuilder Launceston Elliott. Born in India but conceived in the Tasmanian capital, hence his Christian name, Elliott had returned to England with his parents when he was 13. He became a pupil of the professional strong man Eugen Sandow and six years later won a national weightlifting title.

He entered himself for the Athens Olympics in a number of events and was one of the first Britons to compete, finishing fourth in a heat of the 100 metres and eliminated from the later rounds of the sprint. In the weightlifting, his principal event, he came second in the two-handed lifting and first in the one-handed competition. He entered the rope-climbing but withdrew when he could not reach the top of the rope and took part in the Graeco-Roman wrestling. He was defeated quickly in his first bout by a German, Carl Schuhmann. There was no weight limit in the wrestling competition. Schuhmann was only 5 feet 4 inches tall and much lighter than his opponent. Elliott took his loss so badly that he had to be escorted, still protesting, from the stadium.

Even if he was not a skilled wrestler, he was a genuinely strong man with a 50-inch chest and 17-inch biceps. *Sandow's Magazine* of December 1899 reported that he was 'truly a marvellous man' and that he had recently lifted 200 pounds with either hand and narrowly failed to hoist 275 pounds with both hands. Returning home from Athens, he cashed in on his new-found fame by touring the world's music halls with a strong man act, which included a simulated Roman gladiatorial combat. He and his professional boxer opponent once got carried away and battered each other so fiercely that they could not participate in the second house performance.

American strongmen performed well in the 1908 field events. Members of the US team shut out the opposition in the throwing events, with Irish-Americans doing particularly well. Bohola, County Mayo-born Martin Sheridan, who had emigrated at the age of 16, won both the classical discus and the freestyle discus, repeating the successes of previous Olympiads. The freestyle success brought him his third successive Olympic first place in the event, while his classical style win was his second in the Olympics. Altogether, during his career he won five golds, three silvers and a bronze at three Olympiads ranging from 1904 to 1908. He was versatile, a good swimmer and also an exponent of the horizontal pole vault, in which a pole was used to help an athlete gain distance, not height. In October 1907, for all his considerable bulk, Sheridan jumped 28 feet in this event at a New York meeting.

Although he had broken the world record for the freestyle discus throw immediately before leaving for London, by his standards he had been going through a bad patch in the USA. In most of the tournaments in which he had participated he had been handicapped into giving his opponents many yards' start in the different throws, which partly accounted for the problems. Upon his arrival in the UK he remained confident in his ability to raise his game, telling a *New York Times* reporter, 'I can let out a few links yet. They'll have to go some to beat me in the big test.'

Sheridan had good reason to be confident. His career as perhaps the world's outstanding all-round athlete would last for 14 years without flagging. A contemporary wrote of him, 'He was the most handsome of athletes and although he was a giant in strength, he could run the hundred yards in a little more than ten seconds.' Between 1901 and 1911, he increased his discus record incrementally from 120 feet to 141 feet. He was also a resourceful and kind-hearted man to those who did not cross him. At the start of the 1904 Olympic marathon, the Cuban entrant Felix Carbajal had turned up on what was a baking hot day in thick long trousers and street shoes. The Cuban had lost all his money in a poker game on the way and had been forced to hitchhike the last few miles and then compete in his street clothes. Sheridan went to the trouble of hunting down a pair of shears and lopping off the competitor's trousers at the knees, allowing him to run more freely; the Cuban finished fourth.

John Jesus Flanagan, from Kilbreedy, County Limerick, won the 1908 hammer throw for the US, with Irish-born team-mate Mat McGrath coming second. In third place, representing Canada, was Cornelius Walsh, who had been born in County Cork.

Flanagan had emigrated to the USA after winning the 1900 English championship with a world record-breaking throw of 163 feet and 4 inches (he was also credited with a long jump of 22 feet). In the US he had to remodel his technique. Accustomed to throwing a hammer with a stiff wooden handle, he was forced to adapt to a pliable handle. Fortunately he was able to devote some study to this change, having joined the New York Police Force in 1903 and been given a meaningless office job that allowed him plenty of time for training. He was one of the few non-college athletes in the US team. He won the 1908 gold medal with a throw of 170 feet 4¼ inches.

There were no complaints that time about the visibility of the American flag, as again and again the Stars and Stripes emblem was run up on the flagpole in the centre of the arena, but there was some concern about how many people were there to see it raised.

On 15 July, when the strongmen started to win their medals, there were only a few hundred people in the cold and drizzle of the stadium. By the afternoon the number had increased to about 15,000 but there were still great swathes of empty seats apparent all over the White City. The writer Sir Arthur Conan Doyle was moved to wonder if it might not be worth invading the classrooms of London schools and forcing their pupils to watch the Olympiad, thus filling some of the spaces.

There was another Irish athlete in the competition, although one who was to withdraw because he was approaching 40. That was Thomas Kiely, a Tipperary man. At the 1904 Olympics he had rejected Great Britain's offer to pay his way to St Louis if he would compete as a member of its team. Instead, he sold many of his trophies in order to pay his own way so that he could compete for Ireland. At St Louis in 1904, Kiely won the All-Round championship. This was not a competition for sloths, comprising as it did the 100 yards, one mile, hurdles, 880 yards walk, high jump, long jump, pole vault, 56 pounds weight thrown into the air, and the shot put.

The Irish-American cabal formed an influential drinking team during the 1908 Olympics. Rumour had it that the decision for Rose not to dip the Stars and Stripes to King Edward VII during the opening ceremony had been arrived at over a few jars in some ill-lit bar. It was said that the truculent Sheridan in his cups had threatened to put Rose in hospital if he even considered acknowledging the presence of the British monarch. Several years later the same men were still bending their elbows with a will. In an article in 1910, the *St Louis Post-Dispatch* delineated those major track athletes who 'use intoxicants regularly while preparing for their specialties'. Top of the list were Martin Sheridan, John Flanagan, Mel Sheppard and Ralph Rose.

All of them were proud of belonging to the Irish-American club, whether by descent or adoption. Martin Sheridan gave an interview to a reporter in which he said, 'If one were to go right through the team the difficulty would be to pick out those who haven't at least some strain of Irish blood in them.' To the irreverent, the multiplicity of huge ethnic Gaelic throwers were known as the Irish Whales.

In 1908, there was doubt as to whether some of the Irish Whales would be allowed to compete at the White City. Shortly before the US team sailed, New York Police Commissioner Bingham declared that the policemen under his command, Sheridan, McGrath and Flanagan, might not be allowed leave to compete. The Irish-American Alliance were forced to go to the top and pull a few strings with Mayor McLellan before the huge cops could discard their uniforms in favour of athletic clothing. Sheridan then caused more problems by announcing that he was thinking of getting married and might not be able to get away in time. Somehow this problem was smoothed over as well.

At the 1908 Olympics, the Irish were to become floating athletes. When newspapers sneered at the USA for relying on Eire-born competitors a correspondent writing indignantly to the *New York Times* pointed out that 'Great Britain and her colonies were also helped by the Irish. Kerr of Canada is a native of Ireland and Hefferon of South Africa is a native of the same island. Ahearne, Walsh and Leahy, all Irishmen, won points for England.' *Outlook* magazine proudly said that such multi-ethnicity was all part of the American way and that the US team was proud of the fact that it contained Anglo-Saxon, Teuton, Slav, Celt, black Ethiopian and Red Indian members.

Of the Americans, Ralph Rose had won the shot-putting event at St Louis and was literally a heavy favourite to retain it in London. World record distances in excess of 50 feet were predicted of the huge American. Only a few days after Rose's arrival in England, Olympic administrator Theodore Cook watched the athlete achieve 50 feet in training at the White City Stadium.

Rose's character was equally impressive. He was tumultuous and outspoken and had been expelled from Cornell. He had once challenged world heavyweight champion James J. Jeffries to a fight. 'I would not come out the worse for wear were I to swap blows with him!' he boasted. Rose was reputed to eat a two-pound steak and six raw eggs in their shells for breakfast. In the event, it was the weather that won out over his strength and training regime. The rain prevented his breaking a world record at the White City but his winning distance of more than 48 feet was enough. At St Louis in 1904, only one non-American had entered the shot and he had been disqualified. This time, Rose beat contestants in the event from Finland, France, Hungary and Greece.

In second place was Dennis Horgan, yet another Irish-born athlete, from County Cork. He was a very experienced shot putter, the winner of 13 AAA titles and 17 Irish championships in the event. He was fortunate to be able to be present at the White City. In the previous year, as a member of the New York police force, he had attempted to break up a brawl and had his skull smashed with a blow from a shovel. It was doubted whether he would recover, but the 39-year-old Horgan came back to take the silver medal in his first Olympic tournament.

As an example of the meticulous organisation of events on the field, as opposed to the rather ad-hoc administration of earlier Olympiads, in the preliminary rounds of the shot put, each athlete was allowed three throws. Three athletes with best distances at the end of three throws were then allowed three extra attempts. The winner was the one who had thrown the furthest.

Eric Lemming of Sweden, a 28-year-old Stockholm policeman, won the freestyle javelin throw and the javelin events where the javelin was held in the middle, preventing a clean sweep by the USA. At the 1900 Paris Olympics, Lemming had entered six events: the high jump, pole vault, hammer, discus, long jump and triple jump, achieving fourth places in the first two but nothing of particular moment in the others. By the time of the London Olympiad he was specialising a little more.

Both javelin events were distinguished by the variety of techniques used by the different entrants. Some held the javelin in one hand and propelled it forward with the other. Others whirled it about their heads like a hammer and released it at the point of maximum velocity. A few simply bowled the implement. Referring to the multiplicity of styles on display, judge G.S. Robertson, wrote, 'A Hungarian proceeded to take his javelin by its hinder end and, as it were, poke it into the air from the back. A council of war was held on the spot and we decided that the rules were not sufficiently specific to enable us to put a stop to this odd method, which, however, was by no means successful.' It was decided afterwards to strive for some sort of uniformity in throwing styles by banning the javelin held in the middle event from Olympic competition altogether.

The pole vault event ended in a complicated tie for first place between two American athletes, Alfred Gilbert and Edward Cook. Three other athletes tied for third place. Normally there would have been a jump-off for both first and third places but the dramatic closing of the marathon was developing in the arena at the same time, causing long pauses in the pole-vaulting competition as athletes and competitors hurried over to see the events unfolding on the track, forcing the judges to declare ties for the gold and bronze medals.

Even here there were controversies. The pole vault was a notoriously difficult event. Coaches claimed that it took ten years to master the art. Participants developed their own styles and grew accustomed to their own individual poles, which had been evolving in style over the years. Originally, hard ash, spruce and hickory wood up to 15 feet long and weighing a hefty 10 pounds had been used. Then lighter bamboo poles had come into favour. By the time of the Olympics many of the European competitors were using poles with three iron spikes fixed in the base. These could be thrust in to the ground to give purchase. Most of the Americans preferred more solid poles that were jammed into holes in the ground at the end of the run-up. The Olympic officials refused to countenance such holes being dug.

In an effort to gain an advantage, the joint first place winner Gilbert had even purchased an axe for half-a-crown (25p) at an ironmonger's. He had hidden it under his sweater, hoping to dig out a suitable surreptitious socket for his pole. When he crouched to excavate the requisite few inches of soil he was surrounded almost at once by protesting administrators. Gilbert argued back with such vehemence that a policeman was called over. The American athlete demanded to be shown in the rulebook where it said that only spiked poles could be used. He was told that it was the British custom which had to be observed by competitors at the White City event. The hole was filled in.

Reluctantly, the disgruntled competitor affixed iron spikes to the end of his pole, claiming that he could not give of his best with such a cumbersome piece of apparatus. He and a young team-mate named Edward Cook both cleared 12 feet, but Gilbert was not mollified, as his father had promised him $100 if he could jump 13 feet at the Olympics. To make matters worse, there were no mounds of sand or straw to break the falls of the pole vaulters on the far side of the bar. Half in earnest the American competitors threatened to bring mattresses with them to soften their landings.

Cook was equally disgruntled. His coach at Cornell University was only interested in track athletes and Cook practically had to train himself during the preparations for the White City Games. He was accustomed to using a spruce pole and when he came to London he tried to adjust to the bamboo variety, but found it too small and light for his purposes. Cook, from Ohio, was only 19 but showed great coolness under pressure. Onlookers noted that he was one of the few vaulters who did not seem affected by the noise surrounding the finish of the marathon.

Years later he marvelled at the efficacy of fibreglass vaulting poles, which allowed jumpers to scale heights more than six feet in excess of his record. 'They just go out of sight nowadays,' he said wistfully. He had become a bank director and farmer and lived to be well over 90.

Missing from the pole vault competition was American three-time, inter-collegiate champion and claimant to the world record, Walter Dray, who was seen in the stands with his father, watching events on the field closely. The *New York Times* reported that Dray's father had forbidden his son to take part in the event. Other newspapers followed up on the story and several said that the real instigator of Walter Dray's inexplicable absence was his mother, who was afraid that against the best opposition in the world he might soar so high that he would hurt himself on the way back down.

As expected, 34-year-old Ray Ewry won the standing high jump and standing long jump events. As a child, he had spent long periods in bed suffering from polio, but by sheer determination had built up the strength in his legs to such an extent that he was even able to play college football.

Ewry's wife, distressed by the dogged attempts of Matty Halpin to prove that her husband was a professional, had begged her husband to give up athletics altogether and the 1908 Olympics were to prove his swansong. It was the end of a glittering career. Altogether Ewry won eight gold medals in the official Olympiads and had previous won two at Athens in 1906.

The rules for both standing high and long jumps were identical. A competitor could place his feet in any position and was allowed to rock backwards and forwards, lifting toes and heels alternately from the ground, but could leave the ground only once. The *Encyclopaedia Brittanica* of the time also recommended for the standing long jump that 'well-spiked shoes should be worn, for it is in reality nothing but a push against the ground and a perfect purchase is of the greatest importance'.

For all his supremacy in the amateur ranks Ewry was plagued by the claims of professional jumpers, who professed, with no proof, to be leaping much greater distances than the American had ever accomplished. His particular *bête noire* was an English professional called John Darby, from Dudley, who claimed to have out-jumped Ewry in a number of events. It seems likely, however, that Dudley's claimed distance of a standing long jump in excess of almost 15 feet was achieved by the jumper clutching weights in his hands to give him added velocity.

In the 1908 Olympics, Ewry managed a jump of just over 10 feet 11 inches in the standing broad jump (or long jump). Displaying great versatility, enormous thrower M.J. Sheridan achieved third position and gained a bronze medal with a leap of exactly 10 feet 7 inches.

To win the standing high jump, Ewry cleared 5 feet 2 inches. In both events, Greek athlete Konstantinos Tsiklitras won the silver medals. Ewry's Olympic events were discontinued and his St Louis standing long jump of over 11 feet 4 inches would never be equalled.

In the high jump the Olympic competitors were rather put in the shade by the professional, Darby, who claimed that he had achieved a height of six feet with both ankles tied together! There were mutterings that this sort of record could only have been attained by the use of a springboard of some description.

Harry Porter of the USA, a 26-year-old native of Bridgeport, Connecticut, won the high jump with some insouciance, only removing his sweater to make three unsuccessful attempts on the world record after he had won the competition with a leap of 6 feet and 3 inches. Just an inch behind, sharing second place, were Irishman Con Leahy representing the team of Great Britain and Ireland, Istvan Somodi of Hungary and George Andre of France. In order to differentiate between the tied, second-place jumpers, the bar was raised a mere quarter of an inch, but none of the three was able to clear the extra fraction. After some debate among the judges it was agreed that each jumper would be given a silver medal. Throughout the competition a white handkerchief was placed over the bar to help the jumpers on their approach.

Sharing the high jump fifth place was another American, Herbert Gidney of the Boston Athletic Association. He had raised eyebrows earlier in the competition when, after coming third in his heat, he had complained about the prevailing conditions underfoot. As the *Warren Evening Mirror* of 22 July explained, 'H.A. Gidney was defeated by Monson of Norway and Leader of England, but after the other sections had concluded a protest was entered on the ground that the spot where the other sections were contended was more favourable than the first section.' Gidney's protest was upheld and the section was jumped again. This time the American won the heat and went through to the final but could not get among the medals.

Silver medal winner Cornelius 'Con' Leahy had made an unsuccessful bid to represent the USA. A year later he was to emigrate there with his brother. Both made the US national side. In the 1908 competition, Peter Leahy had been eliminated in the early stages, although his personal best of 6 feet 5 inches made him one of the favourites for the gold medal before the event.

Three Americans finished in the final four in the long jump competition, called the broad jump in official reports, causing the satisfied correspondent for the Wisconsin *La Crosse Tribune* to write, 'From the way the Yankees qualified it might have been inferred that they came from Australia, where the kangaroos grow.' The gold medal was taken by Francis Irons, a relative dark horse, with Daniel Kelly in second place and Edward Cook in fourth. The bronze medal was won by the Canadian Calvin Bricker.

The hop, step and jump gold medal was taken by Ireland's Tim Ahearne, representing Great Britain and Ireland, with his last attempt in the competition. In ninth position was Dennis Murray, who had joined with Con Leahy in an effort to be considered for the US team. M.J. Sheridan was also one of the competitors but dropped out early on. Finishing sixth was Native American Frank Mount Pleasant from the Tuscarora-Iroquois tribe near Niagara Falls. His main claim to athletics fame was that he had been one of a team of three from Carlisle Indian College that had taken on and defeated an entire full-strength college side in an open competition. As an outstanding football captain and quarterback he also was one of the first to use the long pass downfield. He was a slightly built man but one of his coaches said of him, 'You didn't dare judge Mount Pleasant by his appearance. Games came as naturally to him as breathing.'

The White City Olympiad was the first one in which the diving and swimming events were held in the same stadium as the track and field events. There were two diving competitions, for men only. The plain high diving contest was held on two wooden platforms, one 5 metres high and the other 10 metres above the board. Each entrant had to make two compulsory dives from each board and a further three plunges from the higher platform. Points were awarded for the degree of difficulty inherent in each dive.

This stipulation led to some unease on the part of the competitors, fearing that they would be expected to take too many risks at this level of diving. Their feelings were expressed by George W. Gaidzik, one of the American entrants: 'Some of the dives called for in the rules are dangerous,' he wrote. 'I doubt that many of those entered in the diving competition will go through with them.' At least one of the other divers proved him wrong, with what could have been serious results.

In the fourth heat, a Briton, George Cane, attempted a difficult double somersault. It went badly wrong. Cane hit the water practically in a belly flop, lost consciousness and sank to the bottom of the pool. When he came to the surface he was floating inert on his face.

Fortunately, a Swede called Hjalmar Johansson, the eventual winner of the event, was alert enough to spot the Englishman's predicament. He dived in and brought the unconscious diver out of the pool. Cane was so badly concussed and shaken up that he spent the next few days in bed. The Swedish team felt sorry for his ignominious exit from the Olympics and generously clubbed together to buy him a silver cup. The official report for the Olympics expressed the hope that the trophy would be a memento of the occasion. He probably had rather a nasty headache as well.

The US representative in the plain diving, George Gaidzik, came fifth in the final, which he only reached after much undignified squabbling. In his heat an official accused the American of benefiting on the diving board from a series of hand signals passed on to him by another American below. There was talk of disqualifying Gaidzik for this breach of the regulations, but the American protested, backed by the other members of his team. The official withdrew his strictures and the matter was treated as a misunderstanding, although there was an implicit reproof in a pointed written suggestion made for future Olympic swimming tournaments: 'It was also thought that difficulties might be avoided in the future if a clause were inserted, forbidding a diver from being signalled to by a friend upon the bank.'

Although George Gaidzik had been a favourite for a medal in the event, and he had scored highly in his heat, his concentration had been disturbed by the bickering and he did not perform nearly as well as he had done earlier in the day. He was also an accident-prone man. Once, when trying to train on the deck of a passenger ship in bad weather, he mistimed a vault over the vessel's rails and badly damaged the knuckles of one hand. He was unsuccessful in the 1912 Olympics and must have found it something of a relief later on to abandon athletics, at least temporarily, for a sojourn studying drawing in Paris.

He did better in the fancy diving event, his speciality. This took place from two springboards, one a metre above the ground and the other 3 metres over the water. A variety of different dives had to be made from each board. Gaidzik was the only non-German to win a medal in this competition. Albert Zurner and Kurt Behrens took the gold and silver respectively, while the American tied for third place with Gottlob Walz.

Snowy Baker, the all-round Australian athlete, also entered the fancy springboard event, but was placed last in his heat. He had not expected to do better. Previously his main diving experience had been garnered at rough and ready country carnivals back home, where his *pièce de résistance* had consisted of being tied up in a sack and thrown into the nearest river, only to emerge miraculously completely unencumbered a few seconds later. On one occasion, however, as he was thrown into the water, he had dropped the penknife he always secreted between his bound wrists to use to rip the bag open. When he did not return to the surface, spectators had to dive in to rescue the semi-conscious diver.

As well as the diving events there were six swimming events in the Olympiad. They were all orthodox races, unlike some of those in earlier competitions. In the Paris Olympics, there had been an obstacle race in which competitors had to struggle over a pole, scramble across a line of moored boats and dive under another set of stationary craft. A more exclusive competition was devised for the first Athens tournament, when a 100 metres freestyle event for sailors only was held.

There were two outstanding swimmers in the 1908 Olympics. Charles Meldrum Daniels of the USA, 'the human fish', had taken two golds, a silver and a bronze at the St Louis Olympics and a gold at the intercalated Games at Athens in 1906. Henry Taylor of Great Britain had also been at Athens, where he had won gold, silver and bronze swimming medals.

The two men came from very different backgrounds. Daniels came from a comfortably-off home and had the time and resources to make a careful study of the art of swimming. He was particularly interested in the stroke known as the Australian crawl, which became popular in the USA soon after the turn of the century. The stroke had originally been naturally used by Solomon Islanders in the Roviana Lagoon of the South Pacific and had been taken to Australia by a young islander called Alick Wickham. Australian swimmers took up the powerful stroke and it began to spread. Daniels modified this method, increasing the ratio of kicks to arm strokes. He soon became the leading member of the swimming section of the New York Athletic Club. His mastery of the new form of swimming became apparent in 1906 when, in his club's 25-metre pool, Daniels set a new American record and equalled the world best time for 100 metres.

Henry Taylor was a much more prosaic character. He came from a poor home, was orphaned early and brought up by a dedicated brother who taught him to swim. Taylor was able to use a local swimming bath on 'dirty day', the day before the water was changed, when the entrance fee was reduced. He won a schoolboy championship in 1898 but after he left school to work in a cotton mill the only swimming practice he could get was in a local canal. He was tipped to do well at the White City Games, as was another working-class British swimmer, Syd Battersby from the Wigan swimming club.

Some of the swimming events were being held for the first time, so the fastest time automatically became an Olympic record. Daniels started brightly by winning the 100 metres freestyle in a world record time. He beat into second place the Hungarian Zoltan von Halmay, who had won the gold medal in St Louis, with

Daniels coming in third. American officials claimed that Daniels had been in the process of taking off his pullover when the gun had sounded to start the race and that the swimmer had had to make up several yards to catch up with the others. Newspapers took up the story but Daniels denied it firmly.

Daniels also entered for the 400 metres freestyle, but withdrew in order to conserve his energy for other events. Henry Taylor won the race by five yards, with the young Australian Frank Beaurepaire in second place and the Austrian Otto Scheff, who had taken the gold in St Louis, coming in third, complaining in vain that he had been fouled.

Taylor and Beaurepaire were expected to contend the 1500 metres freestyle, but Briton Syd Battersby swam the race of his life to split them, coming in three seconds behind Taylor and in third was the Australian. Taylor set new Olympic and world records.

Battersby was a carpenter who was given so much time off for swimming by his boss that in recognition of the fact he presented his employer with a medal, a rare and commendable example of a boss being rewarded for long and meritorious service by an employee. Battersby had so much energy left after his 1500 metres final that, alone of the competitors, he went on to try to post a good time for the mile. Although he had taken a few seconds' breather after the 1500 metres, he still went on to break the mile world record.

The 100 metres backstroke went to a German champion, Arno Bieberstein, while the 200 metres backstroke gold medal was won by an outsider, Briton Fred Holman from the West Country. He set world and Olympic records. He was given a civic reception upon his return home but died only a few years later.

Between events, at the request of the other swimmers, Charles Daniels gave exhibitions of his crafted version of the crawl. He and Taylor then came up against each other in the anticipated 4 × 200 metres freestyle relay. Daniels swam a very fast leg to take his country into second place behind Hungary, but Henry Taylor won his third gold of the competition and was chaired around the field by the other members of the British relay team following the race's last leg, in which he had made up an improbable number of yards on the swimmers ahead of him to win the event for his country.

The race almost ended in tragedy. The much-favoured Hungarian team was in the lead when Zoltan von Halmay started the last leg. However, with two fast swimmers catching up on him, the Hungarian seemed to get disorientated. He slowed down, veered off course and even collided with a wall. He still recovered in time to gain a silver medal for his country.

Having won golds in the 200 metres and 400 metres freestyles in St Louis in 1904, Charles M. Daniels went on to claim the gold in the 100 metres at Athens in 1906 and London in 1908. In 1909 he was named athlete of the year by the American AAU. When he retired at age 26, he held 53 national championships.

Water polo was first played in the 1900 Paris Olympics. The game was slow produce a uniform set of rules – the US version was considered particularly violent and dangerous. The average game was a waterbound fracas in which holding, elbowing and general mayhem made it resemble a form of damp all-in wrestling, with the bodies of unconscious players floating about like so much jetsam. That reputation partly explained why no overseas teams competed in the St Louis competition in 1904. This probably turned out to be a considerable let-off for the absentees. The competition was held in a pond which was so dirty that six of the competitors were taken ill and rumours spread that several of them had contacted typhus.

The White City pool, although by no means sparkling in appearance, did not offer such a threat to the health of the competitors, either in its sanitation or the brutality of its competitors. Indeed, the tournament was a comparatively sedate one. Hungary and Austria withdrew. Belgium defeated the Netherlands 8–1 and Sweden 8–4. Great Britain drew a bye into the final, where its team defeated Belgium 9–2.

By the turn of the century, rowing had become one of the most popular sports in Great Britain and the USA. As early as the 16th century, the River Thames had become one of the most overcrowded inland waterways in the world. So many accidents were brought about by poor rowing and steering that King Henry VIII decreed that in future only properly licensed men would be allowed in charge of boats running through the capital's main artery. His edict led to more than 3,000 professional oarsmen plying their trade on the river before the end of the century, with almost as many bound apprentices learning their trade. The presence of so many skilful boatmen soon led to unofficial races between them and then more organised contests with prizes, champions and patrons.

Two hundred years later, the amateur sport was also flourishing, especially on the Thames. The first Oxford–Cambridge boat race was held in 1829 from Putney to Mortlake, and became an annual event, patronised by thousands of spectators along the river's bank. After another decade, the small, riverside town of Henley instituted its regatta. The opening by the Great Western Railway of a branch line to the town meant that large numbers of spectators could arrive every year to watch the wealthy at their water play. This was not an unmixed blessing as the charming little town also attracted a different sort of patron.

Writing in 1908, author Martin Cobbett in his book *Sporting Notions* deplored the rowdy nature of many of the town's inhabitants during the regattas, 'Nowhere except in such country towns do you find so many labourers, whose only apparent source of income is derivable from standing all day idle in the market place, unless you can call habitual drunkenness a trade, occupation, or profession.' In 1851, Prince Albert became patron of the club, and the regatta was given the 'Royal' prefix. By the time of the Olympics, the regattas extended over four days.

During this period Olympic rowing was also flourishing in the USA, although as in other sporting areas the governing body, the National Association of Amateur Oarsmen, had great difficulty in establishing which of its members were true amateurs and which were not. Matters came to a head in 1904 when a leading American rowing club, Vesper from Philadelphia, entered a crew for an event at Henley. The Americans were defeated but then a row erupted when its members were accused of breaching amateur rules.

The Philadelphians were declared to have employed a professional coach, being lax in their accounting methods and actually accepting money. At an official enquiry held in New York, the club's treasurer was censured and several crew members suspended for a year.

When arrangements were being made for the Olympic rowing events, there was originally a suggestion that they should be based at Putney, closer in to the capital along the river, but this venue was soon overruled in favour of the more traditional and influential Henley. Another row burst out when the Henley Royal Regatta for 1908 was closed to foreign crews, depriving them of the chance to row over the proposed Olympic course. In effect, the autocratic Henley administrators had decided to use the competition as a series of selections for the British crews.

The Americans and some of the other overseas rowing organisations protested, but Henley was adamant. Herbert Steward, chairman of its managing committee, did not sound entirely convincing when he declared that in the Royal Regatta and the Olympic competition it would be unreasonable to expect the club to mount what would be two international regattas so close together in one season. He ended his address by stating that it was the intention of everyone at Henley 'to do all in their power to make its Olympic regatta the international regatta of the year'.

Originally there had been a great deal of interest in the proposed US entry. As early as 1905, the *Buffalo News* had told its readers, 'Buffalo's world champion rower Steven Coppola is looking forward to the 1908 Olympics. Having won the world title in the men's heavyweight rowing in Japan, the 21 year old former student at the West Side Rowers Club hopes to contend for a spot on the Olympic squad about the time he finishes his studies at Princeton.'

By 1908, attitudes were changing. Faced with such a transparent snub from Henley, Americans began to lose interest in the whole rowing competition. Problems had started in January 1908, when James Pilkington, president of US National Association of Oarsmen refuted claims that most of the proposed 30 Olympic rowers would be selected from colleges and universities rather than the more plebian clubs. Pilkington assured his members that selections would be made irrespective of the social position of the competitors. The majority of rowers did not believe him.

As a result Pilkington and his committee found it increasingly difficult to raise funds from the rowing clubs across the country. Those clubs which were willing to contribute were only prepared to do so if at least one of their members was guaranteed a starting place in one of the races. A number of them went even further and demanded that entries from Yale, Harvard, Cornell, Pennsylvania and other colleges be strictly limited. Pilkington refused to give such an assurance.

Almost in desperation, another official, Julian W. Curtiss of Yale, proposed that each major university put up $1,000 and allow their crews to race against one another for Olympic selection, cutting out the clubs altogether. Yale and Pennsylvania agreed to the plan, but the other universities would not part with the money. As at least $4,500 was needed to send the rowers to Britain, the scheme disintegrated. It looked as if the USA would not be represented at Henley.

In the meantime the Royal Regatta continued at Henley. The absence of overseas entries meant that spectators along the banks were fewer than usual, and that the number of moored houseboats containing the more privileged onlookers was reduced to a mere dozen, although the geranium festooned *Miranda,* belonging to the American millionaire A.G. Vanderbilt, certainly stood out among the other small floating hotels. Crews from Cambridge and the Leander club were also missing, as they were training for the Olympics.

Eight nations competed in the 1908 Olympiad rowing, including Hungary and Norway, taking part for the first time, but there were no crews from the USA. At the last moment there was a suggestion that Harvard might compete, but their application was rejected as the deadline of 1 June had passed.

Always delighted to take a swing at the Brits, James E. Sullivan entered the fray. 'I tried to get the Olympic association to give us until 30 June,' he told the press, 'but I was refused. We could not enter by 1 June, as we could not pick our crews until after the big races. If this time had been extended by one month we would have had a crew in the Olympic regatta.'

England was favoured to win each of the four events. John Kennedy, Yale's coach, studied English rowing during the summer of 1908 and concluded that the constant influx of overseas crews competing at Henley over the past few years had done much to invigorate the home country's methods, 'So many different crews – Hungarian, Swiss, Belgian and Americans – have gone to England to compete and have introduced various new ideas.' Crews from Belgium and Sweden were also thought to be in with some chance.

Nations in the competition could enter two teams for each event. The usual Henley course was extended for the occasion to one-and-a-half miles, marked by the addition of piles and booms on each side of the River Thames.

Due to the width of the river, only two boats could compete at the same time and the heats were arranged so that nationals of the same country did not compete against one another in the opening stages of the competition.

The single sculls was an individual event, with a rower pulling on two oars. Two Britons contested the final. Experienced, 40-year-old Harry Blackstaffe had been winning titles since 1897, including the amateur championship of the Thames, the championship of the Netherlands and the prestigious Diamond Sculls. He defeated Alexander McCulloch by almost a length.

Two teams from Leander contested the final of the coxless pairs, with Reginald Fenning and Gordon Thomson winning by over two lengths. Leander also won through to the final of the coxless fours but lost to the boat from Magdalen College, Oxford. Leander came back to triumph in the final of the coxed eights, their eight consisting entirely of Oxford and Cambridge blues, although most of these had been gained so long ago that the team was known as 'the old man's eight'. Guy Nickalls at 41 and C.D. Burnell, who was 36, were the senior members of the Leander eight which defeated a Belgian eight by two lengths in the final. Because of the ban on foreign entrants for Henley Regatta that year, the Belgians had been unable to row over the course, while the Leander side had been practising over that particular stretch of the Thames for weeks.

The motorboat races were a definite disappointment. There were events for three classes: eight metre, 60 feet and open class. But there were few entries, bad weather and sedate speeds, usually of less than 19 miles an hour. The long-awaited return of Lord Howard de Walden and the Duke of Westminster's motorboats from an unsuccessful attempt to defeat the best of the American speedboats proved a definite anti-climax. 'Tommy' de Walden did attract some attention for having the latest in custom-built motor-boats, but he did not seem to know what to do with them. His pride and joy, *Daimler II*, was said by many to be the latest thing in motor-boat design. It possessed three, 90-horsepower Daimler engines capable of producing a speed of 31 miles an hour and, thanks to a judicious placing of the exhaust pipe, ran with a minimum of noise. Unfortunately, upon her Olympic debut in rough seas, the vessel was unable to display its power. The official report said, 'Just before the start *Daimler II* showed a fine burst of speed, but just as the five-minute gun fired, she developed some trouble, and, after hanging about and cruising at slow speed for some time, she turned and went away down the course without crossing the line.'

The peer maintained his standard admirably with his second powered boat *Dylan*. This competed in an open class event taking place in a south westerly gale. Its first race in Southampton Water was abandoned due to the bad weather and the peer did not turn up for the rerun. He contributed to the cause, however, by ordering two more of his vessels, the steam yacht *Branwen* and the steam yacht *Rose en Soleil* to cruise the area in case any of the other motor boats taking part needed assistance.

Each of the races took part over five laps, covering a total of some 70 kilometres. Neither the Duke of Westminster nor Lord Howard de Walden, the only entrants, managed to complete the first of two A-class races, open to vessels of any size or power. The former managed to maintain this standard by being unable to complete the second race in the class, after running up on to a mud spit, leaving the only other entrant, Emile Thubron of France in the *Camille*, the winner.

In the second event, open to vessels of under 60 feet in length, two boats entered. The *Gyrinus*, captained by Thomas Thornycroft, finished the course and won the gold medal. The victory owed a great deal to the efforts of its two crew members, Bernard Redwood and John Field-Richards, who were commended by the press for bailing steadily and with great British aplomb and dignity throughout. Thornycroft had taken a chance of weighing down his boat by taking on board an extra crew member purely for the purpose of getting rid of excess water, but his decision was vindicated. The only other boat in the race was the *Quicksilver*, captained by John Marshall Gorham. He seems to have taken Mrs Gorham with him for the ride, because hers is the only other name down on the crew manifest. Presumably Mrs Gorham's solitary bailing abilities were not quite as well developed as the combined efforts of Messrs Redwood and Field-Richards, for the *Quicksilver* abandoned the race when water coming over the side threatened to capsize the vessel.

Flushed with triumph, the *Gyrinus* also entered the C Class event, for motorboats of less than eight metres. Again, only one other motorboat, the *Sea Dog*, entered and once more Captain Thornycroft and his doughty bailers were successful when the *Sea Dog* broke down with engine trouble, did not complete the distance and had to be towed to safety.

The 12 metre class yachting event not only did not take place in London, but was not even held in England. Only two yachts were entered, the *Hera*, based in Glasgow and the *Mouchette* from Liverpool. It would have been expensive and time-consuming for both vessels to make the long journey to the Isle of Wight, where the other Olympic yacht races were taking place, so it was agreed that the owners would toss a coin to see whether the competition would be held on the Mersey or the Clyde. The owner of the *Hera*,

Thomas Glenn-Coats, eldest son of Sir Thomas Glenn-Coats, was successful and it was agreed that the other owner, Charles MacIver, would sail his yacht to Glasgow where the Olympic title would be decided over the best of three races.

There were ten men in each crew. The *Hera* won the first of the two races convincingly and in the second the *Mouchette* was baulked by a stationary steam yacht, allowing the Scottish vessel to win again, rendering the start of the third race superfluous. The *Hera* went on to a long seagoing life until it sank off the coast of Argentina in 1950.

The remainder of the Olympic yacht races were based on the Royal Victoria Yacht Club at Ryde on the Isle of Wight. Coming from an island race there were many seafaring folk who might have fancied their chances of crewing a vessel in such a prestigious sailing event. They were to be swiftly disabused. An official edict summarised the sort of people wanted in the competition. 'No person can be considered an amateur who has ever been employed for wages in the handling of a sailing yacht or of any fore-and-aft rigged vessel.' It was taken for granted, of course, that such strictures did not apply to naval officers.

With such a rigorous screening process in place, a mere 13 yachts, from five countries, entered the 1908 Olympics. In the seven metre category only one yacht competed. This was the *Heroine*, skippered by Charles Rivett-Carnac and crewed by his wife Frances and two other gentlemen. After the late withdrawal of its only competitor, the *Heroine* completed two separate circuits of the 13-mile course sedately to win the gold medal.

There were five entrants in the six metre class, including yachts from Belgium, France and Sweden. The British vessel *Dormy* won the race, with the Belgian *Zut* second. Another British yacht, the *Cobweb*, beat the Swedish *Vinga* into second place in the eight metre class. In third place was another British vessel, the *Sorais*. The vessel's owner, the Duchess of Westminster, was believed to have been on board, probably as a passenger.

Ten

Track And Wheels

'It is difficult to see how American competition can be welcomed in Europe.'

The Olympic Games of 1908 in London: A Reply to Certain Charges Made by the American Officials

As the days passed in damp monotony at the White City, there were American wins in the 110 metres hurdles, the 400 metres hurdles, the high jump, the long jump, the pole vault, the standing high, long and triple jumps and the relay. There were victories for Great Britain in the five-mile run, the 3200 metres steeplechase, the three-mile run, the 3500 metres walk, the ten-mile walk and the triple jump.

Athletes huddled in blankets in the miserable weather, waiting to be called for their events. The officials, of whom there were many, suffered just as badly. Of the referees, starters, timekeepers, judges, inspectors, scorers, measurers and clerks of the course, few were able to remain under cover for long.

The sprints were won by a South African and an Irish-born Canadian respectively. There were so many entrants for the 100 metres that 17 heats were needed to determine which runners would compete in the semi-finals. This provided plenty of work for the officials charged with the task of chalking the results of each heat on blackboards for the crowd. The competition was watched avidly by a vociferous group of American women sitting close to the Royal box who cheered so wildly that one British spectator commented that they could have been an entire college football crowd.

The South African champion, 19-year-old Reginald Walker, had been able to make the journey to London only after a Natal newspaper backed a public subscription to finance his trip. He attracted some notice by coming second in the AAA championships soon after his arrival, but his relatively slow start was thought to be a liability for him.

Fortunately, Walker attracted the attention of the legendary professional trainer Sam Mussabini, who worked on the South African's start to his considerable advantage. Walker was also assisted by a South African strongman, Tromp van Diggelen, who massaged the sprinter's legs. However, Walker was still not highly regarded. The American James Rector, who claimed never to have lost a race on US soil, was the favourite. Rector came from a distinguished family. One of his grandfathers had been a governor of Mississippi, while another had governed Arkansas during the American Civil War.

Walker did not convince many when he won his first heat in a slow 11 seconds, but in his next race he equalled the Olympic record of 10.8 seconds and the newspapers began to write about him. Rector then achieved the same time in both his preliminary races and the organisers dared to wonder if they might not be going to have a worthwhile final on their hands after all.

It proved to be the case. Over the short distance the lead changed several times. Walker got off to a good start, but at the midway stage the American passed him. Walker then caught up with Rector and the pair ran side by side until Walker pulled away to win the gold medal by just over a foot, equalling the Olympic record.

The victory of a Commonwealth runner over an American appealed greatly to the crowd. Rector later wrote of the occasion, 'The bands were furiously playing national airs, while the bookmakers were calling their bets and the whole stadium seemed to be disordered.'

English runner Jack Morton had been fancied to do well. He had won the English AAA championships for four consecutive years and held a victory over the American Olympic flyer Nate Cartmell. He had also won the Canadian 100 metres title in 1905. By 1908 he was 29 and raced out. He only reached the semi-finals.

Third in the 100 metres final, just ahead of Nate Cartmell, was Bobby Kerr, a former fireman who was born in Enniskillen,

County Fermanagh and lived in Canada. He had been eliminated in the first round of the sprints in the 1904 Olympics, having paid his own way to the USA where he slept on the floor of a friend's house. He couldn't afford to make the journey to Athens two years later. By 1908 he was approaching peak form. He had won the AAA 100 yards title, beating Reginald Walker into second place. In the Olympic 100 metres he clocked the same time as the second-placed Rector.

His moment came in the 200 metres. Kerr took the lead at the gun and hung on to it, although three Americans were gaining on him at the finish. Kerr won in 22.6 seconds. Robert Cloughen was second and Nate Cartmell, so often the bridesmaid, was third. Kerr was carried to his dressing room by a group of jubilant Canadians from the crowd. Later, after a brief visit to Ireland, he returned home to complete a career record of 400 first places, often running under the billing of 'The Fastest Man in the World'. He had a public park named after him and served with the Canadian army in World War I.

For Nate Cartmell it was just another case of what might have been. He had been unfortunate in the final of the 200 metres at the St Louis Olympics. After making a false start he was given a two-yard handicap. A harassed official pointed out the indisputable fact that the track was not long enough to allow Cartmell and several fellow offenders to be placed two yards further back than the rest of the starters. Accordingly, the penalty was rescinded to that of one yard. Even this was too far at Olympic level. The American could not make up all the distance and came second.

On the second day of the 1908 track and field events, Britain won its first gold medal when George Larner, a Brighton policeman and a former soldier who had fought in the Boer War, came first in the 3500 metres walk. Three days later he won the ten-mile walk silver medal.

Larner had won four AAA titles and broken nine world records after taking up the sport at the age of 28 but had returned to his police duties for a two-year layoff before being allowed time off specifically to train for the Olympics. He warmed up, after a disqualification in an earlier event, by winning the AAA two-mile walk. In the ten-mile event he set new Olympic and world best times. He also won the 3500 metres walk.

In each event Ernest Webb came second. Webb had gone to sea at the age of 12 and then joined the cavalry in time to take part in the retreat from Dundee to Ladysmith in the South African war. By the time of the London Olympics he had secured a more sedate occupation in the tobacco industry. Webb went on to win another silver medal in the 1912 Olympics ten kilometre event. Larner went back to his police duties, interspersed with a few gentle cross-country jogs.

The ten-mile walk really sorted out the men from the boys, as there were two preliminary heats before the final. Larner and Webb were placed in different heats and each won his preliminary event. With a time of 78 minutes, 19 seconds, Larner was almost a minute faster than his fellow countryman. He took three minutes off this time in the final. One walker who was eliminated in the second heat was Prague-born Emerich Rath. Eight days later he completed the marathon event in 25th place, with a time of 3 hours 50 minutes and 30.4 seconds. A vegetarian from his youth, Rath was a genuine sporting all-rounder who won the heavyweight boxing championship of Germany, competed successfully in body-building contests, was a pioneer skier and served in mountain rescue teams.

The three-mile team running event final, held on 15 July, the day after the triumphs of Larner and Webb in the shorter walking race, also went to Britain. The race was won by Joe Deakin and the five-man team included Harold Wilson who had won the 1500 metres silver medal the day before, coming in behind the American Mel Sheppard. In the three scoring positions in the team race, Britain came first, second and third. The 29-year-old Deakin, yet another Boer War veteran, won by 30 yards in a sprint finish. Wilson finished fifth. The second placed runner was a Scot, Arthur 'Archie' Robertson, who had not taken up running seriously until 1905. Until then his main interest had been cycling.

The Olympic year was to be a golden one for him. In the space of 12 months he won a gold medal in the three-mile team race and a silver in the Olympic steeplechase. He also won the world cross-country championship and broke the 5000 metres world record, as well as securing a number of Scottish records. Then, still only 30, he went back to his first love of cycling.

Emil Voigt, the AAA champion, won the five-mile race. Born in Manchester of a German father, he had taught in Germany, been a correspondent for the *Manchester Guardian* in Italy and developed a good reputation as a longer-distance runner. He did not drink or smoke and was a vegetarian. He believed that much of the success he attained on the track was due to regular deep breathing and a system of massage.

Only 5 feet 5 inches tall, Voigt had been about to retire from athletics when his late entry for the Olympic trials was accepted. Although he was an experienced cross-country runner he had never competed in the five miles before. He won the trial and at once embarked upon an over-rigorous training schedule for the Olympics. He won his heat but then collapsed with exhaustion. He had also torn some muscle in a foot. Voigt had a plaster of Paris cast put upon the arch of his foot and ran in this in the final, which he won surprisingly easily by some 70 feet.

For several years after his Olympic success, Voigt ran in competitions all over Europe. The five-mile event was never an Olympic event again, so technically Emil Voigt's record of 25 minutes 11.2 seconds still stands. He emigrated to Australia, where he became known for his left-wing views and was a pioneer of local radio broadcasting, specialising in full-blooded commentaries on wrestling matches.

Charles Hefferon, running for South Africa, made a determined effort over the final two laps but faded and had to be content with fourth place. He was to do better in the marathon a few days later.

The 3300 metres steeplechase final contained four Britons, a Canadian and an American. The distance was a compromise between the 2500 metres and 4000 metres steeplechases which were the commonly held events in Britain since about 1850. The earlier races were often handicap affairs, with the stronger runners being made to wear belts weighed down with lead shot.

The White City winner, Arthur Russell, had come second in the

AAA championships when he was only 17 and had continued to win it in 1905, 1906 and 1907. Surprisingly, he had lost to Reg Noakes in the 1908 final, but Noakes had been forced to drop out of the White City event and Russell had taken his place. He ran away from the field over the last lap of the Olympic final to win the gold.

The start of the race was delayed when John Eisele, one of the American entrants and the winner of his heat, arrived at the starting line wearing white shorts instead of the regulation black ones. When he was considered suitably attired the race began. Eisele secured a bronze medal.

Despite the sterling efforts of the British and Empire runners, at the 1908 Olympiad it was the American team that shone in the track and field events. Their outstanding middle-distance runner was Mel Sheppard. A front-runner, he had first attracted attention as a schoolboy competing for Brown prep school in Philadelphia. He was believed to have been the first schools athlete to have run the mile in under 4 minutes 30 seconds. So husky was the precocious schoolboy and so fast his times that there were persistent rumours that he was over-age. Other schools even hired private detectives, posing as census-takers, to investigate his past. The day he celebrated his 21st birthday a local newspaper ran the headline, 'Sheppard now eligible to vote but illegible to run.'

The coaches of the different colleges always kept careful watch on each other's athletes. Writing in *Outing* magazine in January 1903, Caspar Whitney said, 'A band of card-sharpers could not view the acts of one another more suspiciously than do some college athletic authorities.'

A number of clubs wanted to sign Sheppard up, but he opted to join the influential New York Irish-American Athletic Association. Its committee found him a well-paid sinecure supervising street repairs. The athlete claimed to have kept in shape fleeing from irate navvies whose work he had criticised.

Fiercely competitive, Sheppard was suspended after he had seized by the neck and thrown to the ground an athlete called Haskins who tried to pass him. This led to a riot in the stadium, in which Sheppard was struck on the jaw and had to be rescued by a dozen policemen before he was disqualified from the race. In mitigation, the runner had explained that he been tired and irritated after taking part in too many races.

He started winning national American AAU titles almost for fun and was entered for the London Olympics where he won the 800 metres and the 1500 metres in Olympic best times. He also broke the world record in the shorter event, returning 1 minute 52.8 seconds. That race had been specially marked out, with a second tape erected 5 yards and 1½ inches beyond the original finishing line, so that Sheppard could also be timed for a possible world record over 880 yards. However, he slackened pace dramatically after reaching the 800 metre line and had to be satisfied with the record for the shorter distance.

It was only then that the *New York Times* of 15 July revealed: 'Mel Sheppard, the American who won the 1500 race, was rejected last May as physically unfit for the police force of New York. Not unusual, say experts. Might be a fine athlete but might drop dead at any time, says a surgeon who examined him last May.'

Sheppard had little to do with the British runners, however. In a newspaper article he had cast doubt on the honesty of some of them, saying that on at least one occasion a competitor from the United Kingdom had informed him that he had been bribed to come in third and that was exactly what he proposed to do. Sheppard hinted that such malpractices were not uncommon among English runners.

Second to Sheppard in the 800 metres was Emilio Lunghi of Italy, a careful character who had once run a long distance race at Genoa carrying an open umbrella to shelter him from the rain. He was unfortunate in the heats of the 1500 metres. He ran the second fastest heat but came in second to Norman Hallows of Great Britain, an Oxford blue, who set an Olympic record for the distance and thus eliminated the Italian from the competition on the first past the post system.

Lunghi was a 21-year-old naval cadet with a reputation for enjoying the good things in life. In an almost unprecedented personal reference, the official Olympic report chided that the Italian runner 'was not supposed to have trained with particular severity for these games'.

Ivo Fairbairn-Crawford, one of the British finalists who had won the AAA 880 yards championship in 1907, started off at an extremely fast pace. He was 200 yards ahead before half of the first lap had been completed. Harry Hillman, the American 400 metres hurdles runner who was watching the race, claimed that Fairbairn-Crawford had deliberately sacrificed his chance of winning the race by acting as a 'hare', hoping to draw Sheppard into a fast pace so that the American would 'blow up' before the finish. This, he said, would allow Theodore Just, the other British competitor and holder of the AAA 880 yards title with a time of 1 minute 58.2 seconds, to come through and win. Sheppard refused to be drawn and gradually reeled the British front-runner in, so that it was Fairbairn-Crawford who was too exhausted to finish the race. For all his reported lack of match fitness, Emilo Lunghi came in second and also beat the previous best Olympic time.

Theodore Hartman Just, who finished fifth for Great Britain in the final, and another Briton, Harold Holding, who had been eliminated after coming third in his heat, were both taking part in an important scientific athletics experiment at this time. It was conducted by physiologist Leonard Hill, who published his findings soon afterwards in the August edition of the *British Medical Journal*. Just and Holding had been the guinea pigs in Hill's study of the use of oxygen on top class athletes. In his pioneering investigation, Hill concluded that the judicious use of oxygen before a race could produce world record times for good runners, while its application afterwards would help the athletes recover much more quickly and effectively from their exertions.

There were five Britons in the 1500 metres final. Second place was taken by Harold Wilson, a 22-year-old Lincolnshire runner who was the AAA champion. Again, Ivo Fairbairn-Crawford attracted the wrong sort of attention by bolting away at the start and then failing to finish the race. Whether he had panicked or was executing some self-imposed task as the Olympic middle-distance pacemaker was never ascertained. Wilson led gamely into the final straight, but was then overtaken by Sheppard. Hallows finished third. Wilson at once turned professional.

Americans took the first four places in the 110 metres hurdles final, which took place on the last day of the athletics events. For years, hurdles had been hammered firmly into the ground, presenting formidable obstacles, but at the White City they were relatively flimsy, non-threatening constructions, enabling competitors to run all-out with confidence. The winner was Forrest Smithson, from Oregon.

Smithson had attracted a great deal of interest at home by winning local events in fast times. After he had won all the hurdles events at the Jamestown Exhibition he was accepted by Yale, where he won five events at the Yale Fall Games of 1907. However, the runner wanted to put down a marker for the Olympics and left Yale to compete in the New York indoor athletics season. He then returned to Oregon and secured a place in the US Olympics team.

A deeply religious man, Smithson attracted some media interest when it was announced that the hurdler would compete carrying a bible in his hand as a form of protest if the final should be held on a Sunday. There had never been any suggestion of the race being held on the Sabbath, but Smithson was still photographed clearing a hurdle with a bible in his left hand. The final was held on a grass track instead of the customary cinder path. Smithson won from John Garrells with a new world and Olympic record of 15 seconds. The two other leading American hurdlers Shaw and Rand finished third and fourth respectively. Strangely enough, it was the first time all four Americans had competed against one another in the same race.

In the 400-metre hurdles heats and final, Americans Charles Bacon and Harry Hillman played pass the parcel with the Olympic record. Bacon broke it in the first round. Hillman exceeded this time in the second heat, while Bacon is generally held to have set the first official world record for the distance, finishing in 55 seconds to win the gold medal. In the process, he veered off the course and cleared the wrong hurdle before getting back on to the proper track. When the officials measured the course taken by the winning American they discovered that Bacon had run slightly further than the set distance, so to the American's enormous relief his win was allowed to stand. It was to be the outstanding moment of his athletic career. Charles Bacon never even won an AAU championship back home in the USA.

Second place was taken by Hillman, who won golds at the 1904 St Louis Olympics in the 200 metres, the 400 metres and the 400 metres hurdles. He had also competed in the Athens 1906 intercalated Games, when he had been fortunate even to reach the event as he had almost been swept off the deck of the vessel transporting the American team when a huge wave washed across its bows. He entered the 1908 Olympics in the throes of a dispute with the officials of the American National Guard, in which Hillman held a commission. His superior officers decided that it was undignified for an officer to compete in athletic events, especially against other ranks in armoury sports meetings. They gave Hillman the choice of resigning his commission or giving up competition. Hillman went on running. He also survived a dispute between the authorities and the Irish-American Club, when Hillman had not turned up to run in an advertised 600 metre race against John B. Taylor.

After the White City Games, Hillman was to achieve glory once more. In the 1909 100 yards three-legged race, he became the holder, or not unnaturally the co-holder, of the world record. For 35 years he was athletics coach at Dartmouth College, where he dispensed his twin theories for success: swallowing raw eggs and outsmarting the opposition, 'The man who, in addition to his athletic ability, uses his brains and thinks quickly is the one who generally gets away with his races,' he would tell his students.

The last track and field event of the tournament was the 1600 metres relay final. Although they had been neglected, relay races dated back thousands of years. They owed their origins to the carrying of messages across vast tracts of land. The ancient Greeks adopted the *lampadedromes,* or torch races, in which large teams from the different republics carried sacred flames. For a long time the event remained relatively unknown in Britain, the first newspaper account of such a race printed in 1895. At a tournament sponsored by the Ranlagh Harriers, a number of teams passed on a flag from one runner to another.

In 1908, a form of the relay was revived at the Olympics. The 1600 metres medley race was divided into two legs of 200 metres, one of 400 and one of 800 metres. No baton was used. At the end of his allotted portion of the relay, each man touched the next runner. The strong US team of William Hamilton, Nathaniel Cartmell, John Taylor and Mel Sheppard finished seven seconds ahead of Germany, who won the silver medal. Hungary finished a very close third. The official report hinted that perhaps Sheppard had been celebrating his previous middle distance successes on the track a little too wholeheartedly, as in the relay he was 'looking not quite as fit as a few days previously'.

Altogether it was a triumph in track and field events for the USA, but many newspapers believed that their athletes were being cheated by the judges and administrators. One of them wrote, 'It is, of course, clear by this time that our English cousins are going to crown themselves victors in the Olympic Games now being held in London if the thing can possibly be arranged. The spirit being shown by them is very like that of the American statesman who said that as long as he could do the counting, he did not care who did the voting.'

Where the track and field athletes went the cyclists were not far behind. The cycling was conducted in the main arena along with the track and field events and the swimming. From about 1880, bicycle racing on tracks and on roads became very popular in Europe and the USA. Such large crowds attended these races that the sport soon became largely a professional one.

Among the amateurs, cycling was introduced along the route of the marathon race at the Athens Olympiad in 1896. The competitors cycled from Athens to Marathon and then completed the return journey to the stadium in Athens. At the London Olympics there was no road race. All the events took place on the specially constructed White City track. The different nationalities comprising the racers on wheels had their share of grievances. The Canadians protested about the steep banking of the cycle track and the poor quality of the food they were being given to eat.

There were seven events held on the 660-yard track built around the edge of the arena. The shortest event was the one lap race, a distance of 660 yards. There were 16 heats in the first round and four more in the second to determine the finalists. The gold medal was won by an Englishman, Victor Jones, with Emile Demangel of France second and a German, Karl Neumer, winning the bronze medal. At one stage Neumer established a lead of six lengths but Johnson made the distance up and outsprinted Demangel to the finishing line. An outstanding sprinter from Staffordshire, Johnson later won the world championship over one kilometre. His father had also been a cycling champion.

Most of the races took place in the rain and on several occasions the track flooded. The 1000 metres sprint was a shambles. Despite a number of punctures, all the competitors tried to ride a tactical race and proceeded at a crawl in a downpour, despite being shown red flags indicating that they were approaching the stipulated time limit. In the final hectic scramble for the line a Frenchman won by inches, but the race was declared void because of the excessive time taken to complete it.

The tandem race over 2000 metres was won by a French pair, Maurice Schilles and Andre Auffray, who had never ridden together before. F.G. Hamlin and H.T. Johnson, who won the silver medal for Great Britain, complained that they had been hindered by the Frenchmen on the final bend, but their appeal was not upheld.

The 100 kilometres race also had its share of incidents and controversies. The Prince of Wales was to present a special cup in this event, inflaming the ambition of some of the competitors. In one of the heats, a judge from the walking events, Harry Venn, became disorientated and wandered on to the track into the path of speeding Belgian cyclist Guillaume Coeckelberg. The Belgian struck his head on the edge of the track as he fell from his cycle, but remounted and finished the heat fast enough to qualify. Meanwhile, a disgruntled French team had other reasons to feel ill-used, claiming that Octave Lapize, their star man in the 100 kilometre race, had been blocked by several English riders to allow fellow Brit Charles Bartlett to slip through and win. His team-mate Charles Denny took the silver.

The official report was at pains to point out that no official complaint had been received from France over this matter and that in any case any harm befalling the French riders was caused by the foreigners' unsuccessful attempts at deviousness: 'Riding up the banking and slowing down is a tactic imported from the continent, the object being to force the other riders to go in front and give a lead before the finish.'

Lapize recovered from the indignity to enter the 1910 Tour de France, possibly regarding it as being English rider-free and comparatively safe from interference. He was to be disabused. As he toiled despairingly to the top of yet another mountain in the heat of the sun, he screamed at a group of the organisers responsible for plotting the route: 'Murderers! Yes, murderers!'

The cycling race which attracted the most interest at the White City was the three-lap team pursuit over 1980 yards. The English riders defeated the second-placed German side by a margin of ten seconds. Their team was made up of four riders – Ernest Payne was a carpenter, whose main claim to fame was that at a Whitsun race at Bath in 1904 he had been presented with the largest cup known to British sport, extending four feet from the ground. Leon Meredith had a wealthy patron in the form of an uncle, who supported his nephew to such an extent that Meredith was able to treat the sport as a full time pursuit. Together with Clarence Kingsbury and Ben Jones, a Wigan miner who played football twice for Manchester United, the team's victory meant that Great Britain won a total of five gold medals and France took home one.

The closing medal and diploma ceremony got under way with almost unseemly haste before the athletics events had concluded. The presentations took place on 25 July with the commemorative, silver and bronze medals and diplomas.

Anyone who had taken part in the Olympiad as an athlete or an official was entitled to receive a commemorative medal. Diplomas were presented to medal winners and those athletes who had reached an acknowledged standard of excellence but had not won a gold, silver or bronze.

The gold medal winners did not appear at first, but all the others lined up on the opposite side of the arena to the Royal box while the Band of the Grenadier Guards played the national anthems of all the countries represented. Then the drums and bugles of the Irish Guards played the *Advance*. The competitors and officials marched forward towards a number of tables arranged below the Royal box.

It was a highly organised ceremony. The official instructions to the medal winners warned: 'The holder of a prize ticket will walk up to receive his prize between two flags of the same colour as his ticket or he will not receive the award to which he is entitled.'

Silver medals were presented by the Duchess of Rutland, while the Duchess of Westminster handed over the bronze medals. The commemorative medals and diplomas were in the charge of Lady Desborough, who numbered her beaming husband among the recipients. Altogether more than a thousand awards were made.

To add to the social nature of the event the crowd seemed to be largely made up of ladies in white dresses, picture hats and colourful parasols. It was noted that the Americans presented a particularly smart appearance in their track uniforms, while their shooting team wore khaki uniforms with American shields on their breasts. The band played national folk songs and exhibitions of diving and water polo were given in the pool.

At 4pm, Queen Alexandra and several members of her family arrived to the strains of the national anthem and took their seats in time to witness the final of the relay race. After the preliminary presentations, the band then played *See the Conquering Hero Comes* while the gold medallists came out of the dressing room area and marched across the stadium to receive their awards from the Queen.

Eleven

The Ladies

'Our own view of all the athletes sent to these Games from every nation was that each was a picked Olympic representative.'

The Olympic Games of 1908 in London: A Reply to Certain Charges Made by the American Officials

Women had never had it easy in the Olympics. During the ancient Games, respectable women were not even allowed to watch the competition, let alone compete. Olympia was dedicated to Zeus and was a sacred area for men. Any woman who wanted to display her prowess as an athlete had to wait until about 1000 BC, when the Games of Hera were opened for them.

Almost three thousand years later, Baron de Coubertin was just as adamant as any ancient Greek that women should not be allowed to compete in the Games. Their function, he believed, was strictly to encourage male competitors. As late as 1912, he was still saying, 'Tomorrow there will probably be women runners or even women football players. If such sports are played by women, would they constitute a proper spectacle to offer the audience that an Olympiad brings together? We do not think this may claim to be so.'

No woman took part in the 1896 Olympiad, but it was not for want of trying. Contemporary newspaper accounts mentioned an impoverished Greek woman from Piraeus called Stamatis Rovithi, a 30-year-old mother of two children, who hoped to better her lot and gain publicity which might earn her a job or patron by entering the marathon. Described as thin and blonde, she was rejected by the committee on the grounds that her entry had been received too late. Nevertheless, the woman was still determined to complete the marathon course.

As the years passed and the story became embellished, some accounts claimed that Stamatis Rovithi actually ran unofficially alongside the male competitors, as a sort of ghost runner. It seems more likely that she turned up at the village of Marathon some time before the race. She persuaded several local dignitaries to sign a piece of paper acknowledging that the woman had set off on the marathon course at 8am. According to a newspaper account she ran holding her skirt raised to her knees.

She stopped a number of times on the way to drink water and suck oranges and to watch some ships passing off the coast. Either four-and-a-half or five-and-a-half hours after she had left Marathon, Stamatis Revithi arrived at the old military site of Parapigmata, only a few kilometres from the Olympic stadium in Athens. Here she encountered some non-commissioned officers, who signed her piece of paper confirming the time that they had met.

After this, all contemporary accounts end. There were stories that the runner made her way to Panathinaiko stadium and asked if she could be allowed to complete her marathon by running round the track of the arena. She was refused permission and disappeared from history. She became mockingly known as Melpomene, after the goddess of tragedy and disappointments, but this is conjecture. Some claimed that Melpomene was another woman altogether, who also ran over the marathon course in 1896.

At the second modern Olympics in Paris, a few hardy women took advantage of a chink in the armour of male entrenchment in athletics as far as the Olympiad was concerned. The opening occurred at the 1900 Paris Olympics, taking place in the shadow of the newly constructed Eiffel Tower. The governing bodies of the different national sporting organisations were still obdurately set against allowing women on to their hallowed turf. On the other hand, the organisers of the Paris Universal Exhibition, for whom the Olympiad was just another sideshow, were much more relaxed about the admittance of women to any of the events taking place under their aegis. As long as they drew the crowds and did not offend against public decency the fairer sex could just about do what it liked.

A scattering of tough-minded women, about 20 in all, took advantage of this unexpected loophole. It helped considerably that Baron de Coubertin's claws had been blunted by the French Government taking a paternal interest in the Paris Exhibition. The great sports administrator was far too skilful a diplomat to offend those in high places in his native land. He could only look on disapprovingly as a few female athletes took the first tentative steps towards Olympic competition.

They had to be tolerant and not too squeamish. The athletics section of the Exhibition was chaotically developed and badly sited. Events took place on a circumscribed field in which the hammer-throwers sometimes had to retrieve their hammers from surrounding trees. The swimmers were forced to brave the cold of a pool in the River Seine, although the tides of this river assisted in setting some amazing personal best times for the competitors.

A considerable asset for the women was that the lines between the casually organised Exhibition and the extremely rudimentary athletics tournament were so blurred that no one was really sure which events were virtually funfair attractions and which were out-and-out sporting events. It was a problem that was to trouble sports historians for years and lead to some athletes going to their graves not realising that they had won an Olympic title in their youth.

As far as can be discerned, the first woman Olympic title holder was the English Charlotte 'Chattie' Cooper, a tennis player. Cheerful, practical, down-to earth, slightly deaf but something of a chatterbox, Chattie had won the English women's tennis singles five times, starting in 1894.

She learned her tennis at a club in Ealing and was fortunate in having an encouraging mother, as Chattie admitted: 'Many a parent is prejudiced against her daughter having so much freedom, but my mother was lenient (and I consider most sensible) in that respect, and turned a deaf ear to anyone who advised her not to allow my sister and myself to travel about.'

She practised mainly on a court laid out, somewhat haphazardly, in her garden and is reputed to have cycled back matter-of-factly from Wimbledon to her home in Surbiton after winning one of her

The American contingent, led by Ralph Rose, parade at the opening ceremony of the 1908 Olympics. Rose caused a controversy when he refused to dip the American flag to King Edward VII.

The American team withdrew from the tug-of-war competition after losing their first pull to the Liverpool Police side, claiming that the police had cheated by wearing boots.

The Danish women gymnasts caused a furore at the 1908 Olympics with their attractive appearance and fetching costumes. They appeared out of competition in a number of well-attended exhibition displays

Irish-born Martin Sheridan won the freestyle discus throw and the Greek-style discus throw for the USA in 1908 and also gained a bronze medal in the standing long jump.

Canada's Bobby Kerr (centre) wins the 200 metres final in 22.6 seconds. Robert Cloughen of the USA, on Kerr's right is second, and Nat Cartmell, also representing the USA, is third.

Mel Sheppard (USA) on his way to winning the 1500 metres gold medal in an Olympic record time. He also won golds in the 800 metres and the 1600 metres relay.

An exhausted Dorando Pietri is helped over the marathon finishing line by official Jack Andrew. This led to Dorando's disqualification. The gold medal was awarded to Johnny Hayes of the USA.

Albert Oldman, a London policeman, was an unexpected winner of the gold medal in the boxing heavyweight division. He refused all offers to turn professional as a potential 'White Hope'. (Larry Braysher)

British and American winners of wrestling gold medals hold symbolic branches. In the centre of the back row Con O'Kelly, the heavyweight, dwarfs the others. He became a successful professional boxer.

Ralph Rose, the American, receives his shot put gold medal from Queen Alexandra. Rose had offended the Queen's husband, Edward VII, by refusing to dip the US flag to the monarch.

titles. She encountered her brother trimming a hedge. When Chattie informed him that she had just won the championship, he did not reply.

Like all the female players of her day she played in a wide, long skirt, whalebone corsets, stockings and sensible black shoes. Sometimes she would top off the ensemble with a small bowler hat. Always up for a challenge, she entered the tennis section of the Paris Exhibition. She won the women's singles title and the mixed doubles.

In 1907, she played May Sutton, a formidable American, and was the first player to take a set from the visitor on her tour of Europe. 'I was determined to introduce unfamiliar tactics, giving her short balls in order to entice her up to the net. The result was that many of her terrific drives went out.' Then she returned contentedly to Surbiton to resume her life as Mrs Alfred Sterry, who later became president of the Lawn Tennis Association.

Margaret Abbot, an American art student living with her mother in Paris, was not quite as well-organised. She noticed an advertisement in a newspaper about a women's nine-hole golf tournament to be held as a part of the Paris Exhibition. She had learned her golf at a private club in the US and had taken part in a number of Chicago tournaments before leaving for Europe. In Paris, she entered her name and turned up on the day to find that fewer than a dozen competitors had arrived. Margaret had made some effort to wear a vaguely athletic costume but she found that the other women, anticipating something of a hit-and-giggle afternoon, were wearing their usual long, tight skirts and high-heeled shoes.

Not surprisingly Margaret Abbot won the competition with a score of 47 and was given a porcelain bowl mounted in chiselled gold as her prize. Her mother, novelist Mary Ivers Abbot, who entered the competition at the last minute to keep her daughter company, went round in 65. Margaret thought little more about her triumph, regarding her achievement as just a bit of fun and never realised that she had won an Olympic first place. Of much more importance to her was the fact that during her sojourn in the French capital she had been a pupil both of Rodin and Degas.

A Swiss woman, Helen de Pourtales, took first place in a mixed yachting event. Among the other women whose names have survived from the 1900 Games competition were Elvira Guerra in the equestrian competition, the French golfers Mademoiselle Ohniers and Madame Depres and intrepid Madame Maison, a balloonist.

Women competed in archery in the 1904 St Louis Games and were permitted to play in the 1906 Athens tennis events. By 1908, something of a groundswell was developing in the area of women's sports and there were demands for them to be admitted to the London Games as members of the official teams. Altogether it was something of a year for emancipation. Not only did young men turn up for the White City opening ceremony bearing banners declaring 'Votes for Women', but in the same year Edith Berg became the first woman to go in an aeroplane, a passenger in the Wright Brothers *Flyer* in an exhibition in France. Going one better, suffragette Muriel Matters flew over the Houses of Parliament in a balloon, scattering 'Votes for Women' leaflets.

The women who entered the 1908 Olympiad were every bit as doughty as their predecessors, willing to fly in the face of convention in order to express themselves. One of them was Florence Madeleine Cave Syers, better known as Madge, a figure skater from Knightsbridge in London, coached by her husband Edgar. She was only 20 when she noticed that the rules of the International Skating Union, the governing body responsible for the 1902 London-based world championships, made no mention of the fact that the competition was for men only. This was because it was taken for granted. In all sports at the time it was just not done for women to enter anything except all-female competitions.

Madge seized her opportunity and entered the 1902 contest, figuratively clutching the rulebook, and defying the authorities to eject her. She got her way and came a very close second in the tournament. Her skating style was much more flexible than that of most skaters and included elements of dance. The method had been introduced to Europe by an American skater, Jackson Haines. Edgar Syers had adapted the style and taught it to his young wife, with great success.

The World Championship organisers presented Madge with a prize and wasted no time in altering the regulations, making the tournament an all-male bastion again. They claimed, as one of the objections to women skaters, that they could not see the movement of their feet under the long skirts of the day.

Madge Syers bided her time, skating in mixed double competitions with her husband. The British championships did allow both men and women to enter, but to be on the safe side Madge wore a daring mid-calf skirt. She won the first prize. Edgar Syers came second. In 1906 and 1907 special world championships for women were introduced. Madge Syers won the title on both occasions, at Davos and Vienna, and entered the 1908 Olympics. She was easily the best woman in the October tournament and took the gold. Skating with her husband, she also won a bronze medal in the pairs competition.

But those years of intense competition and of constantly having to battle for her rights in the sporting world had taken a toll on Madge Syer's health and she retired from competition after the Olympics. She was only 27. She died nine years later.

The best all-round woman athlete of the era was certainly Charlotte 'Lottie' Dod, who entered the archery competition. She was the daughter of a wealthy Liverpool cotton merchant who had parlayed an inheritance of £5,000 from his father into such a fortune that he was able to retire at 39, having ensured that none of his four children would ever have to work. As a result all of them became superb games players.

Lottie was educated at home by tutors but this did not prevent her becoming an outstanding all-round athlete. Even at a young age, she practised for seven days a week, causing something of a rift with another branch of the family which believed in observing the Sabbath. She took the Ladies' Wimbledon tennis title in 1887 when she was only 15 and went on to win it on four more occasions. She was a strong favourite in 1889, but was enjoying a sailing holiday so much that she did not bother to return for the tournament.

Having mastered one sport it was the pleasant but reserved Lottie's habit to take up another. In 1895, on a holiday in

Switzerland, she adopted winter sports and soon became adept at ice skating and mountaineering, with time off to go down the Cresta Run on a toboggan.

Returning home from such frivolities, with time out for a cycling tour of Italy, Lottie Dod played twice for England at field hockey, but soon gave this up for golf. When the newspapers heard that she had taken up yet another sport, one of them wondered how she would fare:

> Now Lottie Dod, so neatly shod
> Steps forth upon the tee
> On tennis green she is the Queen
> At golf what will she be?

Lottie answered such questions in 1904 by winning the national ladies championship. By the time the 1908 Olympics came along, the versatile Lottie had taken an interest in archery and entered the tournament with her brother William. William had once met the author Rudyard Kipling on a sea voyage, who had been intrigued with the spelling of his surname with one 'd'. 'I suppose what is good enough for God is good enough for Dod,' surmised the writer.

Archery had its antecedents in practical forms. In medieval England the use of the longbow made the English army surpreme. Centuries later, after the end of the Civil War in America, former Confederate troops were forbidden to use rifles. To catch game, rural dwellers became adept in the use of the bow and arrow. By the beginning of the 20th century, however, archery had become something of a genteel minority sport.

The first national archery championships took place in York in 1844 and in 1861 a Grand National Archery Society had been established in the UK. In the USA after the Civil War, J. William Thompson wrote *The Witchery of Archery* and helped to form an archery society. In 1900, the sport was first included at the Olympic Games.

The 1908 Olympics competition was overseen by the Royal Toxophilite Society, archery's governing body. Its committee was solicitous for the comfort of the 25 ladies who had entered. One of the special rules drawn up for the Olympiad stated firmly, 'The gentlemen will not be allowed to smoke at the ladies' targets.'

An article in a contemporary issue of *Badminton Magazine* dealt with the matter of suitable clothing for female archers: 'The lady archer must abstain from wearing frills and laces, as they will assuredly spoil her shooting by catching in the string and ruining what might otherwise have been brilliant shots. Also the sleeves must not be large or puffy, as the left one will invariably catch and not only tear itself but also spoil the shot.'

Bows were made of yew or hickory wood. Arrows had three feathers at their heads. Lady competitors had to loose 48 arrows from a distance of 60 yards and another 24 arrows from 50 yards on each of the two days of the tournament. They wore leather arm guards to protect their arms from the impact of the bowstring flying back after an arrow had been released. Gentlemen had to shoot more arrows from greater distances.

William Dod went on to win an Olympic gold at the White City in 1908, but Lottie had to be content with second place after being in the lead on the first day. Conditions were cold and windy and there were very few spectators. The athletes were hampered in their efforts by the voluminous clothing they were forced to wear. The official report commented sympathetically of their efforts on the first day: 'The ladies commenced at 11am, but had hardly begun to shoot before they had to fly for shelter.'

Easily the best female archer in the country was Alice Leigh, the winner of many national titles, but she had evinced no interest in the White City Olympics. In her absence Lottie Dod had been expected to walk away with the gold medal but she was unexpectedly forestalled by 53-year-old Sybil Fenton 'Queenie' Newall. She was born near Rochdale in 1854, the eldest daughter of well-off parents. In 1905 she moved south and joined the Cheltenham Archery Club.

She won several local tournaments and was something of a surprise choice for the 1908 Olympic team. Despite falling behind on the first day of the White City competition, Queenie Newall persevered and came through to beat Lottie Dod by 43 points. Lottie Dod had a disastrous second day and it was only the fact that she had scored so highly on the first day that enabled her to hang on for second place.

It was the start of an Indian summer for the gold medallist. Queenie Newall won national titles in 1911 and 1912 and continued entering competitions until she was in her 70s. Olympic archery did not have such an uninterrupted run. It was dropped from competition after the first London Olympics and not reinstalled until 1972.

Unlike his sister, William Dod was not expected to do well in the men's archery competition, but he won the Gentlemen's Double York Round some 45 points ahead of Reginald Brooks-King, the silver medallist. In this competition entrants fired a total of 288 arrows from different distances. An American, Henry Richardson, came third. There was a special competition, shooting from 50 metres. In this there were 15 entries from France and only one each from the UK and the US. The French competitors requested that some out-of-competition English archers should shoot with them, although their scores would not count. This was agreed to. The first prize was won by Frenchman Eugene Grisot. On the following Saturday, the French contestants spent a pleasant afternoon as guests of the Royal Toxophilite Society on its six-acre site near Regents Park in London.

Of all the women at the Games, the Danish gymnasts with their spirited exhibition displays continued to be among the most popular. The *Gentlewoman* magazine of 1 August gushed, 'The Danish ladies have taken the town by storm. We were, all of us, Danes in our welcome of them. I mean, of course those charming gymnasts at the stadium.'

The Duchess of Westminster, the aunt of Winston Churchill, was engaged in the competition rather than display – and she was on her way to a medal. The Duchess was an unusual woman. Born Constance Edwina Cornwallis-West, but always known as Shelagh, both she and her sister Mary Theresa had made good matches thanks to an ambitious mother. Mary Theresa had married the wealthy Prince Hans Heinrich of Pless who owned a 600-room castle and had an income of £200,000 a year, while Shelagh had been paired off with Hugh Arthur Richard Grosvenor, 'Bend'or', second Duke of Westminster, owner of Mayfair and Belgravia and reputedly the richest peer in England. It was he whose castle-burgling antics would attract such criticism in 1908. His income was stated to be 'a guinea a minute'. He had inherited his title in 1899, had served until 1901 in the Boer War on the staff, and was in the process of enjoying his wealth and privileges enormously.

Shelagh's mother, 'Patsy' Cornwallis-West, was married to a colonel but owed her influence to the fact that she was one of the mistresses of the Prince of Wales, later to become King Edward VII. The Prince of Wales had been a key element in marrying off Shelagh to the Duke of Westminster. The scheming Patsy had ensured that the Duke and her daughter had been left together on a number of occasions at a house party. She then hurried to the Prince of Wales and informed him with simulated distress that Grosvenor had compromised her daughter by walking in the garden with her.

The harassed prince sought Grosvenor out in a man-to-man chat and had informed the Duke that it was now incumbent upon him to marry 24-year-old Shelagh. The sporting peer was not completely averse to marriage, as Shelagh was attractive, witty and a considerable sportswoman in her own right. The couple became engaged and were married on 16 February 1901, just seven weeks later, at St Paul's in Knightsbridge.

It did not take long for the couple to grow apart. Bend'or was a handsome, restless philanderer and Shelagh soon became tired of her husband's infidelities. For some years they stayed together in a state of polite indifference. Both were interested in sport, especially hunting, but while Bend'or was fascinated by things mechanical and was a pioneer of powerboat racing, Shelagh took more of an interest in yachting.

An oleaginous 1907 article in the New York Times noted, 'She is simple in her tastes and likes country life better than that of the town. She is especially fond of animals, understands them and can break in any young horse with dexterity and daring. She is also fond of gardening and music is one of her pleasures.' Shelagh was also fond of jewellery, particularly her Neeka diamond, as big as a two-shilling piece. Not wishing to be considered ostentatious, the

Duchess of Westminster eschewed wearing it on its own as a pendant, but preferred to fasten it in front of her tiara.

She was worried by the number of overseas competitors threatening to win Olympic medals, so she bought a yacht called the *Sorais* and entered it for the Olympic eight metre class race on the Solent. Some contemporary reports placed the Duchess as being a passenger on board. Others, stretching credibility a little, claimed that she was at the helm of her vessel. A few days later, at the official closing ceremony, she demurely assisted Queen Alexandra and Lady Desborough with the presentation of medals and diplomas.

Dorothy Katherine Douglas, after her marriage in 1907 Dorothy Katherine Lambert Chambers, first came to the notice of followers of women's tennis when she took the all-conquering Charlotte Cooper to a close match in a club encounter, losing 6–4, 2–6, 7–9. 'The match caused quite a sensation,' she wrote. 'We started rather late, in the tea interval, and no one took the least interest in what was considered a forgone conclusion. However, when it got abroad that Miss Cooper had actually lost the first set, people came hurrying round the court in great consternation.'

Douglas went on to become Wimbledon ladies' singles champion in 1903, 1904, 1906, 1910, 1911, 1913 and 1914. She was also runner up in 1905, 1907 and, at the age of 41, in 1920. For a change she entered and won the ladies' doubles and the mixed doubles. She won two All-England badminton titles and represented Middlesex at hockey. She won the Olympic singles title in 1908. Born in Ealing, Douglas was the daughter of a vicar, learned tennis at her school, Princess Helena College, and practised in her garden. 'My greatest amusement was to play up against a brick wall with numerous dolls and animals of all kinds as spectators – really as big a gate as we get now at some tournaments!'

Only five women entered the Olympic competition in 1908 and Dorothy won easily. In the final she defeated Dorothy Boothby, who had won both the ladies' doubles and the mixed doubles at Wimbledon in 1903 and 1904. At the Olympic tournament she had drawn a bye into the final and thus picked up a silver medal without winning a match.

In 1919 and 1920 Dorothy Lambert Chambers lost to the great French player Suzanne Lenglen but continued playing at Wimbledon until 1927, at the age of 48, when she retired to become a professional coach.

Whatever their sport, female athletes of the day had to continue to contend with the voluminous clothing they were forced to wear – long skirts, corsets and hats. Lottie Dod railed against the hidebound males enforcing this restricting female dress code, who 'rather than conceding to the hated rival a glance at her ankle...would have much preferred seen their bride or wife collapse under the burden of their tennis attire'.

Dorothy Lambert Chambers also appealed for more sensible clothing to be worn at tournaments: 'The less experienced are wont to appear in a "garden party" trailing skirt, trimmed hat and a dressy blouse – a most unbusiness-like costume for the game.'

Twelve

Not So Much Winning

'I should like to ask what the American comments would have been if the Amateur Athletic Association had declined to disqualify Dorando. Mr Kirby also seems to think that the action of the officials who assisted Dorando was "cruel, unwise, and unfair" and suggests that they were willing to do anything rather than let an American win.'

The Olympic Games of 1908 in London: A Reply to Certain Charges Made by the American Officials

While many of the Olympic events were conducted before small groups of spectators, the long-anticipated marathon took place in front of a crowd estimated at 90,000 in the stadium. Many more were locked out and offered as much as £5 for a ticket to get inside. Thousands of others lined the route from Windsor Castle to Shepherd's Bush. The event was becoming a cult one.

According to legend, a Greek soldier called Pheidippides had run from Marathon to Athens in about 400 BC, a distance of about 22 miles. He carried news of the Greek victory over the Persians. Crying, 'Rejoice! We conquer!' the exhausted messenger had collapsed and died.

In fact, a more accurate version of the story seems to have been that the Athenians had marched out to meet their enemy, but saw they were outnumbered. Their commander Miltiades had sent a message via Pheidippides to Sparta, a great distance of 150 miles over mountainous countryside, with a request that Spartans march directly to Marathon. The Spartans were engaged in a religious ceremony and, although sympathetic to the Greek cause, could not leave until their observations were over at the full moon. By the time they arrived the Greeks had won the battle and slaughtered over six thousand Persians.

Unknown at the ancient Greek Games, the race became enormously popular towards the end of the 19th century, especially in the USA, with the inauguration of the Boston marathon in 1897. The race as an Olympic event owed its birth to Michel Breal of the Sorbonne University, a friend of Baron de Coubertin. To honour the traditional run of Pheidippides, the academic lobbied long and hard to have the marathon included at the first modern Olympiad in Athens in 1896, promising a cup to the winner.

The idea caught the fancy of both the organising committee and the Greek public, who thought that it would be most fitting if a Greek competitor could win the most famous running event in its country's history. On the morning of the race, 25 athletes lined up on the starting line at Marathon village. Thousands of delighted spectators saw the event won by a 24-year-old Greek called Spiridon Louis, who had been a soldier and was described variously as a shepherd, a water-seller and a postal messenger. Afterwards, he assured listeners that he had trained for the event by fasting and prayer. Louis had spent the first part of the race running at the back of the field. As he began his surge forward, he was encouraged by a mounted policeman who shouted to him, 'There are only foreigners ahead of you!' The exhausted victor was accompanied to the winning line by two royal princes, Nicholas and George. They supported Louis as he walked to the marble steps approaching the Royal box, where King George was sitting.

The marathon winner received the promised silver cup and also an antique vase. There are stories, some of them probably apocryphal, that he was then inundated with prizes, including free shaves and haircuts for life, a lifetime's supply of free clothes, 365 consecutive meals and a vast amount of chocolate. Certainly Baron de Coubertin himself saw a wealthy woman at the finish line take a valuable gold watch from her wrist and send it across to the winner of the race. It was even rumoured that Louis had been offered the hand of the daughter of a wealthy merchant, together with a substantial dowry. However, the athlete was engaged to be married, so could not claim the last prize even if the offer had been genuine.

After this start, interest in the marathon and long-distance running continued to grow. Its major practitioners were usually small, wiry, sad-looking men, with the habit of glancing apprehensively over their shoulders like aircraft tail-gunners of a future generation. Some of them became international stars, often suspected of accepting under-the-counter cash inducements for their not inconsiderable efforts. The 1908 Olympic marathon was particularly keenly anticipated because practically every leading runner of the event had entered the London competition.

Despite this there had been considerable debate as to whether the marathon should even be allowed as an Olympic sport in London. The 1904 St Louis race, also conducted in hot weather, had seen many contestants finish in a poor physical state and others failed to complete the course at all. Even the tough-minded James E. Sullivan expressed his doubts about the race being continued at future Olympiads. 'I do not think that the marathon will be included in the programme,' he said, 'I, personally, am opposed to it and it is indefensible on any ground, but historic.'

The race did go ahead. One of the favourites was Tom Longboat, a Canadian member of the indigenous Onondaga nation who had lived on the Six Nations Reservation near Brantford and the hedonist who had been exiled to Ireland in the run-up to the Olympics. He had won the Boston marathon and great things were being forecast for him. One newspaper predicted, 'If the Onondagu reaches the speed mark expected of him...he will beat the world record at any distance up to 25 miles.'

Longboat had won a number of long-distance races since 1906, culminating in his victory in the 1907 Boston marathon. Mishandled by managers of dubious probity, there were rumours, particularly from the USA, that the Native Canadian was a professional, but his national athletics organisation vouched for his probity.

A strong rival of Longboat's was John Hayes, 5 feet 4 inches tall, 125 pounds and an American son of Irish immigrants. He had a much-publicised day job as an assistant manager in Bloomingdale's New York Department Store. There were even stories planted in newspapers that he exercised on the roof of the clothing company.

In fact he spent most of his time in full-time training, returning to the firm from time to time only for publicity photographs. A typically erroneous article about him appeared in the *New York Sun*: 'Jack Hayes is as Irish as you find them, with black hair, blue eyes, a good humoured and freckled face and a ton of confidence in himself. He has worked at Bloomingdales six days a week since he was 17.'

Also strongly fancied was Charles Hefferon, competing for South Africa, but something of a mystery man. There were rumours that he was a Canadian who had served in the Boer War and had remained in South Africa afterwards. It seems more likely that he was a British immigrant who worked in South Africa as a prison officer. Using a phrase that perhaps could have been better-worded, the *Daily Chronicle* said, 'He went to South Africa during the Boer War and there learnt to run.'

Another entrant who was beginning to make his mark as a distance runner was Dorando Pietri, an Italian confectioner from Carpi in north central Italy, a diminutive man with a drooping moustache. Originally he had been a cyclist but switched to long-distance running after he had witnessed a race including the famous Italian runner Pericle Pagliani. Pietri, who later became fondly known to the public by his Christian name, had started well in the 1906 Athens marathon, but had been forced to withdraw with stomach pains.

A number of changes were made to the course in the days immediately before the start of the marathon. The organisation was in the hands of the London Polytechnic under the direction of Secretary Jack Andrew. The educational institution had considerable experience of arranging long-distance runs for its students.The Polytechnic had also been asked to help with the opening and closing ceremonies of the Olympiad. It made all visiting Olympic athletes honorary members of the Polytechnic, free to use its sporting and social facilities in Regent Street, and it ran a trial marathon from Windsor to Wembley (23 miles). They were sure they could handle the Olympic event.

As time passed and different factions took control, some of that confidence evaporated. A distance of 25 miles from the town of Windsor to the White City Stadium was first mooted. Then the Royal family expressed an interest. A starting point outside the gates of Windsor Castle, the royal residence, was suggested. Then an avenue known as The Long Walk within the grounds of the castle was considered. Finally, a starting point in the courtyard was just about to be agreed, with Edward VII himself as the starter. However, the King was still smarting from the catcalls he had heard from the American spectators at the opening ceremony. He let it be known that he was not interested. It was stated that he had a cold and would not be available. The ever-eager and usually available Lord Desborough took his place.

There was still to be one final change, only a day or two before the start. Some time in the proceedings ten-year-old Princess Mary, granddaughter of King Edward, either let it be known that she was interested in the forthcoming race, or her father, the future King George V, decided that she should appear to take a concern in it. An announcement was made that the 1908 Olympic marathon would commence on the East Lawn, beneath the windows of the Royal nursery, where the Princess was being educated by governesses and finish opposite the Royal box at the White City Stadium

The harassed Polytechnic officials went to work with their, by now frayed, whitewash brushes and tape measures. The distance from beneath the nursery window to the Royal box in the White City Stadium was measured as 26 miles and 385 yards. Years later this became the standard distance for the marathon.

From early morning the route was watered and swept to keep the dust down. Houses along the way were festooned with flags. Thousands of policemen and troops were drafted in to line the way. Competitors were warned that the last possible train from Paddington which would get them to Windsor in time left at 1.03pm. Upon arrival they changed in the waiting rooms of the Great Western railway station. They then handed their street clothes to the baggage handler and made their way in waiting cars and traps to the starting line. There they formed up in four lines and were warned sternly that as they were in England they must take care to run on the left-hand side of the road.

The race began eight minutes late, at 2.38pm, under a gigantic oak tree on a very hot afternoon. A row of scarlet upholstered gilt chairs had been arranged to one side of the starting line for members of the Royal family, next to a table containing a bowl of red roses. Many of the entrants had breakfasted on steaks, eggs, tea and toast, the preferred pre-match meal for long-distance runners. *The Times* announced that the occasion was a triumph of modern technology. According to its report, Queen Alexandra at the White City had sent a signal by electric telegraph to Princess Mary at Windsor Castle. The Princess had then instructed the waiting Lord Desborough to fire his starting pistol twice. Some accounts said that he did so through the window of a stationary motor car.

Some 55 competitors surged forward at the start of the race. They were well equipped for their task. The firm Oxo had been awarded the catering rights for the marathon. Each competitor had been given, free of charge, an athlete's flask containing Oxo. In addition, the runners were offered supplies of rice pudding, raisins, bananas, soda water and milk. They were also issued with reassurances that 'stimulants will be available in case of collapse'. Oxo also set up manned refreshment booths along the route at Ruislip, Harrow, Sudbury and Harlesden, where quantities of eau de cologne and sponges were available for the passing runners.

A few miles along the route each runner picked up two attendants on bicycles, who had been waiting for them. There were trainers among the cyclists, the rest came from the Polytechnic cycling club. Most of the runners approached the opening spell through the town of Windsor quite carefully. The streets were steep and heavily cobbled. To the delight of the large crowds along the way a group of strongly favoured English runners ignored these restrictions and led the way for a while. Even the Anglophobic James E. Sullivan had admitted that runners from the home countries could fill the first three places in the marathon. Some of the more experienced American and European runners, however, were aware that the majority of British distance runners had never competed in a marathon and were inexperienced in their tactics.

Tom Jack, a Scot, led at the start and then gave way to Fred Lord, who stayed in front as far as Uxbridge High Street. Here he was overtaken by a third Briton, Jack Price, who had been running close to Lord. By this time well over an hour had passed and other runners began to leave the British representatives behind. Later the home contestants were blamed by English sports enthusiasts for forcing the pace and burning themselves out. Joseph Forshaw, an American competitor wrote, 'I passed Duncan, the English champion who was expected to win the race, evidently distressed, 12 miles out at Uxbridge...Sprinting the first three miles killed the English competitors.'

Alexander Duncan is officially credited with dropping out of the race after ten miles. As the hot afternoon passed, other runners began to follow his example. Some of them were helped away by their backers or sympathetic members of the crowd. One of the American contestants unwittingly found himself a famous guardian angel.

The runner was Mike Ryan, who later told the *Washington Post*, 'I was overcome by the terrific heat and collapsed at 19 miles and was in pretty bad shape.' At first no one came to the stricken athlete's assistance. Ryan claimed to have sprawled on the ground for a full five minutes before a large automobile drew up. Its occupants got out and approached the American runner. To Ryan's amazement the leader of the group was the enormous Afro-American heavy-weight boxing champion of the world, Jack Johnson.

Johnson had been forced to flee from the USA on 5 June to avoid a charge of violating the Mann Act by transporting a prostitute between states. He was occupying his time with a tour of the European music halls while trying to arrange a contest with the British heavyweight champion Bombardier Billy Wells. The match was to fall through in September when the local Federation of Free Churches objected to a bout between prominent white and black fighters. How he was able to drive his expensive automobile along the marathon route between Windsor and the White City that afternoon is unknown. The way was guarded by many policemen and soldiers and access was prohibited to all vehicles except those officially engaged in policing the runners or taking them off to hospital. It was fortunate for Mike Ryan that the heavyweight had always been an iconoclast. Johnson scooped the exhausted athlete up in his massive arms, carried him back to the car and drove him the seven miles to the Shepherd's Bush stadium and turned him over to the American officials there.

As the remaining runners passed through Harrow, excited boys from the public school cheered them on wildly. After ten miles Charles Hefferon and Tom Longboat were showing well. Seven miles later the leaders were Longboat, Hefferon, Johnny Hayes and Dorando Pietri. Hayes had publicly stated his plan to tuck in behind the leaders. 'I intend to go right out with the pacemakers, keep at their heels until I am ready to finish and then go on and win.'

Longboat was the first of the group to stop, at 19 miles. He was a few hundred yards behind the leader Hefferon when suddenly his legs went and he collapsed. He bounced helplessly off the wheel of one of the accompanying bicycles and lay still in the road. One of his backers tried to revive the Canadian with champagne from a flask, but still the runner did not move. An official medical officer was summoned. The doctor refused to allow Longboat to continue. The stricken athlete was loaded into a motor car like so much baggage and taken off.

Afterwards charges and counter-charges were bandied about concerning the cause of the favourite's collapse. Longboat's trainer claimed that his party-loving charge had been too lazy to train properly. Longboat blamed the heat of the sun and the hard pounding on the pavements for his inability to complete the course. Others, with a touch of hyperbole, said that the road had been too winding for a runner accustomed to the wide-open prairies of his homeland. There were even unsubstantiated accusations of a betting coup by bookmakers eager to dispose, by threats or bribery, of a runner upon whom so much money had been wagered.

J. Howard Crocker, the manager of the Canadian team, had another theory. He believed that Longboat had been drugged. 'I consider it my duty,' he reported, 'to state that my experience in racing leads me to believe that Longboat should have won the race. His sudden collapse and the symptoms shown to me indicate that some form of stimulant was used contrary to the rules of the game. I think that any medical man knowing the facts of the case will assure you that the presence of a drug in an overdose was the cause of the runner's failure.'

Another runner who gave up was Australian Vic Aitken, who had saved Frank Beaurepaire from drowning in the Thames. The Australian managed to cover 21 miles before he collapsed.

In contrast to Longboat, the dapper Swedish entrant Johan Svanberg, who was to finish in eighth position, attracted wide-spread attention for his spritely running and carefree appearance. He had finished third in the five mile final only six days earlier. He was one of the few entrants who actually seemed to be enjoying the marathon race and finished the course in splendid condition. He confirmed his stamina and zest for life by being seen dancing the night away at a ball that evening.

The drama was not over yet. Charles Hefferon was the next to be the subject of controversy on that baking afternoon. The South African, who had taken fourth place in the five mile final, just behind the Swede Svanberg, was still in the lead, with Longboat out of competition. Suddenly he was offered a glass of champagne from a spectator. Ill-advisedly, the South African downed the contents of the glass. Almost at once he started to suffer from severe stomach cramps and was forced to slow down almost to a walk. The Italian Dorando Pietri, who had steadily been gaining on the leaders, took this opportunity to pass Hefferon, several miles from the White City Stadium.

Pietri had almost been prevented from starting the race by scandalised officials who had adjudged his running shorts and vest to be too skimpy. The ubiquitous American coach Mike Murphy had enjoyed confounding the judges by helping the Italian adjust his dress until it conformed to the required standards of propriety.

The huge crowd waiting in the stadium was alerted to the imminent arrival of the leaders by guns being fired at Wormwood Scrubs, the nearest aid station to the course, about a mile-and-a-half away. Almost at once an announcement was made over a megaphone that the first runners were now only ten minutes from the finishing line. An eerie silence fell over the White City.

Pietri's sudden appearance in the lead enthused the crowd by the side of the approach road to such an extent that it cheered

Dorando all along the route to the stadium. This prompted the Italian to increase his speed, instead of conserving his energy for the final lap around the stadium. Hefferon was unable to regain his lost ground and Pietri entered the stadium first, to a wall of welcoming noise from the waiting spectators. The onlookers had a vague idea of what had been going on during the approach to the White City, because men bearing placards had dutifully been holding up information on the changing positions as the news reached Shepherd's Bush.

At this juncture the crowd was swelled by the arrival near the finishing tape of another excited four men. They comprised the Italian team entered for the 1600 metre medley steeplechase. In their number was Emilio Lunghi, the silver medal winner in the 800 metres several days previously. These runners were about to line up for the second heat of their event when they heard that their marathon compatriot was approaching the stadium. In a patriotic fervour the Italians abandoned their race and sped over to give Dorando Pietri their support. In the excitement of what was to follow the Italians never did return to compete in their heat.

The Times of 25 July described Dorando's appearance as he entered the arena: 'A tired man, dazed, bewildered, hardly conscious, in red shorts and white vest, his hair white with dust, staggers on to the track. It is Dorando, the Italian. He looks about him, hardly knowing where he is. Just the knowledge that somehow, by some desperate resolve of determination, he must get round the 200 yards to the tape of the finish keeps him on his feet.'

Completely exhausted, the small Italian turned the wrong way inside the stadium. He was directed towards the finishing line by hovering anxious officials. Dorando Pietri tried to place one trembling foot in front of another. After 50 yards even this effort proved too much. Utterly spent, he collapsed on to the track. Officials lifted the Italian to his feet and pushed him in the direction of the tape. On several more occasions Dorando fell to the ground and was assisted to the perpendicular again. He was on the point of falling for the fifth time when he tottered across the finishing line, aided by Jack Andrew, the chief organiser of the event, who later claimed that he had been instructed by the senior medical officer to support the stricken runner. Andrew had been the subject of an earlier protest in the track and field events for coaching a British competitor in another event, although he was an official at the time.

The doctor who had given the instruction that Dorando Pietri should be assisted over the line was a 40-year-old Irishman, James Bulger, who had played rugby in December 1888 for his country against the touring team billed as the New Zealand Natives. He had then moved to a practice in London and had been instrumental in forming the London Irish RFC. His post at the Olympics was to be the forerunner of many administrative athletics appointments.

Afterwards, when the American officials complained about the way in which Dorando Pietri was assisted, Theodore Cook made an official response on behalf of the organisers: 'Mr Sullivan sees in the assistance given to Dorando a deliberate and official example of anti-Americanism, instead of a very natural feeling of admiration and sympathy for pluck and courage.'

There was a precedent for an Olympic marathon runner receiving assistance. Four years earlier at St Louis, Thomas Hick, one of the American representatives, had been aided to his gold medal by applications of strychnine and brandy. At one stage of his exhausted progess, he had been physically supported by two of the officials, Hugh McGrath and Charles P. Lucas. James Sullivan was in overall charge that day and made no protest.

As Dorando Pietri lay almost unconscious on the side of the White City track, a second runner entered the arena. This was the American Johnny Hayes, who came second in the Boston marathon three months earlier. Hayes claimed to be only 19, but was several years older. He expected to win the Olympic gold medal. The *New York Sun* reported him telling friends, 'I just know I'm going to win, and I wish it were 50 miles instead of 26. The next time you fellows see me I'll be wearing the laurel wreath, or whatever they give the winner, around my ears.' Hayes was almost unknown on the American long-distance running second and had secured an Olympic spot only because he had come second behind Tom Longboat in the previous year's Boston marathon. The *New York Times* said of his run, 'The third to finish was a dark horse, a New Yorker John J. Hayes of the St Bartholomew Athletic Club, who, even by his team-mates, was not thought likely to do so well.'

The young New Yorker had spent most of the previous two days resting in bed and was moving confidently. For 17 miles he was shadowed by a Canadian entrant called Fred Noseworthy. On that sweltering day Noseworthy must have suffered more of a culture and climate shock than most of the runners. For the past seven years he had been undefeated as a snowshoe racer in Canada. The marathon race temperature approached 80 degrees and it finally proved too much for the Montreal-based runner and ice-hockey player. He collapsed with cramp.

Hayes completed the course in 2 hours 55 minutes and 18.4 seconds. Charles Hefferon was next to cross the line, followed by American Joseph Forshaw. Forshaw wrote of the dazzling sunlight in his eyes as he came out of the dark shadows of the tunnel into the stadium. 'I shall never forget my first impression of the crowd cheering wildly as I entered the stadium. It was the most wonderful sight I ever saw.' Forshaw made up ground over the last half of the race but had no idea of his overall position until he reached the last way station. 'Not until I reached the Scrubs did I know that I was well up with the leaders.'

Running at Forshaw's heels for most of the course had been another member of the US team, Lewis Tewanima, a 107-pound Hopi Indian from Arizona. He was a pupil at the famous Carlisle Indian School, which also produced Jim Thorpe, who was briefly to win the decathlon and pentathlon gold medals in Stockholm in 1912 before being disqualified. Tewanima had been raised on a remote reservation where life was monotonous. He would chase rabbits and occasionally run a 120-mile round trip to the town of Winslow, just to see a couple of trains go by. He was selected with 11 other Hopis to be educated at Carlisle, where he learnt the tailoring trade. His running skills were soon noticed and he joined Thorpe on the college team coached by Glenn 'Pop' Warner. On one celebrated occasion, Carlisle's three-man athletics team (including Tewanima and Jim Thorpe) defeated the full 20-man side of Lafayette College.

In what was intended to be a vote of encouragement and approval, noting the progress of Tewanima and the other Hopis, the Maryland *Frederick Evening Post* called them sun-worshippers and pagans, crude members of a lower order of civilisation who had come to the college virtually as prisoners of war but now had evolved into fine athletes and good citizens. Tewanima had been a great favourite with the British spectators watching his training runs at Brighton. They marvelled that such an emaciated man could traverse such long distances apparently effortlessly. Many legends sprang up about the Native American's training methods and diet. Condescendingly he had been nicknamed Chutney Rice, a reference for his alleged predilection to such foodstuffs.

Just before the start of the marathon from Windsor, the US team coach ordered Tewanima to tuck in behind Joe Forshaw, the more experienced runner and then to make a break as they neared Shepherd's Bush. Unfortunately, Forshaw ran a slower race than had been anticipated.

The official report noted that the fancied American was situated towards the rear of the field at the start, with the Hopi trotting dutifully behind him. Tewanima was desperate to surge ahead of the other US runner, but dared not disobey his coach's instructions. His knees, already suspect, became badly swollen and he struggled to finish in ninth place. As the runners battled for the final positions, Queen Alexandra endeared herself to the spectators by jumping up and down with excitement in the royal box, waving her parasol animatedly.

Some time afterwards, through an interpreter, Dorando told journalists, 'I was all right until I entered the stadium. When I heard the people cheering and knew I had nearly won, a thrill passed through me and I felt my strength going. I fell down, but tried to struggle to the tape, but fell again. I never lost consciousness of what was going on and if the doctor had not ordered the attendants to pick me up, I believe I could have finished unaided.'

The streets lining the route of the race seem to have been awash with strong drink. Not only were Hefferon and Longboat plied with champagne, but Joe Deakin, the winner of the three mile team race, was convinced that part of Dorando's eclipse was due to his ingesting too much alcohol as he ran.

'The problem was,' Deakin said later, 'that people along the pavement were giving him glasses of brandy instead of water.' Deakin knew of what he spoke. Earlier he had been forced to abandon a heat of the five-mile race because he had eaten and drunk too heartily in celebration of his three-mile gold.

Following the finish, nobody in the arena seemed to know what was going on. Surprisingly, it took some time for the Americans to lodge an objection about the manner of Dorando's so-called victory. Author and editor James B. Connolly had won the triple jump for the USA in the very first Athens Olympiad. Always full of self-confidence, he had thrown his cap contemptuously a yard beyond the best leap of his nearest competitor and had then gone on to jump another yard beyond that. In his autobiography, he was scathing of the performance of Matthew P. Halpin, one of the senior US officials present at the marathon: 'He was that sort, a little man who went servile in the presence of the great. I pushed him into the arena, all but put the toe of my shoe into his stern sheets. He moved out and falteringly entered our protest. The officials reconsidered their decision.'

The Irish-American Connolly and Halpin had been at odds for years. The triple jumper was a particularly strong-minded man. He had been a freshman at Harvard at the time of the 1896 Olympics. Refused permission to take part in the competition, Connolly had quit full time education and travelled to Greece, the only national champion in the US team.

It took the hastily convened committee two hours to arrive at their verdict in the White City Stadium. In the meantime, the Italian flag had been hoisted above the track. All sorts of conflicting rumours were gaining circulation. The *New York Times* said, 'A report was spread among the crowd that certain British officials had obtained a photograph of Hayes being carried along the marathon course in a blanket.'

Amid all the verbiage after the result had been announced, only the understated Charles Hefferon maintained his calm. When he was asked what he thought of the eventual disqualification of

Dorando Pietri, the South African replied tersely, 'I would rather not win such a race at all than win it on a protest.' He then rather spoiled the effect by complaining that Hayes, who was declared the winner in the wake of the decision against Pietri, had also received aid at one stage during the race. An investigation was unable to confirm this and the matter was allowed to drop.

The British officials in the stadium were more concerned with justifying their actions in assisting Dorando over the line than in making great statements. Their official response to the criticisms was, 'As it was impossible to leave him there, for it looked as if he might die in the very presence of the Queen and that enormous crowd, the doctors and attendants rushed to his assistance.'

Dorando had become a hero. Arthur Conan Doyle, reporting for the *Daily Mail*, had witnessed the Italian's doomed efforts to finish the marathon unaided. The author wrote, 'No Roman of prime has ever borne himself better; the great breed is not yet extinct...The Italian's great performance can never be effaced from our records of sport, be the decision of judges what it may.'

The runners continued to straggle in for hours. Some of them headed for the swimming pool and plunged in gratefully before repairing to the dressing rooms and rub-downs from their trainers. Many of them travelled back to their hotels and boarding houses on the crowded underground railway.

It did not take Matt Halpin long to forget his run-in with James Connolly about his tardiness in appealing and he was soon boasting to newspaper reporters, 'Wasn't it great! We not only won the big race of the Olympic Games, but also got third, fourth and ninth places. What is more our man beat the much-lauded Canadian Indian, Longboat.'

Efforts were soon in hand to recompense the disqualified Italian. The creator of Sherlock Holmes contributed £5 to a fund for the runner. The collection reached £300, effectively destroying the Italian's career as an amateur, such as it was. At one stage Dorando had claimed that he would use the proceeds to buy a bakery back in Carpi. Instead, he turned professional and did not return home for some time. Before he left England, he was presented at the Olympic closing ceremony with a silver gilded cup by Queen Alexandra. There had not been time to engrave an inscription on it, so the Queen had written a personal message on a card. Applause from the crowd lasted at least ten minutes. A few days later the now recovered runner was seen off at Charing Cross station by hundreds of cheering fans. *The Times* reported, 'As the train left the station the Italian national air was sung with great fervour.'

Iconoclastic as ever, writer Caspar Whitney took sour exception to the favours raining down upon the small Italian. 'The subsequent lionising of the man was a maudlin, not to say amusing exhibit of Cockney England gone daft,' he declared.

Queen Alexandra's presentation of the special cup only added to her popularity, except with the Americans. Beautiful and charming, she attracted much sympathy for the way in which she had ignored her husband's philanderings. Years before, she was greeted at England's shores by a ballad from the poet laureate, Lord Tennyson:

> Sea-king's daughter from over the sea, Alexandra!
> Saxon and Norman and Dane are we,
> But all of us Danes in our welcome of thee, Alexandra!

Dorando Pietri was always philosophical about his marathon defeat, appreciating that his dramatic loss had probably gained him more lucrative publicity than a win might have done. He said as much in an interview with the *Corriere della Sera* on 30 July, 'I am not the marathon winner. Instead, as the English say, I am the one who won and lost victory.'

As it happened, the gallant competitor role adopted by Dorando fitted in well with the Olympic theme touted by Coubertin, increasingly worried about the direction the almost out-of-control Olympiad was taking. His aspirations had been put into words during the Olympic period by Bishop Ethelbert Talbot of Pennsylvania in a sermon delivered at St Paul's Cathedral: 'The most important thing in the Olympic Games is not to win, but to take part, just as the most important thing in life is not the triumph but the struggle. The essential thing is not to have conquered, but to have fought well.' This tallied well with Baron de Coubertin's ideals. In a speech he had made in Athens more than a decade earlier he said, 'The dishonour here would not consist of being beaten; it would consist of not contending.'

There was an odd aftermath to the 1908 marathon and it involved an American songwriter. The 20-year-old Irving Berlin had for some time been working as a singing waiter in Jimmy Kelly's restaurant on Union Square in New York. One day he was approached by a comedian who needed to close his act with an Italian dialect song. He offered the neophyte songwriter ten dollars for a suitable lyric. Inspired by the story of Dorando Pietri's London marathon, which was in all the newspapers, Berlin wrote the words for a song about an Italian-American barber who lost his shop betting on Dorando to win and blamed the runner's loss on the fact that he had consumed a plate of Irish stew, not spaghetti, before the race.

The comic lost interest in the idea, so Berlin took his lyrics to a song publisher, claiming that he had already set them to music. The suspicious publisher asked to hear the song being sung. Berlin had intended to find a composer later, but he had to improvise on the spot. He sang his words to a tune he made up as he went along, and was given $25 for his efforts. The song was a minor hit among Italian residents of New York. Part of the chorus went: 'Dorando! Dorando! He run-a, run-a, run-a,/Run like anything.'

There were various realignments among the marathon runners and their backers after the competition. Many of them turned professional, at least those of them who had not already been paid runners for some time did. Tom Longboat temporarily parted company with his manager amid mutual recriminations. Competition between the nations continued to the end. On 29 July, the *Hopewell Herald* proudly announced, 'Under the international system of points, giving five to first, three to second and one to third, America leads Britain.'

Thirteen

Nothing Is Ever Settled

'It is much to be regretted, and we regret with Mr Kirby, that these Games should have in any way failed as a means of bringing the nations of the world into a closer bond; but, from all the evidence before us, that failure belongs only to the nation on behalf of which Mr Kirby poses as a representative, and only to the small, though noisy, portion of that nation which has hitherto believed him.'

The Olympic Games of 1908 in London: A Reply to Certain Charges Made by the American Officials

The closing ceremony of the 1908 Olympiad was held on 28 July, but it continued until 31 October. During that time, in various locations, competitions were held in yachting, rowing, motor-boating, football, lacrosse, rugby football, boxing, figure skating and hockey.

Perhaps inevitably there was a certain air of anti-climax to the proceedings after the conclusion of the track and field events in July. Wounds were slow to heal and corners were still being fought. As late as September of the year, a member of the British Olympic Committee was writing defiantly in *Bailey's* magazine, 'Few greater compliments to English fairplay than the delegation to our great associations of the whole judging in these games have ever been paid.'

There were many suggestions as to how future Games could be improved. None went quite as far as C.B. Fry, all-round athlete and journalist, who was firmly of the opinion that all future Olympiads should be held entirely between the UK and the USA, excluding all lesser nations. However, Fry had a history of embracing lost causes.

Many years later he fruitlessly tried to persuade a bemused Joachim von Ribbentrop, the Nazi Foreign Minister, to channel the menacing energies of the Hitler Youth Movement by introducing its members to cricket.

Fry had played for Southampton in the 1902–03 FA Cup Final and would have taken an interest in the Olympic football competition. Association football had been played at the first three Olympics and also at the Athens intercalated Games, but only as an exhibition sport. At the 1900 Olympiad individual clubs represented their nations in the out of tournament competition. A London team, Upton Park Football Club, defeated Francaise in the final.

There were still many amateur clubs and players, although the professionals were beginning to make inroads. It was an era in which income tax was one shilling in the pound and whisky three shillings a bottle. The comfortable middle classes could afford to let their talented children compete in sport and pay their own way. At the higher echelons of football, the players never worried about where their next half-a-crown was coming from and had plenty of time in which to turn out for their sides.

Some of them, however, were worried about the future of their game, especially the ever-encroaching tide of professionalism. In 1905, Alf Common fetched a record transfer fee of £1,000 when he was transferred from Sunderland to Middlesbrough. What was more, he had been promised a wage of £4 a week. Efforts were made to keep the professionals in their place. At the beginning of the Olympic year the Football Association placed a ceiling of £350 on transfer fees. It proved unworkable and before 1908 was over the rule had been rescinded.

British football at the time was very insular. Until the end of 1908, when it embarked upon its first continental tour, England played only against the so-called 'home countries' of Wales, Scotland and Ireland. Still, all the players who represented Great Britain at soccer in 1908 were true blue and incorruptible, even if some of them did play for professional clubs.

Typical of these players was Vivian Woodward, recognised as one of the best strikers in the game, amateur or professional. He was educated at Ascham College in Clapham and then joined his father's architectural firm. He was seen playing for his school and was picked in turn for Clacton and Chelmsford, always as an amateur. He was not big but he was a very effective goal-scorer, usually at centre or inside forward. He played in an England trial in an inter-area match for the South against the North and then joined Tottenham Hotspur in the Second Division, helping them secure promotion. He scored prolifically and was soon regarded as England's best forward prospect.

In 1903, in an interesting example of the old guard versus the new, Woodward turned out for Spurs against the famous amateur Corinthian Casuals side. Playing for the Corinthians was the former all-round sporting hero C.B. Fry. Woodward totally dominated the game. The *Tottenham and Stamford Hill Times*, perhaps not the most unbiased of newspapers as far as the Spurs were concerned, reported, 'One of the most notable features of the game was the ease with which the Spurs romped around the speediest of opponents. This is particularly the case with V.J. Woodward.' The ageing Fry, on the other hand, was censured for his constant stream of complaints to the referee.

Later Woodward transferred to Chelsea. He first played for the full England side against Ireland in 1903, scoring two goals in a 4–0 win. As an established and well-respected figure he was chosen for Great Britain's amateur side as its captain for the 1908 Olympics.

Eight sides had entered the competition but Hungary and Austria withdrew. In the summer Games, Hungary had won medals in the 1600 metres relay and fencing and competed in many other events. Austria took part in athletics, fencing, swimming and tennis. By the end of the year, however, the political situation had changed. The ambitious Emperor Franz Josef of Austria-Hungary annexed Bosnia and Herzegovinia, thereby lighting the fuse which was to ignite World War I. That left six teams in the Olympic football competition: England, Denmark, Sweden, Holland and two teams from France. The England side was favoured to win the tournament. After all, England had invented the sport and introduced it to the world. Its team of pristine amateurs was revered.

Among the players and cast in the same noble mould as Vivian Woodward was Reginald Kenneth Gunnery Hunt, a theological student who had played at halfback for Corinthian Casuals and was then on the books of Wolverhampton Wanderers, strictly as a part-time amateur. He would leave his studies on Friday night and journey to Wolverhampton, or wherever the team was playing that week. The club was in dire financial straits and not only was the future clergyman fast and energetic, he also came free.

Hunt had made his name in a preliminary round of the FA Cup that season. Playing against Swindon he had twice been knocked unconscious, but on each occasion after he had been revived the student had returned to the fray undaunted and tackling as hard as ever. For his pains, the 24-year-old was selected to play for Wolves against Newcastle in that season's April FA Cup Final. The match took place a week after Hunt had played for Oxford University against Cambridge.

Unfortunately Hunt was also picked to play for England against Wales on the same afternoon as the Cup Final. He opted for his club side. It turned out to be the correct decision. For much of the game Newcastle were well on top, until Hunt, who had been having a quiet match, picked up the ball and tried a speculative shot from 40 yards out. The ball glanced off the Newcastle goalkeeper and went into the net. Much heartened, Wolverhampton scored two more goals and won the game and the cup. Hunt's display was enough to get him picked for England's amateur Olympic side.

England's first game in the tournament strengthened the conviction that they were going to romp to a gold medal in the competition. They defeated Sweden 12–1. The Swedes were bewildered by the home side's constantly changing positional play and fast running. A slight cloud appeared on the horizon when Denmark, emerging as a dangerous opponent, defeated one of the French sides 17–1, with one of their forwards scoring ten of the goals.

England persevered and next defeated Holland 4–1, although the game was not as one-sided as the score suggested and onlookers were beginning to wonder if Vivian Woodward's side was quite as good as had originally been thought. The matter was to be put to the test in the final against Denmark.

Just before the football final was played on 24 October, there was an odd appetiser.

At 1.00pm, the final of the lacrosse tournament was held. Actually, this was the only game played in the competition. Three teams had entered but South Africa withdrew, leaving Canada and England to contest the final. The match was held before the largest crowd ever to witness a lacrosse game in the UK. Because of the proximity of the kick-off of the football final, spectators continued to arrive during the lacrosse match until about 8,000 people were present. This was nothing exceptional for a soccer match but unheard of among the English lacrosse players. The Canadians were more accustomed to playing in front of large crowds. The game was a very popular one in their own country. It had originated among the Iroquois tribe of the Six Nations as a form of war-game played by hundreds of warriors. The sport had been taken up and adapted by North American settlers. In 1842, the first club was established in Montreal. In 1867, a Captain Johnson brought a team from the Caughnawaga tribe to tour England playing exhibition games. They had even appeared before a delighted Queen Victoria at Windsor Castle. The game became established in Britain and by the turn of the century was the principal sport in Canada where there were soon over a hundred clubs.

Lacrosse became an Olympic sport at the 1904 Olympics when two Canadian teams and two US sides entered. Surprisingly, a team of Mohawks representing Canada was eliminated by an American side from St Louis, despite the presence in the Canadian side of such luminaries of lacrosse as Almighty Voice, Flat Iron and Snake Eater.

The other Canadian team, Winnipeg, had a free ticket when an American side from Brooklyn did not arrive to play them. In the final the Winnipeg Shamrock side won the gold medal for Canada by a score of 8–2.

To arouse interest in the game against their unfancied opponents, Canadian officials had been 'talking up' the English side's chances. 'They are big, fast men,' said a Mr Solman of the Canadian party, 'much better runners than the Canadians, can pass and check well, but lack the necessary finesse at critical moments. They need the services of a good coach.'

In spite of the fact that only two teams had entered, getting a team together for the Olympic lacrosse tournament turned out to be surprisingly difficult. The game in Canada was so popular that its better exponents were recruited by professional sides as soon as they emerged in the amateur ranks. In order to pick a team of the best amateurs remaining the Canadian selectors had to scour the country. The men they finally chose were playing for clubs which could have been as much as three thousand miles apart. This meant that many of them had never seen one another in action and it took some time for them to blend together. Until then only individual clubs had represented Canada abroad. The Olympic side was the first truly representative Canadian lacrosse team to visit Europe.

The English side wore red jerseys while the Canadians wore white edged in green and had maple-leaves on the breasts. Lord and Lady Desborough, Lord Roberts VC, the former Commander-in-Chief of the British Army, and the Hon A.J. Balfour, who had been Prime Minister between 1902 and 1905, were in their positions before the game started. Sir George Wyatt Truscott, the Lord Mayor of London, arrived late but it was pointed out by his staff that he had only intended to watch the football.

Few in the crowd at the White City understood the complexities of the sport being played so vigorously before them, but the game turned out to be a thrilling one. Canada took an early lead and by half-time were winning 6–2. England then made a determined comeback, until the score was 9–9. Canada pulled ahead again and eventually won the match and the gold medal by 14 goals to 10. At one stage both teams were a man short. Dillon of Canada broke his stick, so Martin of England and Cambridge University stayed off the field until he could replace it, ensuring England would not gain an unfair advantage in the Canadian player's absence.

When the football final got under way at 3.00pm, this also proved to be a hard-fought encounter and England was severely tested throughout. Woodward and his men received a stroke of good fortune when the Danish goalkeeper slipped and let in the first goal. England scored another goal a little later and hung on to win the Olympic title 2–1.

The players were presented with their medals by the Lord Mayor of London. One of the most contented among the recipients must have been Reginald Hunt. In the space of 12 months he had won an Oxford Blue, an FA cup winner's medal and an Olympic gold. He was to go on to play twice for England. He became an ordained minister and spent many years teaching at Highgate School in London.

Baron de Coubertin was particularly pleased to see rugby football included in the White City programme. He was an enthusiast of the game, having refereed the final of the first French club championship in 1892. As it turned out, the Olympic rugby competition was not nearly as satisfactory for anyone, except the winning team. 1907–08 had not been a good season for England's Rugby Union side. In their championship games played in the first three months of 1908, England had defeated Ireland but lost to Wales and Scotland. In a match played outside the tournament England had beaten France, but almost everyone did that.

If the home countries had united to select a single combined side to play in the Olympics that year they might have mustered a decent side. Wales, which topped the championship league, undefeated, could have provided the wonderfully named Tommy Vile, England had the gigantic forward John Hopley, an outstanding university cricketer and boxer, who was to win the DSO in World War I, and for Scotland there was 'Darkie' Bedell-Sivright, an inspiring leader. There were others as well, but none of the home countries even entered a national side for the rugby tournament, let alone a combined one.

It was a sign of how little-regarded the Olympiad was by some sporting organisations that at the time the White City tournament was being held, the best Anglo-Welsh players were touring New Zealand. A belated, panic-stricken letter from the Rugby Football Union begging some of the players to return for the Olympiad was not even received by the tourists on their travels. The Olympic organisers began to despair of even producing a side for the final.

France, the winner of the competition at the 1900 Olympics, had entered a team but had then withdrawn. The administration of Gallic rugby was chaotic. Despite the amateur ethos of the game the leading French club players were being paid to turn out and constantly poached from one another, incurring the suspicion of the governing body, the International Rugby Football Board, which was agonising over whether or not to admit France into the annual tournament played among England, Ireland, Scotland and Wales. Rather than draw too much attention to itself and damage its chances of making the Four Nations into five, France accordingly steered clear of the Olympics, ensuring an invitation to join the annual tournament several years later.

Fortunately, the combined Australasian side the Wallabies were touring Britain that year, and did not mind an extra game being attached to their schedule. That left only the matter of finding a suitable team to meet them in the Olympic final. With so many of the best players touring the dominions or unable to be released by their employers, the standard was not high. S.M.J. Woods, a former international rugby player and cricketer, was particularly scathing about the average 1908 home countries forward, saying that he was as soft as dough, lacking in basic skills and completely untrained: 'He should go down to the field several times a week and practise with a ball, as it is essential to the proper development of rugby that all forwards should be accustomed to handling the leather on every possible occasion.'

Trained or untrained, the RFU authorities were charged with raising an Olympic side worthy of representing Great Britain. After much flustered debate, the authorities decided to entrust the responsibility to Cornwall. The team had won the county championship in 1907, defeating Durham 17–3 in the final in front of a crowd of 17,000 at Redruth. The county side had lost only one championship game in the whole season, to Devon. Ominously, however, in a friendly match the county side had been defeated easily, 18–5, by the Wallabies in a one-sided game notable only for the fact that the Australian touch judge had managed to break his leg. It was agreed that it was not a perfect choice, as only three of the Cornish side had ever represented England, but its members were willing to make the long journey from the West Country and, what was more, bring a thousand spectators as well. This number may have been exaggerated because in the event fewer than three thousand spectators watched the final.

However, the deal was finalised. The Wallabies had just started what was to become a very successful tour. Before they left home the *Referee* approved of the home country's selection, 'It is a strong combination and will worthily represent Australian rugby union football in the old country.'

The New South Wales Rugby Union, which was backing the tour, did its best to publicise its team. Even before the vessel carrying them from Australia had docked in England, 30 of the 31 players on the tour had lined up on the deck and delivered to the bewildered onlookers ashore in a slightly embarrassed manner what was claimed to be an aboriginal war chant. The one player who had refused to join in was the austere captain, Dr Herbert 'Paddy' Moran. Moran viewed such flamboyant gestures with suspicion, although he was forced to concede grudgingly that the policy 'had a box-office value'.

Moran, a fine player, had his own standards. On the voyage over he had insisted on his collection of sporting butchers, graziers (ranch farmers), warehousemen and miners dressing for dinner every evening. The forerunner of the New Zealand *haka* delivered by the players was claimed to be derived from aboriginal folk, although in fact it had been stolen almost in its entirety from a provincial rugby club back home. Moran dismissed the matter with a resigned shrug, 'We were officially expected to leap up in the air and make foolish gestures which somebody thought Australian natives might have used in similar circumstances,' he sighed, 'and we were also given meaningless words which we were to utter savagely, during this pantomime.' The words in question, which were distributed on sheets of paper for the tour party to memorise, were:

> Gau gau (insert name of opponent) whir-r-r!
> Win-nang-a-lang (thur)
> Mu-e-an-yil-ling
> Bu-rang-a-lang (yang)
> Yai! Yai!. Gun-yil-lang yang yah!

Newspaper reporters greeting the party at Plymouth asked its members what the side was going to call itself during the tour. No one had given any thought to that but when a journalist contemptuously suggested Rabbits as a possible name, the indignant Australians in the group refused to countenance playing under the sobriquet of a pest which had almost ruined so many farmers back home. Moran, acerbic as ever, asked the Englishmen that if stereotypes were to be in order, whether they would like his players to play with the broad arrows of convicts on their arms, in memory of the first English to arrive at Botany Bay. After a number of suggestions, some of them ribald in the extreme, someone came up with the term Wallabies and it stuck.

The newly named Wallabies lost their first international narrowly to Wales, 9–6, but they were to go on and record 25 victories. As their progress continued, their gritty approach to the game began to worry some onlookers, especially the team's propensity to have its players sent off. This caused the *Morning Post* to accuse the Wallabies of 'damaging imperial relations'.

The biggest controversy occurred with the rugged Australian display against Oxford University, when Syd Middleton was sent off for punching one of the students. The next day the *Oxford Chronicle* editorialised sternly, 'Clever as the play of the colonials was, they were so frequently guilty of unfair play that one's admiration of their cleverness was sadly diminished by indignation.'

In addition to Moran there were some good players in the Australasian side. The one who received the most publicity was loose forward Tom 'Rusty' Richards, lauded by *The Times* in glowing terms, 'If ever the earth had to select a rugby football team to play against Mars, Tom Richards would be the first player to be selected.'

Richards was a craggy, globetrotting gold miner, prepared to use his rugby skills to take him around the world and build himself a reputation. After playing for New South Wales, he travelled to South Africa to work in the gold fields there. He played good class rugby for the Transvaal in his new home and had aspirations to be selected for South Africa. When he discovered that there was a seven-year residential qualification for foreign-born would-be Springboks, Richards merely shrugged, packed his boots and journeyed on to England where briefly he played club and county rugby.

He returned home in 1908 in time to be picked for the Wallabies tour of Britain and inclusion in the Olympic Games side. Afterwards, he returned to South Africa. While he was there, an injury-ridden touring British Lions side, discovering that Richard's short club career in England had qualified him, selected the gold miner to play for them in two internationals, making him the first rugby player to represent both Australia and Britain. He ended his rugby career as player-coach for the French club Toulouse.

Only one player in the 1908 Olympic final was destined to win two Olympic golds. This was Daniel Carroll, at 18 the youngest Wallaby. He toured the USA with the 1913 Wallabies and liked the country so much that in 1920 he became player-coach of the US rugby team, largely made up of Stamford University players, who took a surprising first place in the Antwerp Games.

The 1908 final was something of an anti-climax. The captain, Herbert Moran, was absent with a shoulder injury, but was hardly missed. The Wallabies played in blue shirts with the New South Wales logo of the flowering shrub the waratah on their chests and the legend *Australia* beneath it. The match was played in dreadful conditions on a pitch perilously near the swimming pool. The Wallabies were 13–0 up at half-time. During the break, a Cornish official approached Herbert Moran, who was standing on the touchline, and complained that the Wallabies were wearing dangerously long running spikes in their boots and that consequently several of the Cornish players already had serious lacerations on their bodies.

Annoyed, Moran insisted on the English doctor conducting an examination of the state of the tourists' boots. The medic reported that the footwear of the Cornish players was, if anything, worse than that of the Wallabies. Moran looked around in vain for an apology. 'We heard no more from the disappointed Cornish official. He just faded out of the picture,' he commented.

In the second half, the Wallabies continued to prove themselves the superior side. The *Daily Telegraph* correspondent wrote, 'Certainly the day's play showed the winners in a new and very attractive light and it would not be fair to insist on the weakness of the Cornish backs. The pace, the feinting and the swerving of the Australian backs beat them time after time.'

The Wallabies emerged easy winners 32–3. At the end of the game, each man was presented with a silver medal and a certificate by the Olympic authorities. Before the tour had ended, the players in the Olympic final were also each given their gold medal by their proud nation. There may also have been an added incentive for the Australians to do well in a showpiece match like an Olympic final – upon their return to Australia, many of them became pro-fessional players in the newly formed Australian Rugby League. Their captain, Moran, had the last word. When asked what had given him particular satisfaction about the trip, he replied succinctly, 'During a tour of more than five months, while I was with the team, not one of 31 players contracted venereal disease.'

The Cornish side and officials were less highly rewarded. Their post-match celebrations consisted of being given a dinner by the Cornish Members of Parliament.

The day after the final, most of the Wallabies stayed on at the White City to support their compatriot Snowy Baker in the boxing competition. Boxing did not have an easy time being admitted as an Olympic sport. When it was mooted for the 1896 Athens tourna-ment, the sport was rejected at once by the committee as being 'ungentlemanly, dangerous and practised by the dregs of society'. The Paris tournament and the intercalated Games of 1906 also turned their faces against the noble art. It was allowed into the 1904 St Louis Olympiad because boxing was so popular in the USA, but the bouts were not held until a fortnight after most of the athletes had returned home, so the competition became little more than the US national championships.

Before the London Olympics, the Amateur Boxing Association worked hard to have the sport included. It was supported in its efforts by the influential National Sporting Club, promoter of professional contests, with its membership of influential peers. Even so, the boxing event was shunted until the end of the Olympiad. Once again, home fighters predominated among the entries. One newspaper commented tartly on the number of previous English amateur champions who had come out of retirement for the occasion, like old warhorses at the sound of a bugle: 'The majority who have entered are back numbers who do not intend bidding for any more English championships.'

The contests were held over the course of a single day at the Northampton Institute in Clerkenwell, on 27 October. The hall could have been filled several times over, such was the demand for the tickets which ranged from two shillings and sixpence to a guinea. The bouts were of three rounds, the first two rounds being three minutes in duration and the fourth four minutes. There were two judges and a referee. If the judges disagreed, the referee had the option of using his casting vote or of ordering another round to be contested.

Many of the country's leading amateurs, including a number of ABA champions past and present, had turned up for the occasion and there were also entries from France, Denmark and Australia. Among the more interesting entrants was 37-year-old veteran R.K. (Dick) Gunn, of the Surrey Commercial Docks club. An outstanding boxer, Gunn had won the amateur featherweight title in 1894, 1895 and 1896. Eventually, he became so much more proficient at the sport than all the other boxers of his weight in Britain that the authorities requested he retire from active competition because of his 'acknowledged superiority'.

The amenable Gunn agreed and helped in his father's tailor shop, refereed and judged matches and served happily on the ABA Council. He boxed only the occasional exhibition, including one against the outstanding Welsh professional Jim Driscoll. The lure of the Olympics proved too much for him and with the permission of the authorities he threw his hat into the ring again after 12 years of retirement.

Gunn rolled back the years. In the preliminary bouts he defeated a Frenchman and then the current ABA featherweight champion. In the final he outpointed Charlie Morris, twice an ABA champion and a decade younger than his opponent. Morris attacked fiercely but Gunn used all his old skills to keep his opponent at bay.

There was an unexpectedly large contingent from Denmark in the crowd. The group had come to see their man Valdemar Holberg in the lightweight class. In his first contest the Dane was matched against Englishman Matt Wells of the Lynn amateur boxing club, who, although still only 22, had won the ABA title on four occasions. He was so highly regarded by the Amateur Boxing Association that his name had been the first one to be selected for the UK team.

The dividing line between amateurs and professionals was so tenuous that Wells, sponsored by his club, was able to take a week off to be trained by a professional, Jack Meekings, at the Coach and Horses public house at Stonebridge Park in north west London. There he sparred with the American world professional lightweight champion Jimmy Britt.

Although he was expected to do well in his division, Wells was unexpectedly nervous before the start of the competition, which began with the preliminary heats of his lightweight class. In the dressing room before his first contest, another member of the English contingent persuaded the naive young lightweight to share several bottles of beer with him, assuring Wells that it would enhance his ring performance.

Wells was a teetotaller but was so nervous that he allowed himself to be convinced. He downed a quart of strong English Burton ale. As a result he entered the ring with a bad headache and a queasy stomach. The Dane put up such a spirited contest against Wells that at the end of three rounds the referee was unable to separate them and to the dismay of the English boxer ordered that an extra two-minute round be boxed. By then the London boxer was feeling distinctly unwell but he just about scraped through on points. The newspaper reports stated that the last round consisted more of wrestling than boxing by both contestants. Wells staggered back to the dressing room and examined his face in the mirror, and when he 'saw cut lips and eyes and my nose spread across my face I rather wondered what the loser looked like'.

The two doctors in attendance forbade Wells to fight again that day but reluctantly relented when the boxer pleaded to be allowed to go through to the next round. Wells entered the ring again looking, in his own words, like a remnant from a junkman's barrow. The battered and exhausted Jewish fighter came up against a skilful boxer in Fred Grace, who he had defeated in the 1907 ABA final. Wells lost on points and soon turned professional. Grace went on to win the gold medal. Until then, he had never won a major championship but he was to go on to win four ABA championships. In 1920, at the age of 36, he fought in his next Olympics but was defeated early on.

The final of the middleweight boxing championship took place between two of the hardest men in the whole of the Olympic competition. J.W.H.T. Douglas was the Fettes-educated son of a wealthy timber merchant and a boxing enthusiast. At the time of the Olympics he was holding down a sinecure in his father's firm while pursuing the career of a full-time amateur athlete. He was already in the Essex county cricket side. In the 1907–08 season leading up to the Games he had scored 1,167 runs and had taken 83 wickets. A tough, aggressive boxer, a former public schools title holder, he had won the ABA middleweight title in 1905 and had been on the way to repeating the achievement in the following year, when he had been disqualified for throwing his opponent to the canvas.

Douglas had taken his defeat badly. Referee Bernard Angle, a friend of the young boxer, wrote: 'The disqualification in the amateur championship had rankled with him and he had practically retired, but he was persuaded to put on harness again for the honour of the old country.'

Johnny Douglas was certainly determined. He went on to captain his county and his country at cricket and to secure a reputation as a dour, imperious, sharp-tongued leader capable of humiliating the toughest professional and even reducing some of them to tears. He was also a crab-like, defensive batsman, so difficult to get out that the Australians had nicknamed him 'Johnny Won't Hit Today'.

In his opponent in the final he was up against a foe worthy of his steel. Reginald 'Snowy' Baker was every bit as glacial as the

Englishman and a great deal more gifted as an athlete. He had already represented Australia at swimming and diving in the London Olympics, played rugby for the Wallabies and was a gifted rider. He was a wily, ambitious, fearless man who appreciated that the more successful he became as a sportsman the better it would be for his later career. An Olympic gold medal would open many doors for him back home.

As part of the warm-up for the Olympics, Douglas fought a three-round exhibition bout with the world heavyweight champion, Canadian Tommy Burns, at the City Athenaeum, better known as the Thieves' Kitchen in Throgmorton Street. Burns had been expecting a leisurely spar but to his annoyance the amateur went for him from the first bell. At the end Burns was furious but decided it was politic to put a good face on the matter. He pretended to be jolly and roared, 'If this is what you call a sparring exhibition, what is your honest-to-God fighting like down here?'

Some time later that year, in Australia, Burns fought an exhibition in Australia against Snowy Baker, two weeks before the former lost the heavyweight title to Jack Johnson. Baker, a shrewd businessman, was being paid under the counter for the bout. He was much more circumspect than Douglas had been. Placidly he allowed Burns to outbox him before a crowd of 10,000 spectators. In return the mollified Burns told the audience that Baker was every bit as good as J.W.H.T. Douglas had been.

Douglas secured an easier route to the Olympic final, drawing an all-important bye at one stage, but he had also defeated a very tough contender in Rube Warnes, who had already won the ABA title four times and later was to achieve a fifth. Douglas knocked him out in two rounds, a sign that the Englishman was on top form.

The final between Douglas and Baker was said to have been the best bout of the day. Douglas secured the verdict, mainly on the strength of his superiority early on in the bout. The official report noted, 'In the second round Douglas got home a decisive blow on the jaw which took the Australian off his feet, to continue as pluckily as ever.' Douglas went on to secure a narrow points verdict and was presented with a cup by his father, who was that year's president of the ABA.

Great Britain won all five boxing gold medals. The easiest day's work was that of Albert Leonard Oldman, a City of London policeman and former trooper in the Horse Guards who had entered the heavyweight class. An all-round athlete, he had also represented the police at wrestling. He had never won an ABA title, so his entry for the Olympics was lightly regarded. All the same, Oldman, who possessed a massive punch, knocked his first opponent out in about a minute of the first round and secured a bye into the final, where he encountered Sydney Evans, the current ABA heavyweight champion.

He was somewhat handicapped by the punishing route to the final. In the first round of the competition, Evans had knocked out Albert Ireton, who had won a gold medal with the City of Liverpool Police tug-of-war-team. In the next round Evans knocked out Fred Parkes, but in the process damaged his shoulder. Evans was no match for the aggressive policeman. The official report described the final in these terms: 'When Oldman did get to work his execution was something terrific. He crossed Evans with a fine right on the jaw, got him dazed in a corner, and smashed him about a dozen times in the face before Evans could escape.' The bout was over in two minutes. The level-headed Oldman was not carried away by his success and rejected blandishments to turn professional and become one of the White Hopes jostling to challenge the unpopular black heavyweight champion Jack Johnson. Instead, in 1910 he joined the Ceylon police force, where he became a sergeant.

Perhaps all the heavyweight contestants in London had been fortunate, because the best amateur heavyweight in the world, American Sam Berger, winner of the St Louis gold medal in 1904, had turned professional. It was a sign of the gulf between amateur and professional boxing at the time that even the mighty Berger, who had won most of his 40 amateur contests by knockouts, made little inroads among the paid ranks and retired after several years to manage the world professional heavyweight champion James J. Jeffries and then open a San Francisco clothing store.

From his comfortable office above the shop floor he was wont to pontificate on the noble art with such *aperçus* as 'Boxing is an art just as much as music. To excel in it you must have a conception of time, of balance, of distance. The man who attempts to box without such a conception is like a person who tries to be a musician without having an ear for music.' As some of the battered denizens of Cauliflower Alley might have put it, the haberdasher talked a great fight.

In fact, although three of the competitors in the 1908 boxing tournament turned professional, only one became a champion. This was Matt Wells, who had been eliminated in one of the earlier rounds of the lightweight class after his unfortunate pre-bout drinking session. As a professional he had a long globe-trotting career and won the British and European lightweight titles from the highly regarded Freddy Welsh.

The wrestlers competed some time before the boxers. They did not share the fighters' good fortune in competing inside a warm building. Their events took place in the open White City arena on mats, sometimes in the rain. There were two different styles of wrestling, although some competitors took part in both.

The Graeco-Roman style, popular on the mainland of the Continent, did not allow holds or attacks below the waist. The catch-as-catch-can or freestyle bouts did permit these grips. Thanks to an astute English showman called C.B. Cochran, professional freestyle wrestling had been enormously popular in Britain in the first few years of the 20th century. Cochran's protégé, George Hackenschmidt, dubbed the Russian Lion, had drawn enormous crowds in contests against a series of Terrible Turks, Mad Scots and Belligerent Bulgars. By the time of the London Olympics, however, the wrestling craze was in decline. Earlier in the year, Hackenschmidt, who had been earning £25,000 a year, had lost a world championship match of dubious provenance and suspicious probity to the American Frank Gotch, a former Iowan farmer renowned for taking a delight in breaking the bones of those opponents he was convinced were too drunk or ill-equipped to fight back. The first Hackenschmidt–Gotch bout and its successor three years later heralded the grotesque pantomime of fixed fights which was to become professional wrestling for the rest of the 20th century and beyond.

This meant that by 1908, amateur wrestling was largely confined to its earnest devotees and did not attract much public interest nor draw large crowds. The fact did not prevent the White City entrants from gambolling pluckily in the rain as the cyclists and runners hurtled past their ears.

The Graeco Roman competition was as much a lesson in the political geography of Europe at the time as it was a sporting contest. Johannes Joseppson came from Iceland, but his fourth place in the middleweight class was attributed to Denmark, as Iceland was considered a province of Denmark. To add injury to insult, Joseppson also sustained a broken arm in the service of his reluctantly adopted country. Verner Weckman of Finland actually won a gold medal in the light heavyweight division but had to be content with witnessing a placard bearing the inscription *Finland* being waved in defiant celebration in the crowd, as the Russians would not allow its province to use its national flag at the Olympics.

In the lightweight division of the Graeco-Roman wrestling an Italian sailor, Enrico Porro, who claimed to be undefeated, won the gold medal from a total of 25 entrants, defeating Russian Nicolay Orlov on points in the final. The middleweight final was scheduled between two Swedes, Frithiof Martensson and Mauritz Andersson.

Martensson damaged his arm in a semi-final contest and Andersson sportingly agreed to a 24-hour postponement to allow his fellow countryman's injury to heal. Martensson had actually taught Andersson how to wrestle and had defeated him in the final of the 1907 Swedish championship. The delay did the trick, because Martensson went on to win the contest for the gold medal.

Two Finns contested the final of the light heavyweight class, with Verner Weckman taking the gold and Yrjo Saarela winning the silver medal. The heavyweight title was taken quite easily by the Hungarian Richard Weisz, a man whose 50-inch chest and 20-inch neck measurements bore testimony to the fact that he was also his country's heavyweight weight-lifting champion.

Americans won gold medals in the two lightest weights of the catch-as-catch-can competition. George Mehnert was successful in the bantamweight division, while George Dole, the only non-Briton in the entries for the featherweight class, outclassed his opponents. In his entire amateur wrestling career, Mehnert only lost two contests, and one of those was to Dole, who broke Mehnert's undefeated run extending over seven years. He won the American flyweight title four times and the bantamweight championship twice. George Dole and his twin brother Louis represented Yale. Another member of the college wrestling team was A.C. Gilbert, who was co-winner of the pole-vault competition at the White City.

Representing Canada in the bantamweight class was Quebec farmer Aubert Cote. He lost on a fall to Mehnert in 6 minutes and 40 seconds, but went on to win the bronze medal. Cote had been so desperate to represent his country in London that he had mortgaged his farm in order to pay his way across the Atlantic. After his success, the Canadian Olympic Committee reimbursed his expenses.

The lightweight gold medallist was a member of a White Russian émigré family based in Kensington, George de Relwyskow, who wrestled for the Hammersmith Amateur Wrestling Club and the German Gymnasium. He also entered the middleweight class, where his progress was not quite so untroubled, mainly because he was giving away a great deal of weight to most of his opponents. In the semi-final of the heavier weight class de Relwyskow encountered Carl Andersson of Sweden. Both competitors went down on the mat early on, with Andersson on top. At the end of the allotted period of 20 minutes the judges were undecided and the referee used his casting vote in favour of the British team member. The Swedish officials protested, but the adjudicating committee agreed with the referee that de Relwyskow had made most of the attacking moves from his recumbent position on the mat. Andersson was so incensed by the verdict that he refused to take part in the wrestle-off for the silver medal and withdrew from the competition.

In the final of the middleweight division, de Relwyskow was defeated on points by another Briton, Stanley Bacon of the London Amateur Wrestling Society. Bacon was only 5 feet 3 inches tall but was broad and muscular. An all-round athlete he was also the

British civil service middleweight boxing and diving champion and turned out for the civil service rugby team. By the time of the 1908 Olympics he had already won the German and Swiss open championships.

De Relwyskow, however, was the reigning British lightweight and middleweight champion. Bacon went on to wrestle in two more Olympics, while de Relwyskow became a promoter of professional wrestling matches in Scotland, a career that he combined with his trade as a builder and decorator. Both men wrote text-books on wrestling.

The winner of the catch-as-catch-can heavyweight competition was Con O'Kelly, a massive Cork-born member of the Hull Police Fire Brigade. A cheerful, good-tempered man, even his resolution was frayed by an accident at work shortly before the Olympics. A wall fell on him, necessitating a sojourn of several days' duration in hospital. He was off work for almost a month and still had not fully recovered when he entered the British amateur wrestling championships that year. He was defeated by Edward Barrett of the City of Liverpool police team.

O'Kelly was still selected to represent Great Britain and Ireland in the heavyweight wrestling division at the White City Olympics. He won his first bout by a fall and then came up against Barrett again in the semi-final. For the Liverpool policeman it was to be the last day of a fairly busy Olympic schedule even by his standards.

On 14 July he had taken part in the preliminary rounds of the hammer competition and on the following day had thrown the javelin. On 16 July he engaged in the discus throwing and then, because his tug-of-war team had drawn a bye into the final, he had been given a day off. He came back on 18 July to win his tug-of-war gold medal, pulling against the City of London police. There then followed an almost unprecedented three days of idleness before Barrett was defeated in the opening heat of the Graeco-Roman heavyweight wrestling on 21 July. Taking breath on the 22nd, he was successful in the first round of the catch-as-catch-can wrestling on 23 July, defeating Charles Brown of Great Britain on a fall after 3 minutes and 20 seconds. In the semi-final he was defeated in 2 minutes and 14 seconds by O'Kelly, who lifted the huge Liverpool policeman completely off his feet and slammed him to the canvas before applying an arm and crutch hold.

Barrett stayed on long enough to beat Nixon of Great Britain in the contest to determine the bronze medal winner and then wandered off, presumably in search of fresh worlds to conquer. He took part in a few more amateur wrestling competitions and then is recorded as resigning from the Liverpool police in 1914.

Con O'Kelly defeated Jacob Gunderson of Norway in the final to win the gold medal. Gunderson was a resident of the USA and that country's current heavyweight wrestling title-holder, but he was representing the nation of his birth on this occasion. The Norwegian-American was even bigger than the enormous O'Kelly but he was also 11 years older than the Irishman. The two men struggled for 13 minutes before O'Kelly secured the first fall. The effort had been too much for Gunderson and O'Kelly pinned him easily to gain the second and conclusive fall.

A forerunner of the winter sports to be introduced more than a decade later was ice skating. Ulrich Salchow, the Swedish world champion won the men's individual skating competition but not before the Russian entry had walked – or skated – out in protest. The Russian was Nikolai Alexandrovich Kolomenkin, a university teacher. He skated under the name of Panin because members of the middle classes did not usually participate in competitive sports. Four years earlier he had competed in the revolver shooting team event at St Louis. He had taught himself to skate by wrapping towels around his feet to weigh them down and preserve his balance. He was doing quite well in the skating competition when Salchow started hurling abuse and criticisms at him. The Russian protested to the judges who refuted his claim. Kolomenkin-Panin abandoned the contest in disgust.

He went on to win a gold medal, Russia's first in Olympic competition, in the special figures competition for men. In this competition, elaborate designs, plotted in advance, were traced on the ice by the skates of the competitors. Salchow withdrew from this event, claiming to be unwell.

After so much sound and fury the 1908 Olympics ended on a relatively peaceful note with the hockey final. Originally the home countries had intended to enter a UK team for this event but the individual hockey associations complained so vociferously that individual teams were entered by England, Ireland, Scotland and Wales.

Germany was represented by the Uhlenhorster club, the national champions, while the French team consisted of players from a number of clubs. The tournament started with a match between France and Germany, although this is generally regarded as having been a demonstration match and not rightly a part of the official Olympic programme. Germany won by the single goal scored but the onlooker studying the game for the official Olympic report was rather condescending about the efforts of both sides: 'Their one mission is to learn and they acquired not a few wrinkles by watching the British teams.'

England had a comparatively easy route to the final, where it met Ireland. One of the most noted and saddest legacies left by the young England side was the number of its members who went on to distinguish themselves in World War I, some of them making the ultimate sacrifice.

They came from far and wide and had an extensive range of occupations and hobbies. Louis Baillon had been born in the Falkland Islands, where his family owned a farm; Harry Freeman later became one of the doubles-punting champions of the Thames. Eric Green spent many years as a knowledgable hockey correspondent of *The Times* newspaper. The star of the side, Reggie Pridmore, scored ten goals at the White City, almost half of England's total. He also played cricket for Warwickshire.

Six thousand spectators watched the event that was to bring down the curtain on the 1908 London Olympics. All the previous games had been played on the same pitch and there had been a firework display the previous evening, so the turf had cut up quite considerably. England had little difficulty in controlling the game and led 3–0 at half-time. Soon into the second half Ireland managed to score its solitary goal, but that was as much as it could achieve. At some time after 4.00pm in the afternoon of a dull, drab day on 31 October the game ended, with England having won 8–1. The players shook hands and dispersed to the dressing rooms. The spectators went home.

Not many people paid any attention. The newspapers had long since stopped reporting the events on their front pages. All over Britain, life went on as normal. In Barnsley, Second Division West Bromwich Albion defeated the home side, by two goals to nil. On the stage of the Tivoli music hall in London, the bilingual comedian Harry Fragson, who had not yet written his hit song, 'Hello, Hello, Who's Your Lady Friend?', went through his act before a full house of a thousand people.

The 92-year-old Scottish poet Sir Theodore Martin was interviewed on a brief visit to London. Gloomily, he forecast that Socialist firebrands were about to take over the country and that the inhabitants of the capital might yet witness the menacing glitter of bayonets in Piccadilly.

In Edinburgh, the Scottish National Exhibition closed after a six-month run which had attracted more than three million visitors. Misguidedly, the organisers closed the popular Terrace bar early, at 9.30pm. The customers objected vehemently. The police were called in and fights broke out all over Saughton Park. As night drew on, thousands of Hallowe'en parties got under way.

There was one final official duty still to be performed. That night a banquet was held at the Holborn restaurant for those Olympic athletes and officials still residing in the capital. Surprisingly, there were four hundred of them. The restaurant could accommodate such a number with ease – it was one of the largest in the capital and was benefiting from the fact that a rebuilding programme was making the area one of the most up-to-date and fashionable. A slum-clearance scheme had prepared the area for many improvements. The adjacent recently completed Kingsway was the newest and widest street in the city, with a modern underground electric tram system running beneath it. The restaurant's kitchens were renowned for the variety of dishes they could provide at a moment's notice. When a young Indian law student called Gandhi, who had been subsisting mainly on porridge, had called in search of a vegetarian meal for a large party of friends, the Holborn had been the only establishment able to meet his demands.

The last Olympic dinner was presided over almost inevitably by the indomitable Lord Desborough, who was still going strong. He had been there at the beginning and it was only fitting that he should attend at the end. Guests were present from Britain, France, Germany, Australia, South Africa and the USA. At the top table was the Reverend R.S. de Courcy Laffan, Desborough's loyal lieutenant. He made a typically mellifluous speech. Considering the pressure he had been under for most of the year, there was an unexpected core of hope and even determination among Laffan's otherwise anodyne remarks.

He also dealt with the suspicion with which so many had greeted the gathering together of so many different creeds, cultures and countries at the 1908 Olympics. He touched on the undeniable problems which had beset the tournament. But he also pointed out the lessons that had been learnt and the confidence with which the organisers faced the future of the movement, despite the initial misgivings of so many of them. He had come to the Olympic movement to scoff, he told his audience simply, but he had remained to admire. He was sure that there was a great deal still to be done, but there was also much to be proud of. To illustrate his point, de Courcy Laffan quoted from Matthew Arnold's poem *Mortality:*

> With aching hands and bleeding feet
> We dig and heap, lay stone on stone;
> We bear the burden and the heat
> Of the long day and wish 'twere done,
> Not till the hours of light return,
> All we have built do we discern.

Fourteen

The Hero Business

'The Games of 1908 are over.'

*The Olympic Games of 1908 in London: A Reply to Certain
Charges Made by the American Officials*

Although events were to continue for several more months, the
London Olympiad began to wind down after the conclusion of
the athletic events in July. There was a round of parties to celebrate
the conclusion.

Perhaps the most ornate was given on 1 August by New Yorker
George Kessler for Lord Desborough and his committee. It took
place at Kessler's lodge on the Thames. Several hundred male guests
were entertained by Mr and Mrs Kessler. They sat under an awning
on the river bank to be served dinner under the supervision of the
manager of the Savoy Hotel, 'to whom the host gave carte blanche
as regards expense'. The grounds were illuminated by 3,000 electric
lights and thousands of oil lamps and Chinese lanterns.

At the far end of the grounds were painted representations of
the Acropolis and other ancient Greek buildings. After the meal the
guests were taken down the Thames in a chartered steamer to view
a specially presented river fete, with a prize of £100 for the most
handsomely decorated small boat. The evening ended with a
fireworks display along two miles of the illuminated river bank.

Slowly. the American athletes returned home by different
routes. Their fame spread before them. The *Trenton Evening Times*
of 5 August was only one of the many newspapers heralding the
return of the team: 'It was no ordinary championship the plucky
band of Yankee athletes won – it was the most remarkable
demonstration of athletic prowess the world has ever witnessed.'

That summer they assembled twice more. On the first occasion, on Saturday 29 August, 63 of the competitors gathered together for an official civic welcome from the acting Mayor of New York. The Amateur Athletic Union had announced that it was supplying $10,000 towards the cost of the occasion, although a number of newspapers had wondered aloud where the association would find so much money. The athletes and officials assembled in a fleet of automobiles at 46th Street and Broadway and were driven the five miles to City Hall before crowds estimated as hundreds of thousands, cheering and waving flags. The route was lined by policemen and representatives of various sports organisations and athletics teams. Some 150 mounted policemen led the way and khaki-clad soldiers and more colourfully attired members of the National Guard formed an official escort. The ceremony was under the command of General George W. Wingate, the Grand Marshal of the Parade.

At the steps of City Hall the athletes disembarked from their vehicles and stood before the acting mayor, aldermen and various civic dignitaries and prominent citizens, as huge crowds looked on. Team manager Matty Halpin introduced each athlete in turn, in alphabetical order. The members stepped forward to receive specially cast medals in morocco boxes. Ralph Rose was recorded as grinning and blushing like a girl as he climbed the steps to the table, while a great cheer was reserved for J.C. Carpenter, who had been disqualified in the 400 metres final.

The biggest reception of all, however, was reserved for Johnny Hayes, the marathon winner. He had been standing almost unnoticed among the hulking hammer, javelin and discus throwers, but as he stepped forward to receive his medal a concerted shout of 'Hayes! Hayes! Hayes!' went up from the crowd. The band struck up 'The Star Spangled Banner' and the crowd joined in with a will. Hayes walked back to rejoin his team-mates with tears coursing down his cheeks. In his concluding address, acting mayor McGowan, maintaining the theme of the assembly, congratulated 'those of our countrymen who have won victories in athletic sports against the world'.

Two days later the athletes and officials and many newspaper reporters assembled at 8.30am to board the Long Island Railroad vessel *Sagamore* from New York's East 31st Street Dock. Off Sagamore Hill they were taken to the waiting president's summer estate at Oyster Bay in a series of launches and rowing boats. Once ashore, James E. Sullivan, in command as usual, marshalled the athletes into two columns and marched them up to Roosevelt's summer home. Sullivan's position as the unofficial emperor of American athletics had been cemented by the success of the US track and field events. He also continued to serve his commercial masters faithfully, seeing to it that Spalding equipment was used at all the track meets under the jurisdiction of the AAU.

At one point at Oyster Bay reporters began to search diligently for the gigantic Ralph Rose. A rumour was circulating that the thrower intended to lead the impromptu procession up to the front door of the president's house brandishing the borrowed Stars and Stripes, which he had refused to dip in front of Edward VII at the Olympic opening ceremony. There was no sight of the American-Irish athlete, so instead the remaining competitors and officials marched off without him, whistling cheerfully, 'There'll be a hot time in the old town tonight.'

The president and Mrs Roosevelt and their children received their guests at the front door. Roosevelt had always had a soft spot for athletes and athletics. At political gatherings it was not unknown for him to recount the story of how his name had first been attached to the presidency at a sports meeting. According to the president it had happened at an international meeting in 1895, just before the first Olympics, between New York and London athletic clubs. This had probably resulted in the highest standards ever seen at a tournament up to that time. The New York team had won every event.

Roosevelt had bet $5 on Mike Sweeney to win the high jump. Not only had the American succeeded but he had set a new world record in the process. The delighted Roosevelt had tried to cross the track to the central reservation to congratulate the athlete. He had been stopped by the sergeant-at-arms in charge of security, who had refused to allow Roosevelt to walk on the track. Roosevelt took great delight in relating what happened when someone told the sergeant-at-arms that he was impeding the New York Police Commissioner. The official replied, 'I wouldn't care if he was Teddy Roosevelt, president of the USA. He ain't crossing the track!'

At the door of the president's home, the first to be shaken vigorously by the hand was James E. Sullivan. Then the officials and runners were introduced, starting with marathon winner Johnny Hayes. 'Here is the top-notcher!' boomed the beaming president. 'This is fine! Fine! and I am so glad a New York boy won it. By George! I am. I am so glad to see all you boys.'

The well-briefed president had an appropriate word for each athlete as they passed before him. When double medal winner Mel Sheppard shook his hand, Roosevelt recognised him. 'I am right glad to see you – I followed you during the Athens days. Let me see, aren't you a member of the police force?' When the middle-distance runner informed him that he had been rejected by New York's finest, the president snorted with asperity,'I wish I was still Commissioner!'

Roosevelt was in an expansive mood. He was coming to the end of his presidency and had already signed a lucrative contract with *Colliers* magazine for a series of articles he was to write about a planned big-game hunting expedition to Africa. He continued with his congratulations, telling John B. Taylor that the runner had done nobly and calling coach Mike Murphy a national institution. Finally, the president led the way to the library and showed his guests the heads of big game lining the walls. He then made a short speech of congratulation, claiming that he had followed their progress so closely that he was convinced that he could pass an examination on their achievements. He then took them through to the dining room for cigarettes and punch before drawing James E. Sullivan to one side and quizzing him on the events in London. When the administrator tried to describe some of the judging decisions that had gone against the Americans, Roosevelt was diplomatic. 'Well, we've won, and the less talking we do the better. We don't need to talk; we've won. There's never been a team like this one. You fellows have won a place for all time.'

One of the guests shouted for three cheers 'for the greatest president this country has ever had!'. While the walls were still

reverberating from the noise, iconoclastic as ever, the gigantic
Ralph Rose arrived several hours late to cheers and laughter.
Eventually the guests lined up to leave. President Roosevelt gently
tried to give them a reality check. 'Remember that you're heroes for
ten days,' he told the athletes. 'When that time is up, drop the hero
business and go to work.' It was good advice.

Sports continued after the London Olympics. The next
Olympiad was held in Stockholm and was a great success. The
Games lasted five weeks and were a model of efficiency. Lessons
were learnt from London and preceding Games. The International
Amateur Athletics Association was formed to standardise the rules
for track and field events. It was ruled that from then on all
Olympic judges would be drawn from an international pool and
not restricted to officials from the home nation. The number of
women competitors almost doubled. There were political
complaints from the Russians about the presence of the Finns and
from Austria about a Hungarian bid for independence. But
everything on the field and track went smoothly.

Baron de Coubertin did not regard himself as being well
rewarded for his efforts after the first few Olympiads. He was
shouldered to one side at the 1896 and 1900 Olympiads, did not
attend the 1904 St Louis Games, was made to feel unwelcome at the
intercalated tournament in Athens in 1906 and was dismayed by
the controversies thrown up in London in 1908. Still he persevered.
The 1912 Olympiad proved a long-awaited triumph for him. He
sat next to King Gustav at the opening ceremony and was
consulted with due deference by the Olympic Committee. The
1916 Games had to be cancelled because of the War, but Coubertin
lived to see another three Olympiads and to be kept in touch with
events at a fifth and sixth. Ill-health, reduced circumstances and an
unhappy domestic life prevented his ability to attend the Los
Angeles and Berlin Olympiads. He died of a heart attack in 1937.

The White City, the scene of the London Games, continued to
house spectacular exhibitions until the outset of war – including
Japanese-British, the Coronation, the Latin-British, the Anglo-
American. During the war the site was used as a drill ground for
recruits. Textile fairs were held there spasmodically until 1937. In

1927 the track was grassed over to allow for speedway and greyhound racing. Then a new track was laid and the AAA championships were held there annually. The Queens Park Rangers football club played on the ground briefly, as did a professional Rugby League club. During World War II the buildings were used for packing parachutes. In 1949 the area was purchased by the BBC to house its television service. In 2007 it was announced that the Corporation was considering selling the building in a cost-cutting exercise.

King Edward VII died in 1910, only two years after the British Games that had caused him so much personal pain. His wife Queen Alexandra lived on for another ten years. The four men who first debated on board the *Branwen* the possibilities of a London Olympics all went on to lead long and interesting, if sometimes tragic, lives.

For some time after the 1908 Olympics Lord Desborough continued in public life. He was president of the Thames Conservancy Board for 32 years and High Steward of Maidenhead, near his 3,000-acre estate of Grenfell Park at Taplow. He allowed the Oxford crews to use his home as a base for the boat race training. He spent much time nurturing the grounds, planting the seeds of unusual trees he had seen on his travels. He gave ornate dinner parties for the great and the good, where he would lay down the law in his high-pitched staccato voice. Honours continued to come his way. He was made a Knight of the Order of the Garter and Captain of the Yeomen of the Guard.

In 1920, he was disturbed to read his obituary in *The Times*. He had been confused with a recently deceased Lord Besborough. A story went the rounds that an irate Desborough had telephoned the newspaper to complain about the report of his death. There was a stunned silence at the other end of the line, and then the editor had faltered, 'Excuse me, my lord, but where are you phoning from?'

Yet for all his energy, Desborough never really recovered from the effects of World War I, in which he lost two of his sons. In 1926, Lord Desborough's third son George was killed in a car crash. The stricken peer and his wife lapsed into increasing solitude. When Desborough died in 1945 with no male heirs, the title became extinct. An island and a cut on his beloved Thames were named after him.

Another who was at the *Branwen* discussions was Sir Cosmo Edmund Duff Gordon. He continued to exist contentedly enough in the wealthy shadows of his wife Lucille and sister-in-law Elinor Glyn, alternating between London and the Duff Gordons' family seat Maryculter House near Aberdeen in Scotland. It was a pleasant way of life but it was to end abruptly on a dreadful night in the North Atlantic in 1912.

Duff Gordon and his wife had sailed on the maiden voyage to New York of the Cunard luxury liner that was to become the most known of them all, the *Titanic*. The story of how the vessel struck an iceberg and started to sink was reported around the world. There were not enough lifeboats on board and the ships' officers had to fire their pistols to prevent panic-stricken passengers storming them. Somehow in the confusion Duff Gordon, Lucille, their secretary Miss Francatelli, two American passengers and seven crew members pulled away in a lifeboat that had room for 40.

Controversy has reigned ever since about Duff Gordon's role in his miraculous escape when hundreds drowned. Some accounts say that he entered the lifeboat in answer to the pleas of his wife and secretary and that he did not know at the time that the lives of so many others were in danger. However, damning evidence later emerged that as the *Titanic* began to plunge beneath the waves, the tactless Lucille said to Miss Francatelli, 'There is your beautiful nightdress gone!' Hearing this, some of the seamen toiling at the oars grumbled that they had lost everything they possessed. At a later stage, after their rescue, Cosmo Duff Gordon ordered his secretary to draw up seven draft orders for £5 each to recompense them for the deprivation of their possessions.

Debate raged later as to whether this was a generous act of charity or a bribe to the sailors who pulled away from the *Titanic* and had not returned to pick up any freezing survivors in the water. A Board of Trade enquiry exonerated the Duff Gordons of any wrongdoing but many considered Duff Gordon a coward and a blackguard. The pair were ostracised by London society, refused service in fashionable restaurants and even booed in the street.

Lucille's business began to go under. The childless couple drifted apart.

Cosmo Duff Gordon died in 1931. Lady Lucille survived him but never forgot the criticisms heaped upon her in the USA after the *Titanic* enquiry. In 1919, in one of the increasingly numerous court cases in which she became embroiled, she was given a chance to prove her patriotism to the country in which she was currently earning a living by stating how many US Government Liberty Bonds she had purchased. Never noted for her diplomacy, the dressmaker had snapped, 'Why should I buy any? This country means nothing to me. I have had nothing but trouble over here. It is an awful country!'

Another organiser of the Games, Lord Howard de Walden continued his dilettante life in the Arts. Financially secure, thanks to the properties he owned in Central London and elsewhere, he supported orchestras and a bevy of unusual artists known as his 'chicks', bred and raced horses, learned Welsh and wrote plays under the name of T.E. Ellis. He spent much of his time renovating Dean Castle in Scotland, which he had inherited from his grandmother and tending the collection of armour he assembled there. He died in 1946.

Tommy de Walden's friend and fellow motorboat racing enthusiast, the Duke of Westminster, served gallantly in the Middle East in World War I. He enlisted at the age of 35. Waiting until Cowes Week was over he then sailed to France without permission, attached himself to a unit and distinguished himself in heavy fighting there. Maintaining his love of engines he developed a prototype Rolls-Royce armoured car. He was posted to the Middle East and led many dashing motorised raids across the desert. In 1916 he commanded a car-borne raid on a Turkish armed encampment, destroyed its guns and rescued 90 shipwrecked sailors who had been imprisoned by a local Bedouin tribe. He returned to divorce his wife Shelagh in 1919, marry three more times and spend a great deal of his fortune on mistresses. He could afford it. In the 1920s there were over 9,000 shops and houses on his Mayfair estate bringing him in vast sums in rent. He developed increasingly pro-right, anti-Semitic views and, fearing the growing power of Communist Russia, was in favour of a negotiated peace with Hitler in World War II. Bend'or, Duke of Westminster, died in 1953.

Theodore Cook did well from his association with the 1908 Olympics. He wrote a well-received official report of the Olympiad and a tart retort to American criticisms of the Games. Then he became editor first of the *St James Gazette*, a paper 'for gentlemen by gentlemen' and in 1910 editor of the prestigious *The Field*. He was knighted in 1916 for the ferocious and unconditional backing of World War I given by the magazine under his leadership. He published two autobiographies, giving interesting accounts of his association with the first London Olympics. He remained with *The Field* until his death of a heart attack in 1926.

Edgar Seligman, the outstanding fencer in the épée team conveyed to Athens on the *Branwen*, earned his living as an artist but continued his association with the sport he loved. Altogether he won three team Olympic silver medals with the épée, in 1906, 1908 and 1912. From 1913 to 1930 he represented Great Britain at the congresses of the international fencing association. He captained the foil and épée teams at the 1920 Olympics and was overall captain in 1924, when he reached the last eight in the foil competition at the age of 56. The year before, he had won the British sabre championships for the first time. He became vice president of the Amateur Fencing Association and continued his career as a talented artist until his death in 1958.

George Stuart Robinson, who had come to the defence of the British officials against American attacks, became a successful barrister. He was knighted in 1928. When he died at the age of 94 he was the oldest known survivor of the first modern Olympiad. Several of the first paid employees associated with the White City Olympics continued their successful careers. Robert Stuart de Courcy Laffan remained with the Olympic movement until his death in 1927. He took time out to officiate as a forces chaplain during World War I, but then returned to his IOC desk to help plan several post-war Olympiads.

Imre Kiralfy, the Hungarian producer, supervised several more lavish productions at the White City and then took out a lease on the Earl's Court arena in London. He continued working almost to his death in 1919.

The American James E. Sullivan retained his hatred of British officialdom until his dying day, which occurred in 1914, only six years after Wyndham Halswelle and the City of London tug-of-war team had combined to upset him so. Upon his return to the USA he was re-elected president of the American Amateur Athletic Union for a record-breaking third time. A newspaper noticed that in his acceptance speech at the AAU annual convention he had gained no affection for his cousins across the water: 'In the course of his address he flayed the heads of the Olympic Games' officers and the English Amateur Athletic Association. The whole field of alleged mistakes in running and jumping was raked over again.'

At the slightest provocation he continued to give choleric interviews to newspapers, long after the White City closing ceremony, as typified by his remarks to the *Gaelic American*, 'Do you call boo-ing and bah-ing our competitors every time they appear sportsmanlike?' he asked rhetorically. An annual trophy was given in his name each year for the USA's outstanding athlete.

Mike Murphy continued to coach and discover young talented athletes. At the 1912 Olympics he was particularly close to the outstanding all-round Native American athlete Jim Thorpe. He also became a part-time conditioner to ex-President Teddy Roosevelt. Unfortunately, both men were so hard of hearing that they spent most of their time together bellowing at one another in an abrasive timpani of mutual misunderstandings. Murphy died when his son George was only 11 and he did not see him grow up to become a successful song-and-dance man in vaudeville, Broadway and then a Hollywood star of musicals like *Little Miss Broadway* and *This is the Army*, before abandoning show business to become the Republican congressman for California from 1965 to 1969.

James Connolly, the fisherman's son, veteran of San Juan Hill in the Spanish-American War and author, went on almost to make a career of harrassing James Sullivan and the hierarchy of US athletics. His sea stories made him rich and very popular. Twice he ran unsuccessfully for Congress.

Among the athletes, the pioneering Deerfoot, who had done so much to spark off public interest in athletics in Britain with his tour of the country in the 1860s, ended his days in poverty. He returned to the USA to find himself being required to perform more and more outrageous stunts, such as racing against horses and giving other competitors a quarter-mile start in a five-mile race. While he was at his peak he was constantly being asked to lose races deliberately, to bolster betting scams. Then, as he aged, his pride began to be hurt as younger athletes began beating him and he started drinking. It all became too much for the one-time wonder runner. He stole two blankets and then threatened the police with an axe when they came to arrest him. Deerfoot went on the run and avoided capture in the wilds for two years. Throughout this period he was aided by other members of his tribe. There were fears among white residents of the area that this might be a preamble to a Blackfoot uprising. In the end Deerfoot surrendered and was sentenced to 45 days at hard labour. He never raced again. For the rest of his life the one-time fastest Native American of them all was constantly in and out of prison on charges of drunkenness, brawling and assault. He died on the Cattaraugus Reservation in 1897, one year after the first Olympiad.

John Taylor, who had been running last in the 400 metres when the race was aborted, but who went on to win a gold in the relay, was dead five months after the end of the track and field events in the Games. He died of typhoid pneumonia on 2 December 1908. Several thousand people attended his Philadelphia memorial service. His *New York Times* obituary referred to him as 'the world's greatest Negro runner'.

Taylor had been preferred in the Olympic relay to John Carpenter, who had been disqualified in the 400 metres final. The omission upset the runner, who regarded it as a tacit vote of no confidence on the part of the US officials. He drifted out of athletics and no further records can be found of him or of William Robbins, the fourth man in the race.

Most of the White City middle-distance runners soon began to consider their futures outside sport. For a time the cocky, self-assured Mel Sheppard continued to flirt with athletic legality. Soon after his return from the 1908 Olympiad he was brought before a sub-committee accused of exaggerating his expense claims for tournaments. He served a temporary suspension but returned in time to win two more gold medals at the Stockholm Olympics of 1912. During World War I he was in charge of training recruits at several military camps. For a time, in his 50s, 'Peerless Mel' fell upon hard times and worked as a floorwalker in Wanamaker's New York department store. He ended his working life in charge of a large sports complex.

Apart from the marathon runners, only one of the track and field competitors seems to have turned professional. This was an American, Nathaniel John 'Nate' Cartmell. The winner of silver medals in the 100 metres and 200 metres in the 1904 Olympiad, he had secured a gold in the medley sprint relay four years later, as well as bronze in the 200 metres. Famed for a great, crowd-pleasing finishing burst over the last few yards of a race, Cartmell stayed on in Europe after the White City tournament and did well in a few amateur track meetings. This prompted him to turn professional. He spent two years picking up cash instead of trophies and in 1910 returned to the USA to become a coach, first at Penn State and finally at the US Military Academy.

Perhaps the only genius among the gold medal winners at the White City was A.C. Gilbert, who tied for first place in the pole vault. He was a medical student at Yale who had designed his own pole without the usual splits in the end. Instead Gilbert dug a small hole in which to plant a bamboo pole, thus giving him more impetus. He had been enraged when his form of vaulting had been forbidden at the White City.

Gilbert paid his way through college as a professional conjurer. Immediately after the Olympics he visited Paris with a friend. He noticed a number of bamboo poles in a furniture store and bought 50 of them at $1.25 each. He had them shipped to the USA, founded the Yale Bamboo Pole Vaulting Company and sold them to athletic clubs for $25 apiece. He used the profit to update his magic act. Just before he retired from athletics he claimed to have cleared a height of just over 13 feet at a small, unofficial meeting.

Gilbert qualified as a doctor in 1909, although he never practised medicine. One day when he was giving a demonstration of conjuring, someone offered to pay Gilbert to show him the secret of a trick he had performed. Gilbert started to manufacture magical tricks that even idiots could use. This led to his forming a company developing magical equipment. As he was travelling by train to give a conjuring demonstration at one of his stores, Gilbert noticed some workmen welding girders to a tower. This gave him the idea for a child's toy in which metal pieces could be affixed to one another by placing screws through holes. The British company Meccano had already used this idea, but Gilbert's kits were more realistic. He developed the children's construction toy the Erector Set, which was to sell in millions. Before his death in 1961, A.C. Gilbert had taken out more than 150 patents.

Another inventor, although on a smaller scale, was Leon Meredith, who won a cycling gold medal for Britain in 1908 and a silver four years later. After his retirement he developed and sold a racing tyre which made him very wealthy. He also had time to win the national roller skate championship twice and build a very successful roller skating rink in London.

There was quite a high mortality rate among the throwers of 1908. The mighty Martin Sheridan returned to the New York Police Force, attained the rank of detective, first grade, but died of pneumonia at the age of 36 in 1918. His friend and drinking companion Ralph Rose, who had held American records with shots weighing 8, 12, 18, 21 and 28 pounds, was called to the bar in California. He competed in the 1912 Stockholm Games, winning a silver medal in the orthodox shot put and a gold in the two handed shot put. A year later he died of typhoid fever. He was just 29. At the time of his death he was said to weigh almost a hundred pounds more than the 280 pounds he had scaled during his athletic prime.

John Flanagan also came back in triumph from his hammer-winning effort at the White City and a year later broke the world record yet again. In 1910, it all turned to dust for the 220-pounds policeman. His non-job in the Bureau of Licences was abolished. Flanagan was informed that in future he was going to have to walk a beat on the streets of New York. It was too much for his sensitive soul to bear. Flanagan resigned from the NYPD and returned to Ireland. He competed there for a short time and then turned to coaching. With his Olympic record he became an object of veneration at Irish sports meetings.

A contemporary athlete, Tom Barry, spoke of Flanagan's progress at a typical tournament, of 'the ground shaking under his feet. People stopped to look at him. He was like a tiger.' John Flanagan died in 1938 in his mid-60s.

The most persistent of the Irish Whales was Matt McGrath, yet another New York policeman. After coming second to Flanagan in the 1908 hammer event, he appeared in three more Olympic competitions. In 1912 he won the gold medal easily. In 1920, he injured his knee but still finished in fifth place and in 1924, at the age of 45, he won another silver medal. He was not finished yet. McGrath tried out for the 1928 Olympic team but did not do himself justice and was not selected. This caused a public outcry. A subscription was raised to send McGrath to Amsterdam, but when he arrived in Holland, the US Olympic officials would not allow him to compete for the team. He was still rated in the top ten of the world's hammer throwers when he was 50. He died in 1941.

One of the most interesting careers among the big men was that of Michael M. Dorizas, who was often called in the press the 'strongest man on earth'. He had been born in Turkey of Greek parents and attended the University of Pennsylvania, where he attracted some attention by breaking a strength-testing machine during a routine physical check-up. He represented his university at American football, wrestling and track and field. He threw for Greece in three Olympiads. For a time he held the world javelin record and in 1908 he took the silver medal in that event. Dorizas spent World War I as a sergeant and then served as a Greek interpreter at the post-war Paris peace conference. Finally he returned to his old university to become a much-respected professor.

Many of the members of the Irish-American Athletic Association continued to sail pretty close to the wind as far as professionalism was concerned. Within a year of returning from the 1908 Olympics, Martin Sheridan, Matt McGrath and Mel Sheppard had all been suspended temporarily. The two throwers were accused of accepting $500 above their normal expenses at a meeting at Chicago's Forrest Park, while Sheppard compounded a number of offences by flagrantly continuing to run all over the country while suspended. Eventually all the erring but unrepentant athletes were accepted back into the fold.

'Such accusations are astounding, and I don't believe a word of them' was the typical response of James Sullivan, blinkered and loyal to a fault as usual.

Frank Beaurepaire, the young Australian swimmer, won a silver and a bronze at the London Olympics. He was banned from the 1912 Olympiad for taking money as a swimming teacher, was gassed serving in World War I and then, after his reinstatement, he won a silver and a bronze in Antwerp and gained the same swimming medals at the Paris Olympiad in 1924. He toured the world breaking records. In 1922, he received an award of just over £500 for rescuing a swimmer attacked by a shark off the beach at Sydney. He used the money to found a massively successful tyre company, entered politics and for several years was Lord Mayor of Sydney. At his death he was worth £8 million.

Some of the women who had done well in the White City competitions continued with their sporting activities. Lottie Dod took part in more archery tournaments, but never won a major event. Her brother Willie, who had won a gold medal at the White City, enlisted in the army upon the outbreak of war even though he was 47 years old. Lottie worked as a Red Cross volunteer in a military hospital. She lived until the age of 89 and died in 1960.

Shelagh, the Duchess of Westminster, separated from her husband. The terms of their settlement, £10,000 a year, made her a wealthy and independent woman. She opened a military hospital for officers in France at the outbreak of World War I, helped by a magnanimous gift of £500 from the duke. She received the CBE for her war work. She remarried happily but retained her title, causing one newspaper, referring to her real name of Constance, to dub her spitefully 'the constant duchess'. Shelagh died in 1970, at the age of 92. Another long-lived female sportswoman was 'Chattie' Sterry (née Cooper), who had scratched from the tennis entrants in 1908 after originally allowing her name to be entered. She lived to the age of 96. At the age of 90 she flew without any companions from Scotland to Wimbledon to attend an official luncheon at the club.

Almost alone, the marathon runners continued competing against one another, only this time officially for cash. Dorando and Hayes turned professional and replicated their Windsor to the White City race on a number of occasions, with Dorando Pietri usually winning. In their first post-Olympic competition the Italian beat the American by 60 to 75 yards in a sprint finish, before a large, partisan crowd made up largely of Irish-Americans and Italian-Americans.

Dorando abandoned all thoughts of opening a little bakery in his home town. There were pavements to be pounded and hard cash to be earned in the now enormously popular, long-distance races. In a six-month period spanning 1908 and 1909, he took part in nine marathons, of which he won five, and more than a dozen other races. He eschewed the six-day races, held in stadia, where the runners trudged endlessly round and round a track and were allowed to take time out to sleep at night.

In his constant quest for funds, Dorando also appeared in vaudeville with the boxing champion Jack Johnson, but his act was less than thrilling. It consisted of the runner, who spoke no English, looking embarrassed in running shorts, standing on the stage while the master of ceremonies gave an exaggerated account of his London marathon achievements. When human opponents became scarce the Italian raced against men on horseback. For three years he ran all over the world, from South Africa to South America, amassing some 200,000 lire in the process. In his last race in Italy, of 15 kilometres in 1911, he beat Pericle Pagliani, whose efforts had first stimulated Dorando to take up long-distance running.

After his retirement he returned to Italy, where he opened an hotel with his brother. It did not succeed and Dorando Pietri lost most of his savings. He found work in charge of a garage and motor workshop, where occasionally he drove a taxi. He was retained by the Italian government to seek out young marathon runners of promise. Dorando Pietri died in 1942 at the age of 56.

Tom Longboat parted with his manager Tom Flanagan soon after his return to Canada. The *Syracuse Herald* of 31 August said, 'Tom Longboat, the Canadian Indian runner and Tom Flanagan, who has been his manager for the last year or two, have reached the parting of their ways. Longboat says he is through with Flanagan and will look out for his own interests in future…'

There were to be reconciliations and further breaks, but no matter who was looking after the Canadian, Longboat still found plenty of running work as soon as he turned professional at the age of 21. He defeated Dorando in a New York marathon, winning a diamond-encrusted medal worth $500. He beat Dorando again, a short time later in Buffalo. Longboat was then challenged by Britain's leading professional runner, Alf Shrubbs, who told reporters, 'I can beat that over-rated Indian any time!'

He was wrong. Longboat pulled off a spectacular victory over Shrubbs at Madison Square Garden. He continued to draw large crowds for a time, but by about 1912, long-distance running began to lose its appeal for the spectators. In 1916, Tom Longboat joined a Sportsman's Battalion of the Canadian Army. His captain was former trainer Tom Flanagan. He transferred to a fighting unit and served in France, fittingly enough as a runner, conveying messages from the trenches to headquarters. He was once reported as having been killed in action. When he returned home he found that his wife had believed the report and had remarried. He also came home to a world in which professional running was no longer much of a spectator sport. Longboat was forced to work as a labourer in steel mills and then as a road cleaner. He moved back to the Six Rivers Reservation, where he died of pneumonia in 1949.

John Hayes bade farewell to Bloomingdales, the department store, signed up with promoters and took to the open road, and sometimes the indoor tracks, for a living. He presented Theodore Roosevelt with a blackthorn walking stick which he claimed to have carved from a tree he found in the hills of Ireland. For a time he earned good purses. It was announced with a fanfare that the world's best distance runners would take part in a number of elimination contests, culminating in a race for the world's professional marathon championship. His first encounter with Dorando at Madison Square Garden took place before thousands of spectators, paying up to $10 for a ticket. The race was scheduled over 260 laps of the indoor track.

Hayes ran on for years. He also endorsed products, participating in an extensive advertising campaign for O'Sullivan's Live Rubber Heels. In 1912, the Olympic marathon champion was selected as one of the US trainers for the 1912 Stockholm Games. After his retirement from running, Hayes became a teacher of physical education, and then he entered the business word as a food broker. He died in 1965.

Lewis Tewanima, who had come ninth in the marathon because he dared not disobey his coach and run his own race, won a silver medal in Stockholm, but was overshadowed by friend and fellow Carlisle School athlete Jim Thorpe, who won the decathlon and pentathlon events before being disqualified for having accepted $15 for playing a season of semi-professional baseball. Shortly afterwards, Tewanima went back to his reservation, where he eked out a living by raising sheep and growing crops. In 1969, when he was over 90 years of age, he was walking back from an evening church meeting in the dark and fell to his death over a 70-foot cliff. Apart from a brief five years of athletics glory he had spent his entire life on the reservation.

The 1908 marathon left one lasting legacy. The act of extending the race yet further to satisfy the Royal request that Princess Mary might witness the start did not go down well with future generations of long-distance runners. It became the custom as exhausted athletes reached the 24-mile marker in the race for them to shout 'God save the Queen!' or something more derogatory with regard to the Royal family.

Neither Snowy Baker nor J.W.H.T. Douglas boxed seriously again. The Australian Baker, who had won a boxing silver medal and taken part in the swimming and diving, retired from active participation from sports to become a gymnasium owner and boxing referee and promoter. He became an action star in the early Australian silent movie business and emigrated to the USA where he set up an exclusive Californian country club and became a

Hollywood stunt man, supplying horses for Western films as a sideline. He also claimed to have taught movie idol Rudolph Valentino how to kiss properly, which added a whole new dimension to his claim to have been an all-rounder.

Douglas became an unpopular England cricket captain and took an increased interest in his father's timber business. In 1931, he and his father were returning from a trip to Finland when the steamer upon which they were travelling became involved in a collision with another vessel in a fog in the Baltic Sea. Their ship the *Oberon*, sank. J.W.H.T Douglas and his father were both drowned.

Dick Gunn, who had won the lightweight gold at the age of 37, retired for good this time. He went back to refereeing and ran a pub in Westminster Bridge Road. As far as is known he is the only English participant in the 1908 Olympics to have a part in the second London Olympics 40 years later. In the 1948 Games, R.K. Gunn served as a timekeeper in the boxing events. He died in 1961, at the age of 90.

Matt Wells, who had thrown away his chance of an Olympic gold medal in the lightweight class by drinking beer in the dressing room before his first contest, had a good professional career. He won the British professional lightweight title and then toured the USA and Australia extensively. In Australia he defeated Tom McCormick and claimed the world welterweight championship, but lost the title to Mike Glover in the USA in 1915. After his retirement Wells became a publican and a referee. His association with boxing ended sadly after he refereed a 1933 heavyweight bout between Don McCorkindale of South Africa and Walter Neusel of Germany at London's Albert Hall. The German seemed to have won the fight easily but Matt Wells gave his verdict as a draw. There were accusations that the result had been 'fixed' by a betting gang. Wells had his referee's licence taken away by the British Boxing Board of Control.

Con O'Kelly, the jovial Cork-born winner of the catch-as-catch-can heavyweight wrestling gold medal, wasted no time in turning professional. He resigned from the Hull Police Force in order to embark upon a tour of the music halls. Unfortunately, early on in his travels he encountered George Hackenschmidt, the Russian Lion, the best professional heavyweight wrestler in the world. 'Hack' gave

O'Kelly such a thrashing in the ring that the former policeman realised that he would never get anywhere as long as the Russian was around. Obviously a pragmatist, O'Kelly swapped sports and became a successful professional boxer in Great Britain and the USA. He retired to run a pub in Hull. His son Con Junior represented Britain in the Olympics as a boxer, turned professional and finally became a priest.

Walter Winans, the Olympic shooting champion, continued with his life of industrious leisure. Although he had constantly renewed his citizenship, Winans only visited the USA once, and that was towards the end of his life. He won the British revolver shooting title on many occasions. At the 1910 Vienna Exposition, he won two gold medals for displays of big-game shooting culled from more than two thousand animals he had shot on his travels. He died while driving a sulky cart in a trotting race at Parsloes Park in 1920. He was approaching the winning post when he was taken ill.

Winans cried out, 'Stop my horse!' He slipped from his seat, dead, as the horse passed the post and came to a halt.

Emile Rath competed in the ten mile walk and the marathon for Austria. After World War I he opened a sports store in Prague. An anti-Nazi, he was imprisoned by the Germans during World War II and then by the Communists when they took over Czechoslovakia in 1948. After his release he lived rough in a public park before being sent to an old folks' home, where he died at the age of 79 in 1962.

Gradually memories faded as other aspects of life, good and bad, took over for most of the participants in the first London Olympiad. Baron de Coubertin, however, who had done so much to prepare the way for the tournament, always remembered the occasion as an opportunity missed. He wrote: 'It will be necessary to avoid copying the Olympic Games of London. The next Olympiads must not have such a character, they must not be so comprehensive. There was altogether too much in London. The Games must be kept more purely athletic; they must be more dignified, more discreet; more in accordance with classic and artistic requirements …'

Fifteen

Envoi

'It is much to be regretted…that these Games should have in any way failed as a means of bringing the nations of the world into a closer bond.'

The Olympic Games of 1908 in London: A Reply to Certain Charges Made by the American Officials

Casting a shadow over all the participants in the London Olympics was World War I, which broke out only six years after the 1908 Games ended. Hundreds of the participants and officials served in the conflict, many showed great gallantry and some were injured or killed.

A few had it easier than others. Otto Froitzheim, the winner of the silver medal for Germany in the men's singles tennis tournament, continued to play tennis to a high standard. He won the German title. In 1912 he was the world hard court champion. He captained his country in a Davis Cup match against Australia in 1914. World War I had broken out a fortnight earlier. On his way home from the USA, where the tournament had taken place, his vessel was stopped in the Atlantic by a British ship. Frotzheim became a prisoner of war for the next four years.

After the war, things looked up for the tennis player. He captured the German title again in 1921, 1922 and 1925, was appointed the chief of police of Wiesbaden and became the lover of the famous German film-maker Leni Riefenstahl. With such a CV he probably deserved his sobriquet of 'Otto the Great'. He died at the age of 78 in 1962.

Others were much less fortunate. One of the first Olympic athletes to die was Wyndham Halswelle, who unwittingly had sparked off such controversy when John Carpenter had been disqualified for jostling him in the 400 metres final. He raced only once more after his solo 400 metres final and then returned to his military duties. In 1915 Halswelle, by now a captain, was serving with the Highland Light Infantry in northern France near Lille. Halswelle and his men took part in the celebrated three-day battle of Neuve Chapelle, between 10–13 March. Some 40,000 British and Indian troops launched an assault on the well-guarded German line. At first the Allied troops broke through, but they were unable to sustain their advance. Thousands of troops on both sides were slaughtered. More than a quarter of those who had taken part in the attack did not return.

Halswelle wrote after the decimation of his troops during the opening days of the doomed onslaught, 'I counted up the company and found it 61 strong, but I am afraid that there were a lot who never got farther than the first line, and I have lost three platoon sergeants in the first rush.'

Shortly after this Captain Halswelle was wounded. He was treated at a field station but refused to be sent back to a base hospital. He rejoined his company in the front line and almost at once he was shot in the head and killed by a sniper. He was 32 years old.

Jean Bouin, who had been locked up for brawling in London in 1908, became France's leading track athlete of his era. Four years later he won a silver medal in the 1912 Stockholm Olympics 5000 metres, setting a French record that stood for 36 years. In 1914, he tried to enlist in the French army. At first he was rejected because of a heart condition. The runner, still only 26, persisted and finally was accepted. In September 1914, Sergeant Jean Bouin was killed by 'friendly fire' from French artillery while serving near Saint-Michel. An athletics stadium was named after him.

Oscar Lapize, the Olympic cyclist and Tour de France winner, joined the French airforce. He was killed in aerial combat in 1917. Gaston Alibert, winner of the individual épée gold medal, also fell in action.

Henry Wilson, the swimming gold medallist who learned his art in the mill streams of his home town, won a bronze medal in the 4 × 200 metres relay at the 1912 Stockholm Olympics, joined the Navy and and was reputed to have swum around the entire British fleet anchored at Scapa Flow. In 1916 he served at the Battle of Jutland off Scapa Flow. Wilson's ship was sunk in the action, depositing many seamen in the icy waters. For two hours, until they were rescued, Wilson swam continuously from man to man, rendering help and giving encouragement. He survived the conflict to win another bronze medal in the 4 × 200 metres relay in the 1920 Games. Later, he fell upon hard times and was forced to sell or pawn most of his hundreds of swimming trophies, before his death in 1951.

Fred Kelly, a rowing blue, a promising concert pianist and composer, befriended the poet Rupert Brooke during the war. He won the DSC for outstanding gallantry at Gallipoli but was killed in France. Another survivor of Gallipoli was the Australian Rugby gold medallist Tom Richards. He won the Military Cross (MC) storming the Hindenburg Line on the Western Front but was badly gassed in the process.

Just before his death in 1935 at the age of 46, he murmured, 'The gas I swallowed in the war is beating me down steadily.'

Another member of the Wallabies' 1908 side was Syd Middleton, who had attained notoriety by punching an Oxford undergraduate in the Wallabies game against the university. He changed sports and rowed for Australia in the 1912 Olympics before winning a DSO in the war.

In addition to Fred Kelly, a number of Olympic gold medallist rowers served bravely in the army. Collier Cudmore, an Australian, had returned to his home in Australia after the Games. He came back to England to enlist in the Royal Field Artillery, was twice wounded in action and went back to settle in Australia, where he become a barrister, politician and knight. Gilchrist MacLaglen, a lieutenant in the Royal Warwickshire Regiment, was killed in action in 1915. John Somers-Smith won the MC and was killed in 1916. Duncan Mackinnon returned from working in his family business in Calcutta and was killed at Ypres in 1917. Ronald Sanderson, serving with the Royal Field Artillery, was killed a year later. Charles Burnell won the DSO with the London Rifle Brigade. Gordon Thomson joined the RAF and was awarded the DSC for flying low over the Turkish lines at Gallipoli on reconnaissance missions.

A number of the hockey players were in action. Edgar Page, Stanley Shoveller and Reggie Pridmore each won a MC, but Pridmore was killed serving with the Royal Horse Artillery in Italy in 1918. John Robinson was wounded in action in Mesopotamia with the North Staffordshire Regiment. He later died of his wounds.

New Zealander Anthony Wilding had been the world's outstanding tennis player before the war. He had entered the Olympic tournament but withdrew before he played a game. He was killed serving in the trenches in France.

Among the wounded, the wealthy J.J. Astor, who had won a gold medal in the racquets competition, lost a leg in France. Later he became a Member of Parliament and the owner of *The Times*. Despite his disability he also won the parliamentary squash racquets championships on a number of occasions. Joe Deakin, who had won a gold medal in the three-mile team race, was temporarily blinded. He recovered his sight and was still running in his 80s. Lord Wodehouse, a member of the Hurlingham polo team, was twice wounded fighting as a captain with the 16th Lancers, and mentioned in dispatches.

Charles Crichton, one of the yachtsmen to win a gold, received the DSO for gallantry and was promoted to the rank of lieutenant colonel. Herbert Wilson, a polo player, who had won the DSO in the Boer War, was killed at Ypres in 1917.

Noel Chavasse, one of the seven children of the Bishop of Liverpool, was eliminated in 1908, with his twin brother Chris, in the heats of the 400 metres race. He became a doctor, was attached to the London Scottish Regiment and was awarded two Victoria Crosses (VCs) for treating the wounded and helping to carry them from the battlefield under heavy fire. He was killed in France in 1917.

The citation for the bar to his VC was published in the *London Gazette* in September, 1917: 'Early in the action he was severely wounded in the head while carrying a wounded man to his dressing station. He refused to leave his post and for two days not only continued to attend to the cases brought to his first aid post, but repeatedly and under heavy fire went out to the firing line with stretcher parties to search for wounded and dressed those lying out. During these searches he found a number of badly wounded men in the open and assisted to carry them in over heavy and difficult ground. He was practically without food during this period, worn with fatigue and faint from his wounds.'

Noel Chavasse's brother Christopher served as a chaplain in the services and won the MC and the Croix de Guerre. Later he became the Bishop of Rochester. In 1939 he injured his leg severely when he helped rescue nine people who had become trapped beneath an overturned motorboat off the Giant's Causeway in County Antrim, Northern Ireland.

Julian Grenfell, the son of Lord Desborough, was an accomplished amateur boxer but he never became an Olympic athlete. He was a war poet, the author of 'Into Battle' and one of the two sons of Desborough to be killed in battle. Lord Desborough had a monument erected in their memory on his Taplow estate. The sculpture was created by Bertram Mackennal who – in happier, faraway times – had designed the medals for the 1908 Olympics. On one side of the monument was a representation of the god Apollo in a sun chariot. On the other was an engraving of 'Into Battle'. It could have served as an epitaph for all the flowers of the forest who were cut down in the dreadful carnage.

> The thundering line of battle stands,
> And in the air Death moans and sings;
> But Day shall clasp him with strong hands.
> And Night shall fold him in soft wings.

Appendix 1

1908 Olympics Events

Archery (men and women)
Association football
Athletics
Boxing
Cycling
Diving
Fencing
Field hockey
Figure skating (men and women)
Gymnastics
Jeu de paume (real tennis)
Lacrosse
Lawn tennis (men and women)
Motorboating
Polo
Racquets
Rowing and sculling
Rugby Union football
Shooting
Swimming
Tug-of-war
Water polo
Wrestling
Yachting (men and women)

Appendix 2

1908 Olympics Medal Winners

Country	Gold	Silver	Bronze	Total
United Kingdom	56	51	39	146
United States	23	12	12	47
Sweden	8	6	11	25
France	5	5	9	19
Canada	3	3	10	16
Germany	3	5	5	13
Hungary	3	4	2	9
Norway	2	3	3	8
Belgium	1	5	2	8
Finland	1	1	3	5
Denmark	-	2	3	5
Italy	2	2	-	4
Australia	1	2	1	4
Greece	-	3	-	3
Russia	1	2	-	3
South Africa	1	1	-	2
Netherlands	-	-	2	2
Bohemia	-	-	2	2
New Zealand	-	-	1	1
Austria	-	-	1	1

Bibliography

Books

Andrews, T.S., *T.S. Andrews' World's Sporting Annual Record Book*, T.S. Andrews, 1908

Angle, Bernard J., *My Sporting Memories*, Holden, 1925

Anthony, Don, *Minds, Bodies and Souls* (three vols), British Olympic Association, 1995

Arnaud. P and J. Riordan (eds), *Sport and International Politics, 1900-1941*, Spon, 1998

Atkinson, Graeme, *Australian and New Zealand Olympians*, The Five Mile Press, 1984

Batten, Jack, *The Man Who Ran Faster than Everyone: The Story of Tom Longboat*, Tundra Books, 2002

Battiscombe, Georgina, *Queen Alexandra*, Constable, 1969

Bergreen, Laurence, *As Thousands Cheer: the Life of Irving Berlin*, Hodder and Stoughton, 1990

Betts, John Rickards, *America's Sporting Heritage, 1850–1950*, Addison-Wesley, 1974

Birley, Derek, *Land of Sport and Glory: Sport and British Society, 1877–1910*, Manchester University Press, 1995

Blue, Adrianne, *Grace Under Pressure: the Emergence of Women in Sport*, Sidgwick and Jackson, 1987

Brant, Marshall (ed), *The Games: A Complete News History*, Proteus, 1980

Brearley, Giles, *Alfred Liversidge (1836–1921): Swinton's Sporting Hero*, Neville-Douglas, 1998

Buchanan, Ian, *British Olympians*, Guinness, 1991

Caldwell, John, *City of London Police Athletics Club, 1889–1986,* City of London Police, 1986

Chapman, David L., *Sandow the Magnificent,* University of Illinois Press, 1994

Clynes, Ernest, *The Polytechnic Harriers, 1833–1933,* The Harriers, 1933

Cook, T.A. *The Sunlit Hours,* Nisbet, 1925

Cornfield, Susie, *The Queen's Prize: The Story of the National Rifle Association,* Pelham, 1987

Daniels, Stephanie and Anita Tedder, *A Proper Spectacle: Women Olympians, 1900-1936,* ZeNaNa Press, 2000

Dettre, A., *Australia at the Olympics,* Hamlyn, 1980

Diggelen, T. von, *Worthwhile Journey,* Heinemann, 1955

Duff Gordon, Lady, *Discretions and Indiscretions,* Jarrold, 1932

Duncanson, Neil and Patrick Collins, *Tales of Gold,* Queen Anne Press, 1992

Etherington-Smith, Meredith and Jeremy Pilcher, *The It Girls,* Hamish Hamilton, 1986

Field, Leslie, *Bend'or, the Golden Duke of Westminster,* Weidenfeld and Nicolson, 1983

Fry, C.B., *Life Worth Living,* Eyre and Spottiswoode, 1939

Glyn, Anthony, *Elinor Glyn,* Hutchinson, 1955

Godwin, Terry, *The International Rugby Championship, 1883–1983,* Collins Willow, 1984

Gordon, Harry, *Australia and the Olympic Games,* Queensland University Press, 1994

Grayson, Edward, *Corinthians and Cricketers,* Naldrett Press, 1955

Green, Harvey, *Fit for America: Health, Fitness, Sport and American Society,* Pantheon, 1986

Guiney, David, *Silver, Gold, Bronze,* Sportsworld, 1990

Gummer, Selwyn, *The Chavasse Twins,* Hodder and Stoughton, 1963

Haley, Bruce, *The Healthy Body and Victorian Culture,* Harvard University Press, 1978

Hibbert, Christopher, *Edward VII: A Portrait,* Allen Lane, 1976

Hopkins, John, *The Marathon,* Stanley Paul, 1966

Huggins, Mike, *The Victorians and Sport,* Hambledon and London, 2004

Hughes, Thomas, *Tom Brown's Schooldays*, first pub 1857, Penguin Popular Classics, 1994

Jacobs, Norman, *Vivian Woodward: Football's Gentleman*, Tempus, 2005

Kidd, Bruce, *Tom Longboat*, Fitzhenry and Whiteside, 1992

Killanin, Lord and John Rodda (eds), *The Olympic Games: 80 Years of People, Events and Records*, Barrie and Jenkins, 1976

Laver, James, *Edwardian Promenade*, Hulton, 1958

Leder, Jane, *Grace and Glory: A Century of Women in the Olympics*, Triumph Books, 1996

Lemon, David, *Johnny Won't Hit Today: A Cricketing Biography of J.W.H.T. Douglas*, Allen and Unwin, 1983

Levy, Lawrence E., *The Autobiography of an Athlete*, Hammond, 1913

Lord, Walter, *A Night to Remember*, Longmans, 1956

Lovesey, Peter, *The Kings of Distance: A Study of Five Great Runners*, Eyre and Spottiswoode, 1968

Lovesey, Peter, *The Official Centenary History of the Amateur Athletic Association*, Guinness Superlatives, 1979

Lovett, Charlie, *Olympic Marathon*, Greenwood, 1997

MacAloon, John J., *This Great Symbol: Pierre de Coubertin and the Origin of the Modern Olympic Games*, University of Chicago Press, 1981

Machray, Robert, *The Night Side of London*, Macqueen, 1902

Macqueen-Pope, W., *Twenty Shillings in the Pound: A Lost Age of Plenty, 1890-1914*, Hutchinson, 1948

Madol, Hans Roger, *The Private Life of Queen Alexandra*, Hutchinson, 1940

Mallon, Bill and Ian Buchanan, *The 1908 Olympic Games*, McFarland, 2000

Mandell, Richard, *The First Modern Olympics*, University of California Press, 1976

Mangan, J., *Athleticism in the Victorian and Edwardian Public School*, Cambridge, 1988

Matthews, George R., *America's First Olympics: The St Louis Games of 1904*, University of Missouri Press, 2005

Mayne, Richard, Douglas Johnson and Robert Tombs (eds),

Cross Channel Currents: 100 Years of the Entente Cordiale, Routledge, 2004

McCafferry, Dan, *Tommy Burns: Canada's Unknown World Champion,* Lorimer, 2000

Moran, Herbert M., *Viewless Winds: Being the Recollections and Digressions of an Australian Surgeon,* Peter Davies, 1939

Mosley, Nicholas, *Julian Grenfell,* Weidenfeld and Nicolson, 1976

Naughton, Lindie and Johnny Eatterson, *Irish Olympians,* Blackwater, 1992

Newton, Diana and Jonathan Lumby, *The Grosvenors of Eaton; the Dukes of Westminster and their Forebears,* Jennet, 2002

Nickalls, Guy, *Life's a Pudding,* Faber, 1939

Pallett, George, *Women's Athletics,* Normal, 1955

Pearson, Jeffrey, *Lottie Dod, Champion of Champions,* Countrywise, 1988

Salmon, Tom, *The First Hundred Years, The Story of Rugby Football in Cornwall,* Cornwall RFU, 1983

Schmidt, F.A. and Miles, Eustace, *The Training of the Body for Games and Athletics,* Swann Sonnenschein, 1901

Sharpham, Peter, *The First Wallabies,* Sandstone, 2000

Smith, Michael Llewellyn, *Olympics in Athens, 1896,* Profile, 2004

Smith, Ronald A., *Sports and Freedom: The Rise of Big-Time College Athletics,* Oxford University Press, 1988

'Sportsman, The' (ed.), (two vols), *British Sports and Sportsmen,* 1908

Stanton, Richard, *The Forgotten Olympic Art Competitions,* Trafford, 2000

Tomlin, Stan (ed.), *Olympic Odyssey,* Modern Athlete Pubs, 1956

Ulyatt, Michael, *The Fighting O'Kellys,* Hutton Press, 1991

Wallechinsky, David, *The Complete Book of the Olympics,* Aurum, 2000

Watman, Melvyn, *History of British Athletics,* Robert Hale, 1968

Webster, David, *The Iron Game,* Irvine, 1976

Webster, F.A.M., *Athletics of Today: History, Development and Training,* Warne, 1929

Webster, F.A.M., *Olympic Cavalcade,* Hutchinson, 1948

Weintraub, Stanley, *Edward the Caresser,* The Free Press, 2001

Newspapers

The Buffalo News
Corriere della Sera
The Daily Chronicle
The Daily Kennebec Journal
The Daily Mail
The Daily Telegraph
The Daily Tribune
The Frederick Evening Post
The Gaelic American
The Glasgow Herald
The Hopewell Herald
The La Crosse Tribune
The London Gazette
The Manchester Guardian
The Morning Post
The Nebraska State Journal
The New York Sun
The New York Telegraph
The New York Times
The Oakland Tribune
The Observer
The Ohio Evening Telegraph
The Oxford Chronicle
The Pittsburgh Press
The San Antonio Light
The Sandusky Star Journal
The St Louis Post-Dispatch
The Syracuse Herald
The Syracuse Post
The Times
The Tottenham and Stamford Hill Times
The Trenton Evening Times
The Warren Evening Mirror

Journals

The British Medical Journal
The Footballer: The Journal of Soccer History
The International Journal of the History of Sport
The Journal of Olympic History
The Journal of Sport and Social Issues
Olympic Review

Magazines

Badminton Magazine
Baileys' Magazine
Century Magazine
Colhers Magazine
The Field
Illustrated London News
Outlook
Outing
The Referee

Reports and guides

The Fourth Olympiad, Being the Official Report of The Olympic Games of 1908, The British Olympic Council, undated but 1909
The Franco-British Exhibition Illustrated Review, Chatto and Windus, 1908
The Olympic Games of 1908 in London: A Reply to Certain Charges Made by the American Officials, Theodore A. Cook

Index